To Catch a Carp

To Catch a Carp

Tim Paisley and Friends

The Crowood Press

First Published in 1997 by
The Crowood Press Ltd
Ramsbury, Marlborough
Wiltshire SN8 2HR

British Library Cataloguing-in-Publication Data
A catalogue reference for this book is available from the British Library

ISBN 1 86126 081 4

Line illustrations by Frank Warwick.
Photographs by the author and contributors.

Photograph previous page: the author with a Kent thirty pounder.

Dedication

For Mary and Pip, as a tribute to their widely appreciated and
highly praised surrogate mother services to carp anglers before,
during and after the Fishabil sessions, through four memorable
years of *Carpworld* trips.

  And for my friends and companions in publishing, Kevin
Clifford and Chris Ball, for their courage and commitment
during the memorable shared experience of the creation of the
first carp and specialist weekly, *Carp-Talk*.

Typefaces used: text, M Plantin; labels, Helvetica.

Typeset and designed by
D & N Publishing
Membury Business Park, Lambourn Woodlands
Hungerford, Berkshire.

Printed and bound by The Bath Press.

CONTENTS

ACKNOWLEDGEMENTS

Thanks to John Dennis and Ken Hathaway of Crowood Press who had sufficient confidence in me to commission this work on the strength of my enthusiastic ramblings about it.

Thanks to my contributors who have so expertly covered those areas of carp fishing I feel least equipped to deal with: Rob Hughes and Simon Crow, Rod Hutchinson, Martin Clarke, Kevin Nash, Paddy Webb, Mike Willmott and Frank Warwick. Their contributions are based on an understanding gained from thousands of hours of carp fishing, and their efforts are appreciated by author and reader alike.

Thanks to Frank Warwick who converted my barely recognizable rough drawings into perfectly comprehensible works of art. Frank's own carp-fishing expertise has made his assistance invaluable.

Thanks to Jemima for her back-up proofing work. Proofing is my least favourite part of the writing and publishing process, as Jemima discovered when she sat down to plough her way through all 100,000 words of this book! Thanks also to Sandra for her invaluable assistance in setting and correcting much of the text, and for translating Rod's and my spirited efforts from tape.

Thanks to my many friends, acquaintances and carp fishing companions whose own ideas have gone a long way towards making much of the material on which this book is based possible, in particular Rod Hutchinson, John Lilley, Tony Baskeyfield, Kevin Nash, Jim Gibbinson, Julian Cundiff and Dave Chilton.

Thanks to those many individuals and firms who have given me practical support by way of tackle and bait sponsorship over the years, in particular Bill Cottam and Richard Skidmore from Nutrabaits; Dave Chilton of Kryston; Kevin Nash; Steve, Kevin and Kevin from Mainline and Mainline Connection; Terry and Rob Eustace from Gold Label Tackle; Max Cottis and Cliff Fox from Fox International; Danny Fairbrass from Korda Leads.

My apologies to those who have not been acknowledged and who recognize something of their own ideas in here, and those who have given me support and sponsorship which has temporarily evaded my faulty memory.

Thanks to all of you who buy this book to read it. I hope you are enriched by the experience: you are the inspiration for it.

Finally thanks to Mary who, remarkably, finds having me at home locked in my thoughts and my study writing about carp fishing marginally better than having me away from home three days a week living the experiences that make the writing possible! As I keep pointing out to her, carp fishing is work to me therefore I have to go and do it. Not that she ever utters a discouraging word, bless her, even when I tell her that she really will have to fill a few more pages of advertising for the following month's *Carpworld* as I drive off for a few days of arduous relaxation in one of my favourite swims.

PREFACE

The realization that there was a need for this book slowly dawned on me when I gradually started to accept that the term 'carp angler' covers as many differing categories as does the familiar expression 'worker'. There are startling differences in types of waters, sizes of water, degrees of pressure, commitment, available time, distances travelled, financial resources, knowledge, experience, understanding and physical capabilities. All these aspects influence the type of carp fishing pursued by a wide variety of what we conveniently refer to as 'carp anglers'.

The actual catalysts for the book were two very separate occurrences – the panel evening and the reaction to the Carp Leader, both of which I refer to in Chapter 1. As editor of *Carpworld* it is necessary for me to ensure that the magazine caters for as wide a cross-section of the carp fraternity as possible. In terms of entertainment this is not unduly difficult. In terms of instructional, practical and tactical material it had not occurred to me that there was a problem. The fishing the majority of carp writers engage in, and therefore write about, is of limited application if the majority of the readership cannot exactly relate to what they are reading, because they perceive carp fishing as something very different. The situation is worse still if they do not perceive it to be something different and practise the inappropriate advice they accept as law.

This book recognizes that the time spent carp fishing and the venues it is practised on are major influencing factors on tactics. A four-hour evening session is a very different type of carp fishing to a two-day session over a pressured weekend. Twelve-hour sessions on day-ticket waters require a very different approach to four-day sessions on very similar waters. Carp fishing when time is against you is a much harder prospect than long sessions when time is on your side. Gravel pits are a very different prospect to clay pits or meres of a similar size.

I have always categorized instructional writing about carp fishing as technical and practical. I have now added a crucial third category – tactical material. We all have the same baits, rigs and tackle available to us; but most of us recognize that even given exactly the same resources, some carp anglers are much more successful than others. Knowledge, experience, understanding, ability – and tactical awareness – are the base on which successful carp fishing is built.

With the help of excellent additional material from Rod Hutchinson, Kevin Nash, Paddy Webb, Frank Warwick, Rob Hughes and Simon Crow, Martin Clarke and Mike Willmott, *To Catch a Carp* attempts to add the dimensions of tactical awareness and understanding to the wealth of excellent practical and technical carp fishing material that is already in existence.

Tim Paisley
January 1997

1 TERMS OF REFERENCE

My last technical book on carp fishing was *Big Carp*, published by Crowood in 1989. Since then I have done an enormous amount of carp fishing, given innumerable slide shows, written a great deal of technical material in the periodical publications *Carpworld*, *Carp Fisher* and *Carp-Talk*, and written technical and practical material for a number of other publications. In addition, I have contributed an annual article to Nutrabaits' twelve-monthly publication *Bait*. So why another technical book on carp fishing now?

Well, somewhere along the line in a life which, rather wonderfully, involves sleeping, eating and living carp fishing, the realization came to me that most carp-fishing writing lacks direction. We have never been better served in terms of carp publications, writers and wealth of material, but here's the but! Most writers write of fishing for, and catching, large carp, and base their observations on the methods and time scales involved in such fishing. This truism was first brought home to me during a (so-called) 'panel of experts' at a carp meeting. I was on the panel and we were fielding a question on bait quantities. First star to reply suggested 18lbs of bait a week as a starting point... I winced, and wondered how many people in the audience could afford, prepare and have the time to use eighteen pounds of boilies per week. I made a quick rough estimate and came up with the answer 'One': the friend of mine who was answering the question!

I had a few minutes to consider my reply to the panel question about bait quantities, and when my turn came I based my comments around the theme 'put in as much bait as you can afford when you're not fishing, and as little as you can get away with when you are'. Four or five years

on I think that formula stands up well, but it is a theme I will elaborate on in a number of the chapters that follow. Leaving aside location, I am convinced that bait and bait application hold the entire key to successful carp fishing, and I am equally convinced that each individual angler must make his or her own assessment of the rights and wrongs of type and use of bait in his or her own special circumstances.

The realization brought about during the 'panel of experts' evening was emphasized soon after. I received an article by an aspiring carp angler who felt that his recent success was the basis for an article. He and a couple of his mates had gone to a local water for a night's fishing. Up with the bivvy, out with the rods, whack in 5lb of bait each. I wondered why they had done that even as I read the piece – and still wondered when I had finished it. No action during the night; one carp at ten in the morning just when they were packing up. Fifteen pounds of bait for one carp. You read; you analyse as you read. First thought was that they had put in far too much bait. Second thought was they they had put in the right amount of bait, and that the feeding spell on that water was from ten in the morning onwards. Either way, they had got it totally wrong the moment they set foot on the bank. Knowing when the carp feed is as big a part of the formula as knowing what they feed on, and where they feed on it. I am convinced that most carp anglers reduce their chances of catching within minutes of arriving at the lake through slavishly putting in too much bait as soon as they arrive to start their session.

Looking back over my own fishing I am quite certain I have made more mistakes over bait application than over any other aspect.

Given that the recognition of the diversity of the degrees of carp fishing practised by the growing legion of carp anglers started to filter into my thick skull five years or so ago, it took me quite some time to take the bull by the horns and actually direct an article towards what I now perceive to be the majority carp-fishing audience – the short session angler. What's a short session? Two nights downwards. Been there, done that. If I rarely fish sessions shorter than three nights now I have, like most of my fellow writers, paid my dues and suffered the pressure and frustration of long days travelling to, fishing and returning from day-only ticket waters. The next stage on in my fishing consisted of late Friday afternoon arrivals for sessions on ticket and syndicate waters, sessions which were terminated by the need to be back in harness by Monday morning at the latest – and preferably earlier if circumstances dictated me making at least a token effort at being a domestic human being.

I wrote of day-ticket and short-session considerations in an article entitled – somewhat bizarrely, I guess 'And Then I Went and Spoilt It All' in the January 1996 issue of *Carpworld*. Now as a rule, writers write in a sort of vacuum. You have to be your own biggest critic in terms of getting it right, because as a rule, the only time you get feedback is if someone disagrees with you, or you make an indefensible error. The article was one of those rare animals, one which brought an astonishing response because it was perceived to be helpful! Over a period of twenty years I have become something of a realist in terms of assessing the validity of my own material, and I consider that the article was no better, and no worse, than many technical pieces I have written. Why the startling response then? Apparently because it was directed at a much bigger percentage of the readership than I'd visualized when I sat down to write it, and secondly because it was possibly a percentage which was starved of material dealing with their specific set of problems.

The audience reaction made me sit down and reassess the direction of my own writing. I am certainly not alone in understanding that each season, each water, each session (and even each fish) present their own sets of problems, and that these problems then have to be considered in the light of the available time and finance scale. Writing for a magazine, even on a regular basis, is limiting with a subject as diverse and changeable as trying to catch carp. My writing is, inevitably, coloured by my own experiences. I fish as much as possible, but I now recognize that my fishing mirrors that of a more limited percentage of the readership than I thought. I started to form a clearer picture of the type of material I had to write to reach as wide a cross-section of the carp-fishing public as possible, and the only way I could present that material in one volume was in a book.

Crowood have published my two previous technical books, *Carp Fishing*, 1988 and *Big Carp*, 1990. Early in 1996, I rang that lovely man John Dennis and asked him if there was room in his publishing company's portfolio for another Paisley technical treatise on carp fishing. There was, and this is it. My original brief for *Carp Fishing* was 25,000 words. The final wordage was increased by negotiation, and while I have an abiding affection for what was my first published book, its size, my own experience and the stage carp fishing itself had reached at the time, all limited the scope of the book.

Big Carp is a lovely book, mainly because of the spectacular line-up of high-profile writers who kindly supplied a large percentage of the material. And again, while I was more than happy with the end product, the timing of the book was something of a frustration. The chapter 'Big Fish Summer' spells out the fact that I was coming to terms with new methods after a period of comparative inactivity. Towards the end of the chapter I had this to say about my experiences on the Mangrove:

On the Mangrove just once or twice I felt I was unlucky, and we all feel like that periodically when we are fishing for the big fish. But when I sit down and analyse it all dispassionately, the noticeable thing is that my bad luck almost always comes when I am not really on top of what I am doing.

An 'unlucky' season is often the prelude to a very, very good one, as long as you learn from the experiences and the frustrations you suffer. When you switch methods, or bait, the 'fine tuning' can make all the difference between success and failure.

I knew at the time that I was coming to terms with catching carp on a consistent basis, and since that summer I have had a series of successful seasons, summer and winter. I have total belief in the baits and the methods I use, and while I have detailed the basis for success in some magazine articles, I am pleased to have this opportunity to spell them out in permanent record form. Pressure changes carp, and while what I have referred to in the past as the 'variables' (the changing aspects of carp fishing we each have to analyse and come to terms with ourselves) have to be continually assessed to keep one thought ahead of the carp, I have come to recognize that there are certain ongoing situations and tactics to which the carp has little defence.

Tackle has improved immeasurably. The bait boffins have made all things possible on the bait front. Throwing sticks and bait rockets have developed from being fringe benefits to being absolute musts in the carp-fishing armoury. There are more carp, more carp waters, and an increasing army of very talented carp anglers who devote long periods of their young and energetic lives to the catching of monster fish. Yes, I know; they are the minority. Most of you want to know how you can catch your share of the carp in the limited time you have available, and on a budget which takes account of the fact that some priority has to be given to the running of a family and home – and which is not subsidized to the tune of a thousand pounds plus per annum in bait and tackle!

Hopefully, what follows will cater for the requirements of most carp anglers. In fact, the group I can offer least help to is the one which contributes most of the carp-fishing material you read in the magazines – the young tigers who drive themselves to the brink of penury and ill-health in pursuit of the monsters most of us will never aspire to. For the majority of us, carp fishing is a much simpler and demanding project than waging war on one or two target monster fish. Like most of you, when I am planning a season, or a session, my first objective is a simple one, reflected in this book's title: *To Catch a Carp*.

I am delighted that a number of carp anglers for whom I have a very high regard have contributed chapters to the book. Rod Hutchinson, Kevin Nash, Martin Clarke, Mike Willmott, Rob Hughes and Simon Crow, Paddy Webb and Frank Warwick are all consistently successful carp anglers and writers. Their specialized chapters cover subjects I feel I lack the experience and knowledge to cover in depth, and their expertise in the fields they cover in the book make this as complete a technical book on carp fishing as I feel it reasonable to put together at this time.

I look on all these contributors as being at the top of the tree. Their accumulated knowledge and experience of carp fishing is massive and we can all learn a great deal from them. The carp angler's worst enemies are indecision, lack of confidence and lack of belief. You must buy knowledge and experience with time. Banks are the currency and the experience is based on the successful analysis of results – good or bad. Readers must understand that every contributor to this book and to magazines sits at the back of a set of rods just as they do. Before they get to the water they have done everything in their power to make catching a probability. They then cast out and hope, and think, and analyse and agonise. Reputations count for nothing to the carp. Cast out and you are on your own. Not catching is part of the learning curve on the route to writing about catching. Everyone has spells when they don't catch.

I'm labouring that point because I think some carp anglers want too much help and expect too much too soon of their carp fishing. They don't understand that for all of us the bottom line is sweating it out behind a set of rods and learning the hard way. There is a very fine line between success and failure, and some of you will be very close to success without realizing it and without knowing that you are making progress. Whatever help you get from magazines and videos and books can only make you successful on the basis of your own observations and analysis. Becoming successful creeps up on you. The buzzer that never sounded starts to sound occasionally, but to start with it might only be the difference between not at all and once a weekend. In carp-fishing terms, that can be a lot. Getting it right for one fish is the starting point to getting it right con-sistently – as long as you understand why it has started to happen in terms of why it hadn't been happening.

That is the basis of understanding, which is what this book tries to promote. Somewhere in here there will be the key to open your mind to a greater understanding of catching carp.

Experience and knowledge are hard earned, but understanding can come to you in an instant, as startling as the enlightenment of Paul on the road to Damascus. I can put my finger on two such moments in my twenty-six years of carp fishing. The first was Andy Little referring to bait as a 'food source' when we were putting together the *Carp Baits* video. The second was seeing a carp head and shoulder in what I sud-denly realized must be a feeding spot. I'd known about bait being a food source for years; I'd know about carp visiting regular feeding spots for years. But I hadn't understood.

I hope that somewhere in what follows there will be something that helps you understand just what it is you have to do to catch a carp.

Reputations count for nothing to the carp. Cast out and you are on your own.

2 BASIC APPROACH

I am quite sure, from talking to people and from correspondence, that carp fishing for the majority of what we can loosely refer to as 'carp anglers' is bivvying up behind a carp-rod set-up. I am not going to try to defend that to those on the fringes of carp fishing who are critical of the concept of modern carping. I get a bit bored by pompous bleatings that a proper carp angler stalks his prey, is adept with floaters and would not dream of sleeping behind the rods. That is a minority view, and as none of us is going to try to condemn stalkers and floater anglers (I do both anyway) I don't go along with the minority condemnation of the buzzer and bivvy life.

Bivvying out by the water not only captures the imagination, but it is a pleasant way of life, too. To me, and thousands like me, it is carp fishing. The trouble is that it is not always the most effective way of catching. The stalkers and the floater fishers are right. We should get off our butts more often, ease our way into the middle of the odd bramble bush and lower a tasty morsel onto the nose of the big carp we are likely to stumble on in the bramble margins. But many choose not to. Carp fishing is the great escape: an escape to hours and days of nothingness but existing and carp fishing. It is the way the majority of us carp fish, largely through choice, but very often because it's a choice that's forced on us by bankside pressure and a noticeable absence of obliging fish haunting the margins or willing to take floaters.

The difficulty is that because static carp fishing is an inefficient method of catching carp, the angler has to have a considerable understanding of what is happening out in the water in front of him, out of sight. Success or failure in bivvy-session fishing stems from the degree of understanding, or successful guessing, the angler achieves. To understand he has to have an accumulation of knowledge, experience, tactical awareness and intuition which enable him to anticipate the likely reactions of his carp to what has gone before on the water, what is happening at that precise moment, and what is going to happen in the immediate and long-term future.

There's nothing very original in what I have said there. It has all been said before, but it's the guts of carp fishing and can't be emphasized enough. Trouble is it is not what some of you want to read. Give us a rig, give us a bait: that's what carp fishing's all about. Given the right rig, and the right bait, you think you'll conquer the world, which misses the point. You will not. Without understanding, you will fish from crisis to crisis, achieving the odd temporary success when the carp get very silly, or you stumble on a temporary solution through desperation.

Give us a bait. No sweat. I'll give you a few, in fact, and we will revisit the subject at greater length shortly. Big Fish Mix, Grange CSL Mix, Lockey's Savay Seed Mixes, Nashy's Sting or 'S' Mix, Hutchy's this that or the other ... I could pick up the phone to any bait dealer in the country and put together a bait in which I would have confidence for the season ahead, provided I knew something about the water I was going to fish, and the methods and baits which had put the carp in that water under any sort of pressure over the preceding seasons. That's the first consideration. For instance, fishmeals. They are prolific carp catchers, some better than others. If you are going to use them, you want to know what their track record is on the water in question. Are they going, or blowing? Good fishmeal baits have a long life, and it is not always easy to pick up the signs when their effectiveness is diminishing, but such is their effective life that I am inclining to the opinion that it is the attractors which blow a bait, not the base mix itself. (I am singling out fishmeal baits here because they can make life much simpler for a confused carp angler. Carp get on them quickly, and stay on them.)

I have seen conflicting opinions about the importance and effectiveness of prebaiting, and it's important to understand why there are differing opinions on this very basic subject. In a nutshell, all baits don't go on catching over a period of time. Inadequate food value or overstrong attractors can drastically reduce the life of a bait. Once you have chosen a bait, it will help your confidence – and your results – if you can get to prebait and assess the reaction of the carp to the bait over a period of time. There is a reaction cycle of carp to a newly introduced bait, which it helps to understand.

Given that most of us are fishing fairly pressured waters, the carp will start by feeding on a newly introduced bait with cautious curiosity. When you are putting the first baiting into the water, don't introduce it all at once; introduce it gradually. Start with fifteen to twenty baits, then build up. Why? Because it helps to encourage an element of competitive feeding from the start. Put out a thousand baits at a time and a shoal of carp can take their time browsing over and snacking at the baits. A steady introduction of bait over the course of a day builds up the competition element, and the degree of enthusiasm for the bait too. The first day you introduce the bait you will probably come away with the impression that the fish are eating the bait, but probably without sufficient enthusiasm to get caught on it – at that stage. If the carp show excessive enthusiasm about the bait the first time in I have reservations that the attractors may be too strong for a long-term bait.

In prebaiting, you want a build up of enthusiasm for the bait. You are demonstrating to the carp that what you are offering them is a food source, and building up their confidence in feeding on that food source by making it readily available to them. 'Familiarity breeds contempt.' Individual carp will vary enormously in the degree of familiarity with, or confidence in, a bait they need to have before they will accept one attached to your end tackle. Some fish will be catchable on the first bait they encounter; some may be cautious about the first hundred; others the first thousand; others will never pick up a bait, even though they may be present with other members of their shoal eating this strange food source. If it doesn't smell like food, the carp will not treat it as a food. Some carp are virtually uncatchable because they are cute; others because they just don't recognize baits as food.

The more times the carp are able to eat your bait in an unpressured situation the more confidence they will develop in it – provided it is an acceptable food source in the first place. If you want examples of the success of prebaiting and continued baiting Ian Booker's interview in *Carp Fisher 12* spells it out. My successful summer of 1992 described in *From the Bivvy* was also based on a steady baiting campaign, although in my case I was using Nutrabaits' Big Fish Mix, which was already established on the water. In that instance, I wanted the carp to become addicted to my own version of a bait that a percentage of the fish had already accepted as a food source. Carp-fishing literature is littered with stories of successful baiting campaigns, and most of my carp-fishing confidence comes from fishing with a bait I know the carp have accepted as a food source.

Don't get confused about the reason for establishing a food source. I am not talking about prebaiting a swim here. When I prebait, I apply the bait to three or four favoured swims, and I start when the water is warm enough for the fish to be feeding strongly. I don't prebait an individual swim within three or four days of going fishing unless I know for certain I am going to be fishing that swim. Once the season gets under way, all my baiting up is done while I am fishing, or as I leave the water (in the latter case provided no one is following me into the swim, or is fishing an adjacent swim).

The more enthusiastic the carp become about your bait, the more avidly they will feed on it.

But be warned. Establishing a bait does not guarantee immediate success. Carp will eat bait most days, but there is a big difference between carp feeding on a bait and carp feeding strongly enough to get caught. An established bait gives you the confidence to catch, but it is very much a starting point. Bivvy angling is built on confidence. You know the carp will feed on your bait if you can get it in the right place in the right conditions. You have to know the bait is acceptable because getting the rest of the equation right is not anything like a foregone conclusion.

It may help to consider the reasons for a bait not continuing to work over a period of time, or never being taken by the carp with the required degree of confidence – or enthusiasm – for you to consistently catch them. I see a certain amount of scepticism about the long-term/short-term bait concept, but I have got total acceptance of it, as have many others. On the other hand, I accept that anyone new to carp baits must find this categorizing of baits difficult to come to terms with. Briefly, I'll explain why your bait may not work as well as you want it to in the certain knowledge that many of you will have grave doubts about some of what follows!

Look at it this way. To pressured fish, a new bait may be a potential source of danger until acceptance, then confidence, is achieved through familiarity. The three main reasons for a bait never being fully accepted as a food source are:

1. Inadequate food value, which means that the bait is relying mainly on the strength of the attractors to produce results. 'Inadequate food value' does not necessarily mean too low a protein level. Carp need protein, vitamins and minerals, fats, and a limited carbohydrate provision. Attractors make bait smell like food. An apparent food source which fails to live up to the promise the attractors make can have a limited life and lead to a reducing level of enthusiasm in the carp's feeding on it.
2. Too many additives, too high a flavour level and the addition of preservatives, may limit the life of a bait. Results may be immediate, then become spasmodic, then fade away.

These baits can work early in a long session, then stop working. If the additive levels are not acceptable to the carp, then the food value will not matter. The carp are reacting against the overloading of artificial, unnatural ingredients. Be warned. This can happen immediately, within days, or within weeks.

3. Underfeeding. If you want your bait to be accepted as a food source, you have to convince the carp of its value as a food, which means introducing enough of it on a regular enough basis for the carp to reach the acceptance stage, then the enthusiasm stage. When you are fishing against established baits, it may take longer for you to break down the carp's resistance to a new, suspicious food source. The more different baits there are going into a water, the more confusing the situation is to the carp, and the longer you may have to persevere to achieve the sort of results you are after.

Have a clear idea of exactly what you are after – what you are trying to achieve through your prebaiting. What I am after is, that when the carp finally encounters my hook bait it will give a sigh of relief and say to itself 'Ah, here's another one!' You are trying to achieve what Roger Smith describes as 'A momentary lapse in concentration', on the part of the carp, which is not to suggest that prebaiting is the only way to achieve this rewarding moment, but it is certainly a way, and it is the way my carp fishing and that of many other carp anglers is based around.

On most waters, a prebaiting campaign need not mean the introduction of huge quantities of bait. Use your common sense. A regular introduction of a pound of bait every few days into known feeding or holding areas may well suffice, but the less bait you introduce at any one time, the longer you want to keep it going in before you start fishing with it. Feed your local birds if you have any doubts about the value of prebaiting. Birds react very quickly to a new food source. Make nuts or seeds available to them on a regular basis and there will be a fairly rapid build up of different species feeding on your offerings – some of which you will not have seen in the garden before. But if the local cat is waiting for them the first time they come to feed, they may never accept your offerings as a food source. The appearance of the odd cat after a week or two may make them wary, but will not necessarily scare them off. A series of bad experiences with the cat may well result in them shunning your offerings, even though they are still perfectly valid as a food source.

It is not too difficult to convert this situation to carp and baits. The end tackle is the cat, and if there is end tackle in the swim the first time you introduce the bait, it will make the carp edgy. Catch one at the first time of asking and their resistance will start to build up. The greater their confidence in the food source by the time you start fishing for them, the less adversely they will be affected by captures. And once you start catching, it is essential that you keep the bait going in. This is where the introduction of bait at the end of a session comes into its own. It is a particularly effective tactic where pressure is concentrated into the weekend period. The carp are aware of the presence of anglers, and in normal circumstances react adversely to the 'weekend pressure syndrome'. More noise, more pressure, more beds of bait, more bait available. Keep the bulk of your bait in a freezer box for a prebaiting session as you are leaving the water. It's my experience that weekend anglers cannot get off the water quickly enough once Sunday morning comes. This works massively to the advantage of anyone who recognizes the period of reducing pressure as the ideal baiting-up time. Late Friday afternoon arrivals often have to set up not on the fish, but close observation of the happenings on the water over the weekend should make the location of the fish clear to you. This gives you the chance to bait up where the fish are, and leave them to gain more confidence in the bait in an unpressured situation.

Establishing this tactic as an essential part of your fishing will enable you to fish with a minimum of bait the following weekend, and you will soon find that stringers or single baits strategically placed will bring you far better results than the mandatory mix or two fired in over nervous fish on Friday afternoon or Friday evening, at a time when a number of other well-meaning anglers are busily firing in their mandatory mix or two of baits. Do not then become confused by the success of the 'single-bait or stringer syndrome'. If it starts to work, it is because you have established your bait and have kept making it available to the fish. The more successful your bait becomes, the more important it becomes to keep it going into the water. In these circumstances, the success of the single hookbait or stringer is simply a manifestation of the 'Ah, here's another one!' tactic.

To some of you it may seem that I am labouring this concept of establishing a successful bait, but I know how essential it can be for consistent success. I've watched carp at Birch Grove feeding on bait during the close season when they are under no pressure, and on occasions have been astonished at their reactions to baits and baiting situations. One particular close season three or four years back stands out in my memory. I wanted to start the season on fishmeals, and introduced two different versions (different attractors) to ensure that I came up with a version which would be accepted by the carp over a period of time. Both versions were readily eaten by the carp on the first introduction, and over the first weekend (I was down for Mangrove and Birch Grove work parties) they got through 10lb of bait, which was introduced forty or fifty baits at a time. By the third weekend, the reaction to one version of the bait was far stronger than to the other which, rightly or wrongly, I presumed was down to unacceptable attractor levels in the less-favoured version. I dropped that version and continued baiting up with the favoured one.

At this stage of the close season, the gin-clear water was starting to colour up slightly through bottom-feeding activity, and when I went down the weekend before the start of the season, I expected this coloration to be intensifying. It wasn't. The water was gin-clear again, a cool wind from the north-west having apparently slowed down the build up of feeding activity. When I started introducing bait into the designated viewing spots, it became apparent that feeding activity had almost stopped! The bait they had been coming straight in on and tearing up the bottom for the previous weekend lay for twenty minutes before a single carp came in to investigate. There was no end tackle in the swim and the carp had been feeding on the bait for well over a month by this time, but the first carp in started rolling baits around with its nose to test them for safety! Seriously discouraging. Enthusiasm built up as more carp started appearing, and while they didn't get round to tearing up the bottom that day, they did keep eating enough of the bait to convince me that I'd got a valid food source, and that their reluctant feeding was caused by the conditions. On the other hand, it has to be said that I didn't see one carp taking bait with enough enthusiasm to have got caught in an angling situation. Feeding activity just was not strong enough to cause that momentary lapse in concentration which leads to a carp making a mistake and getting itself hooked up.

Such had been the enthusiasm for the bait during the previous month that I'd no doubt it was a winner, as the start of season results later proved, but the thought of those lethargic carp being affected by the cool north-west wind always reminds me (as if I need any reminding) that when it comes to catching carp, all we can do is stack the odds as strongly as possible in our favour, then wait for the carp to complete the equation. Understanding that they can be totally switched off is as important an element in the static carp-fishing battle of wits as understanding what it is that makes them catchable in the first place.

What does the word 'bait' bring into your mind? Probably different things to different people, depending on your carp-fishing involvement. But I think it is fair to say that to the majority of the readership 'bait' will mean boilies of a fairly standard size (in the 18–20mm range) probably laced with one of a limited number of successful flavours. You only have to read the numerous catch reports in the weekly *Carp-Talk* to confirm that fairly uniform tactics are being used from area to area and water to water. And why not? Over the past ten years or so, variations on this limited theme have accounted for the capture of thousands of carp in this country and abroad.

But it may make life easier for you if you recognize that prebaiting and fishing are two different animals. When you are prebaiting, you are trying to establish a food source, and it helps if you narrow the range of fish feeding on the bait to those fish you hope to catch on the bait. Alan Smith of Kent first alerted me to the tactic of prebaiting with tennis-ball size of baits. This was on the Tip Lake at Darenth in the early 1980s, and Alan was using HNV baits and essential oils. His close-season baiting was done with very big baits to minimize the attentions of the Tip Lake tench which love HNV baits and essential oils (as do eels). Once the season started, Alan reverted to baits of 18mm, but his prebaiting campaign had done the job, and his first five fish of the season were all carp in excess of 26lb.

I have used the Grange Mix with CSL for most of my fishing during the last couple of seasons, and when I came to bait-up during one close season, I copied Alan's tactics – because I know that virtually every species of fish that swims is just as enthusiastic about the Grange with CSL as carp are! The tactic worked just as well for me as it did for Alan, and I had my best start ever fishing Birch and the Mangrove on the back of the big bait baiting campaign, reverting to more normal-sized baits for my actual fishing.

I now extend this tactic through into my winter fishing too. I use tiny baits for most of my cold-weather carping, but I bait-up with 18mm baits when I am leaving the water in the hope that they will survive the attentions of the bream. I think this question of differentiating between the food source and the angling situation is important. The carp is recognizing the bait by its smell. Size, colour, shape and application are angling considerations, and my preferred carp trap is a small bed of tiny baits, a situation we will discuss at greater length in Chapters 13, 17 and 29.

To achieve the sort of results you will be seeking in a variety of situations, you are going to have to give thought to the application of your chosen food source: in other words, the baiting situation. Carp fishing is very convenient when

Alan Smith from Dartford in Kent, a consistent catcher of big fish and an angler with invaluable and original ideas on prebaiting and ongoing bait application principles.

the carp are responding to a bed of 18mm baits within range of a powerful catapult, or throwing stick, and that will be the limit of the thinking and capabilities of many of you. Here are some of the alternative situations that you may have to consider, and should be able to cope with.

1. Your normal baiting situation at ranges up to 100 yards. A catapult will not achieve this. You need a bait rocket (spod) or a throwing stick. If you can't make 100 yards with 18mm baits from a throwing stick (some baits are denser than others) scale up to bigger baits. If you cannot use a throwing stick, then learn. It is an essential part of the carp-fishing armoury.
2. You need a marker float and a spod rod. These two additions to your armoury can be almost as important as the rods you fish with, because they make catching on them possible. The

modern bait rockets will achieve over 100 yards comfortably, and you do not need a beach caster to use them. I am happiest spodding with an 11–12ft rod of 3–4lb test curve, the model I use being called the Spodnik, designed and built by Alan Young, who designed and builds my Carpseeker rod range.
3. A scattering of boilies at whatever range has a limited life as a successful baiting situation, however effective the bait. Once situations of this type are showing signs of passing their sell-by date, change to one of the other proven successful baiting situations, which include:
   • Fishing with or over hemp or other seeds. Most effective in the margins where you can keep topping up the swim, or where you can use a boat to bait up, but a bait rocket will enable you to fish this method up to about 100 yards.

Four-rod set-up. Two rods fishing, plus a marker rod and a spod rod. The marker and spod rods make it possible for the other rods to catch.

- There are plenty of alternatives to hemp available now, both in seed and pellet form. I have had success over Hinders Partiblend, Nashy's Ball Pellet and Micromass (my own favourite background feed) and various types of pellets, including those marketed by Rod Hutchinson, Quality Baits, and Reponse Pellets marketed by Mainline.
- Scaling down the size of the boilies to make the carp work harder at its feeding. Keep an open mind as to the size of the baits which may be required to achieve the required reaction: 14mm baits are an easy option, but may not be small enough to encourage the required preoccupation. I have been using baits as small as 4–6mm in much of my fishing over the last few years, with consistently successful results.
- Read up on the various groundbait articles that have appeared in the last few years. Ken Townley has contributed a great deal

of thinking on this front, and you can either follow his ideas, or adapt them to your own line of thinking. Crumb is popular but is difficult (and messy) to fish at range without a boat. I like the concept of baits that break down very quickly, as with many of the pellets and with Micromass. They are easy to use with the bait rocket mixed with groats, hemp or other seeds, or on their own, or in combination, with PVA bags.

I am skimming the surface here in outlining a few baiting alternatives. The important thing is that you find a bait and a baiting situation which suits you, in which you have total confidence, then fine tune the method until it produces the sort of results you are trying to achieve. The fine-tuning part is important because it is what makes your method different from all the other methods in use. It is your edge, based on your own originality. If all your fishing is based slavishly on ideas in books and articles, then you will always be fishing with the ideas of others. Recognize that a great many of the carp you are fishing for will only fall to a situation that includes an element of surprise, and the more unique the surprise element is in your own fishing, the better your results are likely to be.

Each time you go to the water, remind yourself that there will be a limited number of carp in front of you willing to get caught. The more predictable your baiting situation is, the easier you make it for the carp not to get caught. You have got to make the fish careless. Getting inside their heads from a static bivvy situation is an exercise in observation, calculation, application and – once the hard work is done – anticipation. The more pressured the carp become, the greater your own personal edge in bait effectiveness, baiting situation and hookbait surprise will have to be.

A number of friends commented that they were disappointed by the literary content of my last book, 'From the Bivvy', which is fair enough comment, but rather misses the point of the book. It was actually intended as a practical book to assist the bivvy-bound carper in his or her thinking, and the whole approach to their fishing. Like any other practical book it becomes dated, but the methods described caught me a lot of fish during the nine months in question. The fact that I have since had to think it out again as I go along is just a reflection of the way in which pressure affects carp. What has happened for the past two or three seasons on your waters is not necessarily a basis for your fishing for the season ahead: it is the basis on which to plan the changes you may have to make to keep one step ahead of the build up of caution in the carp caused by captures and the operation of the pressure cycle.

Bivvy life behind the rods; the favourite form of carp fishing for many.

3 SOME PAINLESS BAIT THEORY

Some carp anglers want to know something of the theory behind the effectiveness of carp baits. Others just want a bait which will work. This is the first of a group of chapters on bait (*see also* Chapters 4 to 6), dealing with the theoretical and practical principles behind successful baits, and dwelling on some of the considerations which need to be applied when it comes to designing a bait to do a specific job for you.

I think it is entirely natural to be intrigued by the wonders of carp being stimulated by and attracted to certain substances (and combinations thereof) and the phenomenon of nutritional recognition, which is the natural instinct for recognizing what is and what is not food. This is not to suggest that to catch carp you have to understand anything about bait, science, nutrition, digestion, fish physiology or the numerous other aspects of science related to the workings of nature. You do not have to know anything about these subjects, but some people get pleasure from trying to understand something about them, and others feel that in some circumstances, having a little understanding of the basics principles involved does help.

The change from maggots and casters to the world of carp baits can be a traumatic one. It was for me, and I see the necessary change having a similar effect on others. There is a confusion in the mind between our feeding principles and those of the carp (and many other natural creatures). We are sight feeders and feed on what we are taught to eat. Carp are instinctive feeders, their recognition and location of food being largely based on smell. That's it in a nutshell.

I was nearer forty than thirty when I first read the marvellous writings of Fred Wilton in the *Third BCSG Book*, but I didn't think they were particularly marvellous at the time. In fact I thought Fred's theory that carp would respond to a food source which fulfilled its natural nutritional requirements was a load of cobblers, and said so at some length in a *Coarse Angler* article 'Protein, Carbohydrate or Just Food?' which was published in 1977. In retrospect, the article was a stunningly ignorant appraisal of the situation because at the time I did not even know the difference between a protein and a carbohydrate. I suspect that is the position many aspiring carp nutritionists find themselves in when they want to explore the carp-bait minefield.

When we argue that nutritional recognition in carp is not possible, or logical, we are actually saying that to our intelligent minds such a highly developed thought process is not possible. That's right, because it is not a thought process. It is a survival instinct bestowed on carp by nature, and many wild creatures have this same instinct. In fact, the lower the life form and the lower the level of intelligence the more necessary an instinctive recognition of food becomes. I spent some head-banging months reading up on nutritional recognition back in the 1970s and the most extreme example I found was of a type of African ant which needed to eat one plant to provide themselves with the necessary enzyme to obtain the necessary nutrients from another form of plant, the second plant containing their main dietary requirement. Their instincts dictated to them what they should eat, not their intelligence. So it is with carp.

In the mid-1970s, I had a problem which has been eroded by time. I read the writings of Wilton and duly trotted off to the reference library to read up on his radical, heretical theory that carp could recognize and in some way assess the value of a food source. Nowhere in the library was there a book which mentioned nutritional recognition or any similar phenomenon. In fact, it was almost impossible to find a textbook that made any mention of carp in those days.

I realized that I would have to come to terms with an understanding of nutrition if I was to understand the phenomenon of the recognition of same, so I set about making myself familiar with those expressions which slipped so easily and so authoritatively off Fred's pen. I needed to understand what proteins, carbohydrates, fats, vitamins and minerals were, what their functions were, and what foodstuffs fell into the various categories.

Learning about human nutrition is the starting point, provided you bear in mind that carp nutrition and human nutrition, while having the same basics and many similarities, are different. The main difference is a subtle one and is still an area for lively debate among those who claim to have some understanding of carp nutrition, but keep confusing me by repeatedly displaying in print that their knowledge and understanding is flawed.

I have not found a better book on the subject of nutrition than Magnus Pyke's *Success in Nutrition*. This is a paperback in the 'Success Study-books' series and was first published in 1975 by John Murray, 50 Albermarle Street, London W1X 4BD. If you can get hold of a copy it will spell out all you need to know about human nutrition in an easily read format. Find it, read it, digest it, but remember that there are two major differences between humans and carp. Carp do not have a stomach, which reduces their efficiency with the sort of solids our stomach acids will break down, and they do not have the same metabolic (nutrient conversion) system that we have when it comes to converting carbohydrates to energy. The carp's nutritional requirement for carbohydrates is very limited compared to ours and fats are their prime energy source.

Grasping that there are a very limited number of categories of nutrients in the range of foods available is revealing in that you soon realize that many of the bait ingredients you see listed are in fact duplications of each other. For a functional nutritional bait, you need quality protein, vitamins and minerals, and a quality fat source. Is

that it? You may well ask! Yes, that is it, in nutritional terms. In attraction and stimulation terms, in angling terms, in physical bait property terms, you are only just beginning, but in nutritional terms it really is as simple as that.

You will see percentages quoted whenever a bait debate develops in the carp press. Forget them. Percentages quoted are based on dietary requirements, and most carp waters see such a cross-section of baits that, as a rule, the ideal percentages of the various nutrients are not achieved. Guidelines are: 1 per cent of the diet to be vitamins and minerals in the approved quantities quoted in the table; 25–50 per cent protein, depending on the quality and the percentage which survives the preparation of the bait; and 10–20 per cent fats (largely oils), again depending on the quality and the survival rate. There have been instances where recommended dietary percentages were exceeded through common usage of a bait, or a type of bait. This happened with the excessive use of peanuts (which I would cheerfully ban from all carp waters), and the excessive use of fish oils in fishmeal baits, but as a rule, the diversity of baits in use and the availability of natural food reduce the chances of exceeding a dietary percentage to a minimum.

What does the balance of the bait consist of if the essential nutritional requirements add up to 70 per cent at the very most? Oddly enough I have never seen any of the percentage quoters address that particular conundrum! The answer is that there is inevitably a great deal of carbohydrate in most baits which goes to waste, which is why low food-value baits are referred to as 'crap baits', because that's what carp do with them. It is what we all do with the wastage in our diets.

How do you advance your bait knowledge from there? I am not going to repeat the technical material contained in the huge bait chapter in *Big Carp* here, but I do think there is much valuable information in that chapter. From there I would recommend that you hitch your wagon to the carp periodicals and the bait company catalogues. Many of these companies are run by carp anglers with a very comprehensive grasp of what makes up a good bait, what the dietary composition of the individual ingredients is, and what the thinking is behind each item which is included in the bait. Nutrabaits have formed Club Nutrabaits (at an annual subscription of £2.00!) and aim to publish a periodical bait magazine to keep their members informed and instructed, plus fact sheets on various technical and practical aspects of bait. The writings of Fred Wilton were the starting point on bait, and the principles he discussed are still very valid, but the material does date back well over twenty years, since which time knowledge has advanced, ingredients have improved, and there has been a shift in emphasis in the evaluation of ingredients and the composition of baits.

In addition to the bait catalogues, many of the bait barons write for the carp periodicals on a regular basis, including contributors to this book Rod Hutchinson, Kevin Nash and Mike Willmott, who are renowned for their knowledge of bait and their successes on their own bait recipes.

Besides the written word, there are a couple of super videos available which are devoted solely to carp baits. Angling Publications have a two-hour *Carp Baits* epic which features some of the leading lights in the carp-bait world and takes a comprehensive look at the theory, making and use of carp baits. In addition, Nutrabaits have a one-hour bait video which is well worth watching and will be very enlightening for those of you who are new to the carp-bait confusion.

Much of the published work on the carp's reactions to amino acids and related chemicals which have been shown to trigger a feeding reaction in carp have been published in the form of scientific papers, some of the more enlightening papers having also been collected together and published in book form. Toshiaka J. Hara has long been recognized as the leading authority in this particular field and he has compiled two books of research papers, details of which are shown in the Appendix to this chapter. I am not sure how available these books are, but if you really want a copy I am sure you will get in touch with the publishers in an effort to track one down.

I wrote a great deal about the science of attraction, and the possible mechanics of nutritional recognition in the early to mid-1980s. This was an area I studied with massive intensity in an effort to understand how it was possible for this instinct to work. If you set off down the same trail I will warn you that you need a scientific background or you will become bogged down. Science passed me by at school. My powers of retention were – and still are – very limited, and I was never a very conscientious student anyway: smelling the roses was always more important to me than having any understanding of how they grew. But when I first started to take an interest in the theory of carp baits I became very curious about the instincts of carp, and I whiled away a few thousand hours of my life trying to grasp the mechanics of a concept that no one studies in detail because it just is not meaningful research.

The most important practical knowledge I have gained from struggling with books on fish physiology, biochemistry, biophysics, chemoreception, and so on, is that through ionization, a chemical relationship can exist between the carp's receptors and a solid. You will read vague descriptions of the effectiveness of attractors 'leeching out of the bait', or suggestions that the bait has to break down in some way for the carp to smell it. These concepts have validity but they are not the full picture by any means. How do you smell a rose? It emits chemicals and your receptors recognize the chemical cue (the smell). The rose does not dissolve, nor does scent, or aftershave. Fish and chips have to be warm for you to smell them, but they are not breaking down, and you do not have to see them to know where they are, or what they are.

Water is 'liquid air', and the carp is made aware of its food sources in just the same way that we recognize and are able to identify certain smells. Attractors react with water to trigger the food scent, but they do not necessarily dissolve in it. That is the basis of attraction and stimulation. To me it is logical that the best attractors somehow mirror the smell of a carp's food sources. Not exactly, or all carp would eat boilies, but closely enough for boilies to have become an almost natural food source to thousands of carp over the last few years.

Knowing what food smells like is one thing. Accepting the presence of an instinct which enables the carp to actually assess the value of the food it eats in nutritional terms, is a different matter. But in theory, it is easily enough explained. Humans experience hunger, and that hunger is appeased by eating. We have a stomach which we fill with food and our hunger goes. To me, hunger in carp is a nutritional need, and they eat to appease their nutritional hunger. A diet which fulfils their nutritional needs will appease their hunger. A diet which doesn't, won't.

There has been much argument about the respective values of various carp baits, but on no water I fish has there ever been enough of one bait introduced for it to have had a chance of becoming the food source for the water. It is my experience from observing capture patterns and the contents of carp sacks that when carp feed, they take on board most food sources that are available to them. Through experience they will learn that some food sources are more prized than others. Where this applies to baits those they most readily accept will be those on which they are at the greatest risk of being caught.

I will repeat that it is not necessary to have any of this knowledge to catch carp, but acquiring the knowledge is a harmless enough pastime for those who have got to take the theory of baits further than simply knowing what will catch carp. For me, having a clear picture of why something catches is an enormous help in understanding short-term, long-term and seasonal variations in the effectiveness of a bait. In many minds, there is some confusion between a food source and a smell source. For instance where does Strawberry Ethyl Alcohol flavour rate in a list of the carp's dietary requirements? The simple answer is that it does not rate at all. The flavour is the smell source and is used to draw attention to the bait, which is the food source. If the carrier of the flavour has little or no nutritional value the carp will, in time, start to disbelieve the message given by the flavour, the promised food source will be eaten with growing reluctance, and in time the effectiveness of the bait will diminish. We will look at the angling effects of this common situation in Chapters 4 and 6.

Suggested Reading

All written material on carp fishing may be valid to the line of thought and planning you are trying to pursue. *Carpworld* and other monthly magazines, *Carp-Talk*, and bait catalogues and rig books represent a wealth of up-to-date material which will keep you informed of recent developments.

I think I possess every carp book that has ever been published, and while I do not read them regularly, I know what is in them, and where to look if I have a problem which may have been covered in print by someone in the past.

It is with material in connection with fringe areas of carp fishing that readers have the greatest problems, particularly authoritative material on bait-related topics and sciences. The following is a guide to the areas which cover aspects of bait. This will almost certainly be minority reading, but will be of huge interest to that minority. This is an avenue I painstakingly travelled down for a few years of my carp-fishing life, and which I found engrossing and enlightening.

The books I list below may be difficult to get hold of now, or there may be more suitable literature available now. I was searching for relevant material ten to twenty years ago, and I am sure great progress will have been made with both sciences and literature in the meantime.

Aquaculture My source was *Recent Advances in Aquaculture*, but there will be up-dated sources. Aquaculture covers carp foods, and their nutrient breakdown percentages, and conversion rates in generalized fish-culture terms. This material was the forerunner of the bait world, but I suspect the bait world could be of more help to aquaculturists than vice versa these days.

Biochemistry This massive subject covers the scientific guts of the matter. Water, pH, ionization, amino acids, organic acids, fats, carbon chains, enzymes, etc. The function and classification of all these chemicals and elements are defined in biochemistry books. In 1981, Keith Sykes kindly gave me a copy of *Lehninger's*

Biochemistry, a huge volume which hurt my head for many years, but which enabled me to fit a few pieces into what is still an incomplete jigsaw. I think there will be lighter, equally comprehensive volumes available now. Water and pH are very difficult areas to come to terms with, but you need some understanding of them to have a grasp of the overall picture here.

Biophysics I cannot believe I wrestled with this area. I wanted to understand the actual mechanics of the workings of amino acids as a source of recognition, which is biophysics. To me this is the next-to-last piece in the jigsaw. Not recommended reading, but revealing if you can grasp the principles.

Chemoreception There is a wealth of material on research into the chemical recognition relationship between carp and their food sources. Chemoreception is, broadly speaking, underwater smell. Scientific papers cover substances and chemicals which stimulate the carp's food sensors at the receptor site. For many years Toshiaka J. Hara was the leading authority in this important research field, and he has published two fascinating collections of scientific papers, as follows:

Chemoreception in Fishes (1982). Published by Elsevier Scientific Publishing Company, P.O. Box 330, 1000 AH Amsterdam, The Netherlands.

Fish Chemoreception (1992). Published by Chapman & Hall, 2–6 Boundary Row, London SE1 8HN.

Fish Physiology My source was a book titled *Introduction to Fish Physiology* by Dr Lynwood S. Smith. There is some detailed carp-related material in it covering receptors, digestive systems and metabolism (food conversion), in addition to non-metabolic aspects. The book was published in 1982 by TFH Publications, their English outlet being TFH (Great Britain) Ltd. 13, Nutley Lane, Reigate, Surrey.

Nutrition Essential reading to an understanding of why carp need certain nutrients. My source was the brilliantly simple *Success in Nutrition* by ex-television science presenter Magnus Pyke. Explains the need for nutrients, what nutrients are, what nutrients various foodstuffs contain, and gives tables showing percentages of the vital acids, fats, etc. in the nutrients. It also explains the function of vitamins and minerals and enzymes.

Major booksellers and libraries are now fully computerized and can tell you if a book is available, or still in print, even if they do not stock it.

I summarized much of the above material, and categorized bait ingredients, in the big 'Bait' chapter in the Crowood book *Big Carp*, which is why I have not dealt with it as a separate chapter in this book.

In the paragraph on biophysics I mentioned the 'next-to-last piece' in the jigsaw, which was as far as I could get – in a very basic sort of way. For those interested, to me the last piece in the jigsaw is an area where there had been no published research into that I could find. This covers the identification of the receptor site, the linkage to the enzymes, and the actual scientific explanation of the simple mechanics of nutritional recognition. I managed to explain this in my head as a lock-and-key effect between the peptide chain of the food source and the peptide chain of the receiving enzyme. My thinking was that there can be nothing random about the sequence of the amino acids in proteins, which in turn may explain why some amino acids are massively significant to carp, while others have little or no significance at the receptor site.

The major problem inquisitive bait-buff carp anglers have here is that there is no single academic subject which embraces all the areas listed here, which is why all the threads have never been woven together by a scientific authority. It is an area waiting to be fully explored and fully explained and there is no reason why a carp angler should not produce a major scientific paper explaining a largely unexplained phenomenon. On the other hand, there may now be material linking all the above subjects together. Good hunting.

4 WHAT'S IN A BAIT? UNDERTONES AND OVERTONES

This chapter is an attempt to marry the theory of bait with some of the practicalities. As a rule, I want a bait to do two things. I want it to attract the carp to the bait, and I want it to fulfil the carp nutritionally when it eats the bait. In certain angling situations I will want the bait to fulfil a slightly different role. I will want it to attract the carp, then stimulate it into picking up the bait, with less thought given to the nutritional fulfilment once the bait has been taken.

As a session angler looking to have my baits in the water for long periods of time I am aware of a problem which goes far beyond the simple job of selecting a food-source bait, then adding an attractor, then fishing it. The problem is that a bait starts to change physically and chemically the moment it goes into the water. For instance; what is the effective life of your flavour once the bait has gone into the water? And given that a flavour attracts through ionization, at what point after you have put the bait into the water will it be at its most effective? Is there a point at which there is no attraction from the flavour, and at that point is the carp still attracted to the bait, and able to identify it as the bait you have conditioned it to accept? To have confidence in your bait you need some understanding of its make-up.

Through the 1980s when I was fishing over silt, these were the thoughts that started to bother me more and more, and started to focus my thinking on the physical properties of the bait and the attractors. I started to think of liquid flavours as overtones – instant and reducing in attraction – and bait ingredients as undertones, some of which are there for nutritional purposes, and some of which start to become a source of attraction once the bait has been in the water for some time. I stopped relying on the source of attraction

Bait making, a necessary chore. I always carry a variety of types of hookbait for making subtle changes in presentation, and to stop the carp trap from becoming too predictable. Here I'm making hookbaits, buoyant bottom baits and pop-ups.

as being an unstable liquid additive, and started focusing on ways of increasing the attractiveness of the base mix itself, by the addition of attractors other than flavours and ingredients with a reputation for attracting in their own right. I started to think of overtones as what comes out of the bait, and undertones as what stays in there and takes over as the source of attraction once the overtones have started to lose their effectiveness.

The theme of this book is that much of the writing about carp fishing that has gone before is minority oriented. This is confusing for those who are not part of the minority the advice is most suitable for. Bait is such an area. We all think of bait in certain convenient categories. But just how meaningful are those categories for your own type of carp fishing? Ready-made? Birdfood? Fishmeal? What do the various categories mean to you in terms of the job you may need your bait to do? Selection of the type of bait to be used tends to be random, and based on considerations which may, or may not, be meaningful in the context of the individual angler's bait needs.

Given just one basic bait mix, it is possible to come up with at least four different types of bait through permutation of the base mix, additives and attractors. Not four different baits, but four different types of bait designed to do different jobs. The type of bait most suited to your fishing will depend on a number of factors. I will identify just five of them.

- Length of session. It is no good fishing the weekend with a bait that gives its best results in the third or fourth day of use. Conversely, it is no good looking to spend a week in a swim with a high-powered attractor bait which will fish the swim out long before it is time for you to go home.
- When you are fishing overnight sessions, you must give some thought to the effectiveness of the bait at the time the carp are likely to feed on it, which might be at ten in the evening, or might be at ten the following morning.
- The actual physical properties of the bait may be just as important as the food content and the make-up of the attractors. Degree of pressure, fishing range, type of bottom and depth of water may all be determining factors when you are considering the size, density, colour and shape of your bait.
- How far away is the water you are going to fish, and how long will your sessions be? Certain baits need careful storage, and if you set out on a week-long session with a perishable

bait, you have to have freezer facilities built into your set-up, or available at or near the water you are going to fish.
- Attractiveness of the bait and the attractors to other species. This may not determine the actual bait you will use, but it may determine the size, and even the colour, where you have to try to minimize the attentions of bream, tench and eels.

The bottom line with bait is that you need it to catch fish in the circumstances in which you fish, and only you, and those familiar with your fishing and your water, can make a realistic assessment of those circumstances. I now find it impossible to think bait without thinking about the circumstances in which the bait will be used.

For the reasons enumerated above, I have always tried to write about bait in terms of principles rather than specifics. Grasp the principles, assess the likeliest type of bait for your own individual angling circumstances, then start considering the specifics.

When you are considering the make-up of a bait, there are up to eight categories of ingredients to consider. I'll itemize them, and make suggestions regarding those you are likely to find in a ready-made bait, or a ready-to-mix base mix, and those you may have to incorporate into your bait yourself.

The main categories of bait ingredients are:

- Basic food ingredients.
- Liquid food ingredients.
- Taste enhancers and other powdered stimulatory additives.
- Powdered food ingredients/attractors.
- Liquid attractors.
- Bulking ingredients.
- Preservatives.
- Vitamins and minerals.

Let us look at the various categories in greater detail.

1. Basic food ingredients include milk powders, egg powders, fishmeals, soya, blood, meat

and other bulk powders which form the base mix and add to the nutritional quality of the bait, but have limited or no attraction properties in their own right.

2. Liquid food ingredients (many of which have attraction properties): Minamino, Multimino, Corn Steep Liquor, Liquid Liver, Liquid Molasses, Cod Liver Oil, Fish Oils, Essential Oils, Vegetable Oils. The addition of any of these liquids adds to the food properties of the bait. Products like Minamino and Multimino appear under the brand name of many individual bait companies (you can smell the similarity), and there are other individual derivatives of liquid foods with added flavours or taste enhancers, like the Sense Appeal range, for instance. The important thing is to recognize that these are not flavours, they are attractors/foods, and are essential additives for increasing both the food value and the attraction properties of your bait.

3. Powdered taste additives: taste enhancers, which are added to the bait to evoke a response from the carp's taste receptors. These are based on those nucleotides which are known to be meaningful to the fish in identifying a food source. In our terms, these are to improve the taste of the bait. In carp feeding terms they are to improve the acceptability of the bait at the testing stage.

1. Powdered food ingredients/attractors: I will make clear the differentiation between these and the basic food ingredients. These are items which add to the food value and the attraction value, but are added to the bait at lower levels than the bulk ingredients itemized under category (1): they include crushed hemp, Robin Red, betaine, amino acids, powdered kelp, taste enhancers, molasses, dried seaweed, dried brewer's yeast, green-lipped mussel extract and various other extracts which are concentrated, and should be added to the bait in small quantities.

5. Liquid attractors: liquid flavours and taste enhancers. To my mind, they do one job in the bait, and that is to attract the fish to the smell source and help convince the fish that the bait is in fact food. Some flavours may have some food value but I look on these liquids as attractors which add little or nothing to the food value of the bait, and can detract from it if added at too high a level.

6. Bulking ingredients: no food can be 100 per cent nutritional, and a bait is no exception. There are a number of bulk ingredients in use in carp baits which are there to make up the balance of the 100 per cent. These may be added on the basis of cost limitation, or to make the bait mix and roll successfully: obvious examples are semolina and ground rice.

7. Preservatives: chemicals and sugars added to the ingredients to preserve the bait without having to freeze it. An example, in human terms, is the difference between long-life milk and fresh milk.

8. Vitamins and minerals: nutritional additives which may have some significance in terms of attraction. Most bait companies have a vitamin and minerals mix, or include one in their base mix. They are also available from health shops in tablet, powdered and capsule form, pet shops and farm shops. Many of the vitamin mixes available were originally designed for horses, dogs, pigeons or other household or farmyard animals or birds.

I will make a rough assessment of the various bait alternatives on offer, with some regard to the categories listed above. These descriptions are broadly based and some baits may offer more, or less, than I suggest here. These comments are concerned with principles rather than specifics. If you want to be absolutely specific about your own bait, you will design your own.

Ready-mades have to be competitively priced and easily prepared. Their structure is based on four main considerations. They have to be attractive to carp, they have to be competitively priced, they have to be physically structured so they can be rolled by machine (although not all ready-mades are rolled by mass production machines) and they have to be preserved. These considerations mean that most ready-mades are high on liquid attraction and taste stimulation, low on food value, high on preservatives and long on shelf life. The liquid attraction gives a promise of food, the taste stimulants give short-term confirmation of the presence of food, the preservatives are necessary to stop the bait from going off, the bulk ingredients are of limited food value.

Ready-mades may tend to have a short life as a bait. For the most part, they will not be good overnight baits because the overtones are stronger than the undertones. Any one bait fished continually in any one swim will probably start to lose its effectiveness after three or four days of usage as the carp learn that the promise of food being advertised by the attractors is not being fulfilled. It may pay to take more than one version of a ready-made on a longer session.

The advantage of these baits is that they are instant, readily available and you can carry them round for months without worrying about them going off. The disadvantage is that the level of initial attraction leads to an inevitable tailing off in results, both on long sessions and over a period of time. It seems to take carp on certain waters some time to realize that these little balls of food which promise so much do not necessarily fulfil their promise. There is an initial period of success with high-flavour/low food-value baits which tends not to be maintained by later versions of low food-value baits.

When boilies first became fashionable we were told that all we needed for success was a mixture of soya and semolina, a few millilitres of flavour and some sweetener. These baits caught, with some flavours being far more successful than others.

The next stage up from these 'crap' baits was the same line of attack, but with the addition of a high level of *liquid food*, Nutramino and Liquid Liver being the first liquids used to boost the food value of the bait without much change to the soya and semolina base mix. The problem with a bait of this type is that all the food value and the attractors are in liquid form, which will limit the bait as a source of attraction once it has been in the water for some time. The primary attraction will be strong, there will be a food element, but there is no locked-in attraction or food value for long-term static baiting situations. This type of bait can be improved further by the addition of a vitamin mineral ingredient, which a great many anglers are in the habit of adding to all their baits to improve the nutritional content.

Once carp have been under pressure from low food value baits for some time, they start to become increasingly discriminating about their bait selection. Their instinct for assessment of these new food sources becomes sharpened, baiting situations become more sophisticated, and more thought and greater care is given to the design of the base mixes themselves.

Birdfood baits, fishmeal baits, protein baits, HNV baits, all-season type mixes and fishmeal mixes all depend on the *base mix* fulfilling the nutritional requirements of the carp to a greater or lesser degree. Recipes based on base mixes recommend the addition of liquid foods and flavours to

The author with a Kent thirty-pounder caught on a milk-protein based HNV.

supplement the protein, fat, carbohydrate and vit-amins and minerals provided by the base mix. The base mixes themselves will now often include taste enhancers, and secondary attractors like betaine, amino acids and other substances known to be the basis of 'natural attraction'.

The move towards sophistication has been a move towards the bait which fulfils all the angler's requirements. The designers of baits are largely successful carp anglers and they rec-ognize what is needed to catch carp in the whole range of situations. Once a bait has moved on from the initial soya/semolina base, how signi-ficant are the various categories in terms of nutrition and attraction?

Rightly or wrongly I look on the next step up from crap baits as being *birdfood-based baits*. 'Bird-food' is too all-embracing, really, because even within the range of birdfoods there is a strong vari-ation in what you will buy in terms of nutritional and attraction qualities. Most bait makers give some indication of the contents of their base mixes now, and if they do not, then ask them. Most of these baits contain a range of seeds in addition to the nutritional and bulking ingredients. In-built attraction comes from enhancers, and the best will have some sort of vitamin and mineral content. Add liquid flavours and liquid foods and you have primary and secondary attraction, a bait which will attract from the second it is introduced into the water, and will still have a level of attraction, and food value, the following morning.

Champions of birdfoods emphasize the fact that their loose structuring results in a stronger level of attraction than from some of the denser baits, including straight soya and semolina bases. These are very popular baits which norm-ally have a lower nutritional content than the best fishmeal and HNV baits, but which still allow you to fish a bait which includes all the main categories of ingredients and nutrients under consideration here.

Fishmeal baits have become massively popular and have accounted for the capture of literally thousands of carp over the last few years. They represent the most natural of all the baits in terms of in-built nutritional content, attraction

qualities, vitamin and mineral content and taste appeal. They are universally accepted by carp because they have been universally used, and they need a far lower level of attraction added to get them working than most other baits.

As with birdfoods the term 'fishmeals' covers a multitude of baits, some of which are far more effective than others. The fishmeal level, the quality of the ingredients and the addition of unique items which give an individual bait the edge over its rivals are the points which make one bait stand out from others. The marketplace soon gets to know which are the stand out baits through catch reports.

There are only two points I will add about fish-meal baits. One is that it is possible to add too high a level of oil when these baits are in common use on a water (when every one is using them.) 10–20ml of oil is enough. To go above that level may be dangerous to the health of the fish. The second point is that some of these baits very near-ly stand alone in terms of attraction. Overload with liquid flavours, and you may shorten the life of what is an excellent long-term bait.

HNV baits were more popular in the 1980s than they are today, although there are still tons and tons of the best protein and HNV mixes sold each year. The principle of an HNV bait is that it is designed to fulfil all a carp's nutritional requirements. Milk, egg and soya protein, liver powder, vitamins and minerals, natural attract-ors, vegetable or fish oil and essential oil as the label, attractor or point of identification. Prebait-ing is essential, as is freshness of bait when used.

Overnight attraction undertones is the ele-ment which needs careful thought with these baits. Bill Cottam and I designed the Nutra-baits' Addits range, and started using flavour/essential oil combinations to boost the attractor value of these baits without overloading with liquid flavours when we were developing Hi-Nu-Val in the mid-1980s. Lean towards attrac-tor food additives rather than straight attractors when looking to individualize your own version of this type of bait. Most popular in autumn and winter when fishmeals are said to be less effec-tive than during the warmer months.

Richard Skidmore with one of his numerous Mangrove fish on the Big Fish Mix. He proved it was still working well long after I thought it was losing its effectiveness.

There are now many effective base mixes which do not quite fall into any of the above categories. All-season or four-season mixes tend to be protein baits with some built-in attraction. There are some very successful baits based on yeasts, and some equally successful ones based on a combination of fish and liver baits. All these latter categories pay high regard to both the nutritional and the attraction quality of the bait, and are very successful carp catchers.

For the best part of ten years I spent many hundreds of hours experimenting with ingredients, making my own base mixes, then rolling and boiling my own baits. At the same time, I spent thousands of hours studying the theory of carp and their food sources. I never felt there would be an ultimate bait, but I did feel that there was always a great deal of room for improvement in the baits that were commercially available in the early

1980s. But such were the advances made in bait during the late 1980s and early 1990s that I think it is very difficult to improve on some of the best base mixes now available over the counter. You can fish some of them with total confidence, secure in the knowledge that if you get your part of the carp catching package right, your bait will do its job for you.

The one area where there is still room for experiment is in individualizing your own bait to make sure it suits your angling circumstances: instant attraction, long-term nutrition, overnight stability, or a combination of all three. If you cannot find a bait that does precisely the job you want of it, then perhaps there is some guidance in these notes to clarify your thinking on just what it is you want from your bait, and some thoughts on how you go about achieving it.

5 INSTANT CARP BAITS – ROD HUTCHINSON

Originally from Grimsby, Rod now lives nearby in the Louth area of Lincolnshire, and is the owner of his own tackle and bait company. Undoubtedly one of the greatest carp anglers of all time, Rod's record on waters in this country and on the continent is second to none. A regular contributor to angling and carp magazines for over twenty years, Rod has also had a number of books published. Although an authority on all things carpy, Rod's name is most strongly linked to the research, development and design of carp baits, attractors, flavours and enhancers. As I know Rod to be an angler who does not like to sit around too long before the buzzer sounds I took my tape recorder across to his home in Louth and we supped a couple of drinks while he taped some words of wisdom on instant baits and short session fishing.

T.P. *These days, Rod, much of the published material on carp fishing is written by session anglers and therefore the baiting situations, and the baits described, tend to aim at session anglers. You've seen both sides of the coin and you always advocated that in your type of fishing, you like the bait to be as likely to catch within ten minutes or half an hour of it going into the water as after three days. What would your advice be to people who have got an afternoon or an evening a week to fish, or one night at the weekend – where their time is very limited and they want an instant result?*

R.H. Well, basically, you make your bait as attractive as you can; you want it to work that instant. With some types of bait it's a case of upping the flavour range; maybe with other types it's more a case of spraying or dipping your baits, something like that. Basically you are trying to give instant solubility, so that flavour is leaking out from the bait the second it's hit the water. Such a bait is probably at its best for no more than about three hours, but in short session fishing that's it, it's more fishing for bites; you're not trying to stop a shoal and, for this type of fishing, you don't use a lot of bait.

When you say a bait of that type is probably at its most effective for three hours, are you talking about a heavily loaded bait there, or a dipped bait?

Yes, a heavily loaded or dipped bait. A heavily loaded bait is going to be effective for a longer period. If you are session fishing, I think they have a very good chance that it will still be going after three days, but I just believe in making a bait as attractive as you can from the outset.

In different situations – you know the big reservoir we fish in France? – the worse the conditions, the better the fish feed, but there are times when you can't get your bait out because you have to take it out by boat a lot of the time. If you get a gale for two or three days, like this year – Mallie Roberts and I were there in that hurricane. You've got a water full of crayfish and your ordinary bait is not going to be there after a day. We use Clawbuster baits, which are the hardest baits you can make. That bait has taken a long time to develop – it's certainly taken since 1987; there's a long history on the thing.

There we have a bait which we wanted to stay out for four days, at times. To be quite truthful, these baits aren't at their best once they soften up a bit. With very hard baits, to get the best from them, and to get bites early on, you are dipping and spraying and when you make the bait you are overloading.

Talking to you before we started doing this, you thinking on instant baits goes much further than boilies.

That's right.

I think you look on pellets as being very instant, so therefore how can someone who is going for short sessions use pellets? Let's start with pellets. A man who is going for a short session, how does he go about getting the fish in on pellets?

Well, the way I use pellets, I go for rapid breakdown pellets. There are different ones on the market – you know, ones which last longer, but mine are designed for my style of fishing. They break down very quickly; they send the aroma, the scent, the taste into the water because they break down immediately. All the ingredients we use in the pellets are cooked. This is a particle thing, you know, I think attraction is about solubility. I think everything in attraction is through messages through the water.

Like when we were talking about particles. My favourite bait of all time is maple peas, because I've caught more fish on it than any other bait. I absolutely love it and there is not a lake in the world where they are not going to have maples. I think all these things work best when they are cooked or particled; like maize – maize and sweetcorn – there's no doubt what's the most instant. Sweetcorn is probably the most instant bait in the world but, having said that, maples are too. Once you have cooked them, they are as instant as anything, but you have to cook them to release the flavours in there. Particles are at their best then; they've all got oils in and I think you thin out what oil is in there.

Like hemp – most people use hemp but they would not dream of using that raw, would they?

No, but I do see it happen, particularly where you get the bigger lakes; people say, 'Oh just throw it in there raw.' They think the fish will respond to it and eat it in any condition. They won't. The last time we went back to the big French reservoir, the Orient, the water was

down and there were maples and hemp growing everywhere because they'd not been cooked! The water level had gone down, the sunshine had got on them and they were growing all up the banks; everywhere. That's dead serious. Just because they hadn't cooked it. The sad thing is, they didn't get the best out of that bait; there's no way in the world that there would have been cooked hemp left there, because the other species wouldn't have allowed it to happen. With the maples, the roach would have had it, the bream would have had it.

Particles are at their best cooked.

And used in small quantities for short sessions?

Yes. Rather like boilies; a 400g bag of boilies is plenty for a short session, and with particles, a gallon is a lot more than you would generally use in a short session. If it's cooked, or been prepared right, a dozen catapults is a lot of bait. short session fishing – I know we're talking about bait but the main thing is – in short session fishing you don't sit at one end of a lake waiting for the fish to come to you. The main thing is you put yourself in the spot where you think you've got the best chance, so there are fish around in the area anyway. I like to dot baits around, about the size of a tennis court; spread it over that sort of area; I like fish to have a taste for it and in short session fishing, you have to have the mental attitude of 'the fish are feeding'.

I'm the same as everyone else – you go on a long session and you tend to think, 'Well, they're not feeding, I'll wait,' but somewhere there is always a carp feeding; they don't all stop feeding for the same period. There are times when most fish are feeding and you try to tie short session fishing into that; you hopefully fish when fish are feeding. I think you have to fish with that attitude, put yourself in an area where there are fish, or where there should be fish and that's it. I think the more fish that are feeding, the more bait you can put in. It's as simple as that. Even particles, they will go through them like a dose of salts if there's a load of fish there.

With boilies, if you are doing a day session, I would say a pound of bait is plenty.

Let's just go back to boilies. I would take it ready-mades are attractor baits. Is that fair comment?

Let's be fair about it, I can't comment on anybody else's bait, but I make ready-mades to be instant baits out of the packet.

Ready-mades from the packet; someone going to make their own attractor bait, how important is the base and how do you go about putting together your attractors for something you just want to chuck out and bump, catch a carp?

I honestly think that depends a lot on the time of the year. If carp are feeding ravenously – I hate this summer, winter thing, you know, categories; I was brought up in Lincolnshire where you can fish at all times of the year. To me, probably the best six weeks of carp fishing, well, the best month is the last two weeks of May and the first two weeks of June; fish are feeding their heads off, you can put a lot more in; you can get away with a lot more and at that period I don't believe that the base is going to play that significant a part because it's the time of the year when they first come onto heavy feeding.

I think as the year goes on, maybe it becomes a lot more important, especially through the summer. The harder the fishing becomes the more the base begins to matter. But right at the beginning of the angling pressure period, I don't think it matters too much.

You've got a lot of people, they're going to go out, they're pleasure fishing in summer. You're going to make an attractor bait that's going to catch a carp wherever you go, whenever you chuck it out. You say to the kid, 'Look, I know I'll catch carp with this. I don't know whether you're good enough but, if you are, this'll catch you a carp.'

If I had one mix where I would go throughout the year and say this was an attractor base – I think people will be surprised by this – it would

be Promix 50/50. I make no bones about this, I wrote about it in the beginning; people used to refer to semolina baits as crap baits, casein baits as high protein only. Now, they both caught fish and there were times of the year, when fish were feeding very, very heavily, when the semolina baits were equally as good as the others, if you were using the attractors on the same dosages. Then, as the year got older and particularly as it started getting colder, October time, the protein mix would out-fish the other one. We used to fish them alongside each other and I put that down to the fact that in winter you need more solubles and the protein mix had got the caseinates in, which are solubles. When you boil a bait you are cooking it, which – again – is making what's in there more soluble.

Just explaining this base mix, the lads were buying the two and mixing them together so, really, you got the Promix 50/50 – being half a semolina base and the other half a caseinate base.

There was a gang of us, including my Dutch mates, testing lots and lots of flavours out and everybody came to the conclusion that the best base mix to use was Promix 50/50, I think it would catch without flavours because of its caseinate content, because that base, in itself, is attractive.

So you are starting off with an attractor base, and then you are going to add to it? What are you going to add to it? What are your attractors going to be, your liquids that you add, your taste enhancers?

Well, you know you've got an attractive base. I must admit, for short session fishing I try to make the ultimate attractor bait. I put (and this isn't generally known) there are different names for it, we call them appetite stimulators and people think powders, this and that, it's mainly a taste ingredient which, in all fairness, is right. But you know, one-third of the things I make called 'appetite stimulators' are – again – based on solubles, so I have always got that soluble input.

With different sorts of flavours, you can go higher. All flavours are on some sort of base, either the flavour itself being derived from a concentrate (as in a fruit) or being derived from an essential oil. They are then put into a certain sort of base and you've got carriers from heavy sugar syrups, which are very good for creams and things like that, going up to propylene glycols, glycerol being a sugar syrup. The thicker that is, the less water soluble it is. What a lot of kids don't realize is that glycerol is the least water soluble of all the commonly used solvents, so that's not going to give you a lot of attraction. If you are using that type of flavour, you will probably double the flavour level to get the desired result.

So it will depend on the base of the flavour how much you put in for instant attraction?

Yes. It depends on the base and the flavour you are using. If you add 1ml of an EA or 10 drops of an Essential Oil; those are things you can easily overload. I don't use Essential Oils in summer any more. Ethyl Alcohols I do; I like the solubility, I like the 'woomph', it's out there, coming out of the bait and pulling them down. I like to use them in conjunction with other things.

If you took a glycerol bait and it said 'use at 10ml', for instant attraction you took it to 20ml; you are just improving it a bit, you are not going to overload it because the solubility of that flavour is not great. Those sort of flavours were from the boiled sweet industry, years and years ago, where you put a little bit in and it lingered. It's food culture and it's just how things have progressed.

Something like Chocolate Malt – I wrote a story years ago about the Dutch lads using it at 50ml and catching stacks of fish, based on a very simple sugar base. The less soluble, the higher you can go with it. Everybody has their personal favourites and I suppose my most instant bait is the Chocolate Malt, I love it. In summer, on a short session, I will use it at about 20ml.

What base is that, Chocolate Malt? You say simple sugar...

It's a simple hydrolysed sugar base.

So what is in the Chocolate Malt bracket? You say Chocolate Malt is your top one.

I don't think he realized it at the time, but I'll be fair about it because maybe he had some criticism at the time because all the people there were using that sort of flavour – can you remember Geoff Kemp always said, 'Use the Cream at 25ml'. There was a certain amount of propylene glycol in that at the beginning but at that time, when it first came out and was used as a solvent, it was much more viscous, a lot thicker than what is used in the food industry today. Thinking about it, what Geoff recommended was right. That's how it was; use it at the higher level, but what it all came down to it was because the base of that flavour wasn't water soluble.

He caught a lot of carp on it, let's be right!

Loads of carp on it, yes.

So your flavour, you want one of your simple sugar bases.

Yes, a simple sugar base at high level or if you're using – say you've got a favourite food – EAs [Ethyl Alcohols] I tend to combine them now and put a couple of ml in with something and they work lovely at that. They go 'woomph', straight out of it...

An alcohol base with the sugar base?

Yes. Use it in conjunction.

Like Strawberry and Cream?

Yes. Strawberry and Cream, that has been a big bait over the last few years.

But you use the two different bases?

Yes.

A dramatic picture of Rod with a big French fish and stormy big-fish conditions showing in the background.

Julian's favourite is Strawberry and Cream EA, isn't it?

Yes, but I'd use the different bases. I don't have any secrets – for short session fishing, 2ml of Super Cream EA makes a terrific difference to anything; it's absolutely brilliant. When I say to the lads, 'You can use it in a fishmeal,' initially they are doubtful. You tend to think you've got to use this flavour with that bait, and that flavour with this bait, but the fish don't know what it is; it's just what reaction it's having on them. Use a good bait… It's trying to create a reaction straight away. If everybody's using fishmeals, bung the attractors in which will get them to your fishmeal first.

Fishmeals in themselves, do you consider them an attractor base?

I do, but I am going to go against things here. In recent years – we know we had the craze of filling them up with oil, didn't we? – It's been proved in recent years, in fish farming, that high levels of oil, they don't like. What happened there, fishmeal was so good, or it was working at times of the year when it was working *despite the oils*. I don't believe you want fish oils at high levels. You can go as far as you like down the line towards what you think is the perfect bait. You've been in the bait industry and you know what you can get. You can buy fish caseinates now; you can buy pure fish protein; you can buy all of these things. Everything is available; you can buy de-oiled fish, so they are all there.

I personally don't think I can make a better fishmeal bait than Superfish, I can't; I took that as far as I could. You can put another attractor in but it's got mussel, squid and crab in – three of the biggest carp pullers in, all together; small amounts, but pure protein.

Do the fish recognize the attraction from that base in a five-hour session? Is it adding to your flavours and your enhancers?

I don't know. What I do know is, I put fish solubles in. The solubles are there for fish to recognize straight away. We're talking about short session fishing here and for short session fishing you try to make your bait as good as you can. You can make anything better, no doubt about that. If you are buying the bait out of the bag, that's as good as the product can be for that price and that's what people have to understand. Martin Clarke has recommended some great baits but people may not realize that to put some of the ingredients he recommends into ready-mades what price they would be paying per bag. So you make the best product you can for the price.

I do like the sprays. If I'm using ready-mades and I'm fishing a short session, I'll spray them up to make them even better. The sprays are classed as water soluble; we put in – I won't go into the brand names but they do call them 'food polymers'; they cling – and they are supposed to. They are basically used in the animal biscuit industry, where they spray everything on and it's there to keep the flavour on for a decent time.

I'll come back to the bait in a minute, but while you're on sprays, because you've got a bait which says it's 'strawberry' – or whatever flavour – will you go for a different spray, or the same spray?

I don't think that would matter too much. I think in the first instance I would go with the flavour of the thing. People see us fishing, you can't hide what you are doing; 90 per cent of the time we're on Monster Crab or Chocolate Malt. Probably our third choice these days is Scopex and Mulberry. We always start off spraying with

that one. I explained that the Chocolate Malt, which is a thick base, not all that water soluble, you can get away with a high level. In the spray form, we have obviously made it as water soluble as we can and we start with that.

However, you do get this thing, you know – 'Oh, the lake's on strawberry at the moment.' It happens, doesn't it? There are times when you put strawberry out but then it changes; it slowly goes off and it seems that the first person to do something different first, that's the next hit. That's when you try doing it with the cream, or doing it with – one that's very popular on the continent, not as big here in England, funnily enough – Honey Nectar which Kevin Maddocks has pushed for years. That goes lovely with fruit. I'd use it with a fruit or a cream.

It's the old story – maybe there comes a time of overkill where a method's lost its novelty: lots of fish have been caught on it and we know it; it gets to that point where they are getting cautious and at that time, spraying a strawberry boilie with something different; soaking it in anything to give it the sweet edge again. The fruit flavour is still there in the background but it's no longer representative of the label they have come to regard with caution.

Liquid foods like Liquid Liver and Fish Oils, Minamino or whatever people sell it as these days; Sensappeals, that sort of thing, are they valid to add to the bait as additional attractors?

They are all a bit different in what they are and what their bases are. They are definitely worth having in there. It's easy for me, because I know what these things are but – again – I go more to the attraction of it than I would the nutritional property.

That's what I'm saying, do they attract?

Yes. I think you go along with what basically are the best bases. You talk about Minamino – it's a proven good additive to a bait. I still think the name is a bit misleading but, as much as anything, that's adding a lot of sugars.

The Liquid Liver. Talking about my own products I have the Amino Blend Supreme. The liver itself is in a state of predigestion, which is going to release things but on that short-term thing, I look upon that, and Sensappeal as more nutritional things. From my products Amino Blend Supreme, I know that is 90 per cent water soluble, which is a lot of difference. Minamino is good because that's got a soluble sugar compound base to it, which is very water soluble.

Again, it's just down to the solubility of the product. If people like a product, maybe they'll learn how to use it, the best levels, when it works best, how long it takes to work, that sort of thing.

Can people test solubility themselves by pouring it into a glass of water to see what it actually does?

I would say so, yes, to see if it clouds up – or some products float. If they are floating, it's not having an awful lot of solubility about it. You can pour thick drops into tanks and see them not break down but often, if they go down as globules and then you watch it and see how it breaks down. Yes, I think you can test solubility.

So your main thrust is going to be from your taste enhancers and your flavours that you talked about. An oil is going to stay separate from the water...

Well, generally, oil will float to the top. Some of the other things – you will see the globule growing as it grows apart and other things will disappear quickly. Those which disappear quickly are your most soluble. Simple as that.

Most of us have got a simple concept that the warmer the water is the better the bait attracts. When it's very warm you can smell things much more strongly than when it's cold.

Yes, that's very true.

So we are probably more confident of instant attraction in summer, when the water is warmer than we are in winter? Is attraction or stimulation valid in the colder water?

I believe it is and I wish I could scientifically explain this but I can't. I can give you the concept. You can do this in tanks; we've got a stock pond where we throw things. I tell the lads to chuck all their boilies when they come back from winter and we do a netting in the spring. Certain types of bait have not been eaten, so there are still some types of boilie there after a long period. If we did it a month later – it might be eaten, even after that stage because in their natural environment the carp are eating a lot of decaying food. Even plants are giving off a certain amount of protein and goodness, cellulose and sugars, as they are decaying. Everything has its right time and I think there would have been food value there which they could recognize at a later stage, or some attraction to it. But we were certainly taking boilies out that were three months old. I don't think they've harmed anything; carp tend to eat things when they want to eat them.

The whole thing is like the old tank test. Nowadays it can be decried a lot because you feed them what you want to feed them and it's not a natural environment, but then you see foods that don't do anything for them. I used to have a big tank in the garage and I didn't have any heat on in winter; some foods were just left completely alone and other things got eaten. You were just trying to see if there was anything which created a reaction.

Certainly, over the years I have always done better when I've added some sort of spice in winter. It could be in nearly any form, I mean, when you think of most spices you think of Essential Oils but spices in Ethyl Alcohol have worked very well, and powdered spices have done very well.

I believe in winter you must aim to put your bait next to a fish's head – that's the main thing you try to do – find out where the fish are and try to put a bait next to his head. Now, if you can get a bait close, you are in with a very good chance. If it doesn't take that bait – I don't like that word 'trigger' – I think there's a stimulus and I think it's a chemical reaction in the water. Very acidic things seem to work in winter; acidic fruits do.

Like Strawberry?

Not just Strawberry. One of our better ones – with my company, if we sell something it's working. Nouvelle Fizz, Autumn Harvest – all very acid berries. Very acidic baits seem to work very well. It's almost like the bait in the water is creating a sort of electric pulse, like you get in a battery when you put alkaline with acid, you create an electric field and I think the sort of baits which work in winter react like that. To make it work well, you use a bait – and we're talking about short session fishing again – which will allow that linkage.

All over the years I've always said, with my base mix the most important thing to me, in winter, is having a caseinate in there; I like a lot of solubles in my base mix in winter; I want things to come out, so don't use things that only become soluble in high temperatures. Most of the time I use the Promix 50/50 straight out of the bag, because it's got a good caseinate content, but if I was making a bait up from the first stage, I would push the caseinate content as high as I could for the bait to roll.

So you are less interested in the solvent or the base in winter and more interested in the flavour?

Yes, I think you want an acidic flavour in winter.

In your Carpworld *tapes you mentioned Ultraspice a lot.*

Yes. It's been my number one bait in the winter over the years. My mate Charlie always says, 'The only question this year is what do we add to our Ultraspice?' We started off with it and, on Savay, it has been documented. You mixed Scopex with Ultraspice, you did this, you did that but, all the time, everything was mixed with a spice. Then – this is harking back, Fred Wilton did it before me; I think the reasons were different but he did it with Essential Oils. I think the first one we really found in winter which positively boosted your chances was cinnamon. Actually, everything to do with cinnamon because every part, the whole tree, the leaves, the bark, the root; they were under different names but everything in there was good. Even the Ultraspice has cinnamon in there. Clove is another good one. If you're stuck in winter, use a spice combined with a very acid fruit.

Do you boost the levels in winter or do you stay with the normal levels?

I don't like large amounts of Essential Oils, the reason being, I've never done any good on high levels with them. I think 12ml is a lot of Essential Oil. When we were testing them all, 18ml was the top whack anybody caught on a regular basis. I like them with citrus-based flavours because it's really the easiest medium to use, limes, lemons, oranges. I like to use these in conjunction with a small amount of Essential Oil and I think, between them, there's a kind of electrical field. There are some fish out there with which you are trying to create the stimuli to wake them up to feed. In that type of flavour – in summer we do use EA but a lot of the others are based on propylene glycol alcohol, which is the next most soluble one in the chain.

You read a lot about emulsifiers. Are you an advocate of emulsifiers?

I'm not trying to be careful but what I am trying to do here – we all go through life, each year you, hopefully, learn a little bit more and when we were first trying to get a feeling for the potential of Essential Oils, we were trying to break them down. What people have to realize is that there was nothing before this. You know, I went through that great bait revolution of the 70s and 80s, so you were learning about things. I think we tended maybe, to use them at too high a level in the beginning but with an oil, what people have to realize is that an oil isn't water soluble. When we started putting larger amounts of emulsifier in, the bait worked better. Nowadays, it's come down to

Rod Hutchinson with a big southern fish caught on an instant bait within half an hour of casting out. This fish, in excess of 30lb, grew to over 50lb in weight!

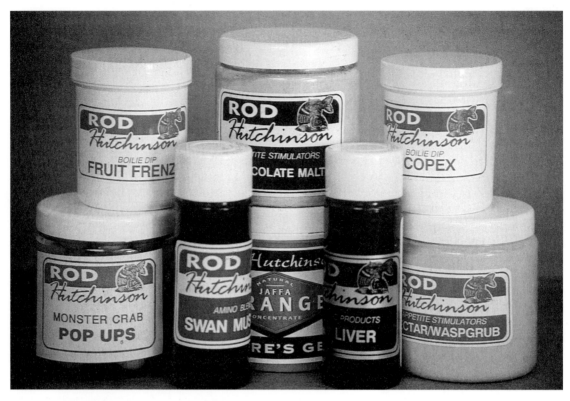

Instant success in a bottle – if you get everything else right! Rod was one of the pioneers of flavours and taste enhancers, and his bait products have been making the catching of carp easier for carp anglers for over seventeen years.

two different things. I would certainly say that emulsifier isn't doing any harm and it's probably helping that oil leak out sooner. You are not trying to attract over a great area in winter. The more you talk to people who are very successful in winter – it's where you put your bait. You've got to be on the spot because you're not going to draw them from 50 yards away, but if you've got your bait within maybe 10ft of that fish, you're in with a chance. An emulsifier will give that Essential Oil a better chance of working.

I see you advertise your Protaste as an emulsifier, a sweetener and an enhancer, so that's like an additive that can do all the jobs.

Yes, I think if you look at most of the things I do now – you know, what we call the 'natural sweeteners' are expensive products, protein sweeteners in the trade, aren't they? But they do break down, they emulsify; they are used in the confectionery industry and they are good products. They definitely bring out the best of the flavour and enable you to use less of that flavour.

Thanks for talking to us.

6 THE LIFE OF A BAIT

What is the life of the bait they are using? This is a vexing question for many. How many carp can they catch on it from one water before the bait starts to lose its effectiveness, before it starts to 'blow' in carp-fishing parlance? There are a number of variables which make a simple answer difficult. I will relate a few experiences and throw in some rough guidelines which may help you to make your own assessment.

I will emphasize one basic guideline to clarify some of what follows. At each end of the bait scale you have two extremes, at one end a high food-value bait with low/moderate attractor levels, and at the other end a low food-value bait with high attractor levels. The first is aimed at achieving medium to long-term success following a baiting campaign and continuing regular introduction. It is designed as a food source and the attractors are kept moderate so they don't counteract the food value of the bait by upsetting the carp's system in any way. In human terms, chicken is a food, korma chicken a mildly spiced food which most people can cope with without it upsetting them and vindaloo chicken a heavily spiced food which a small minority of humans of my acquaintance enjoy, although even then it does not seem to do their system much good! I can enjoy and benefit from a diet of chicken. I will occasionally eat korma chicken or chicken tikka massala. I steer well clear of chicken vindaloo.

In carp-bait terms, chicken vindaloo is the other end of the scale to the long-term food bait. It is the instant bait that Chapter 5 deals with. The food value in the base Rod Hutchinson recommends is an aid to instant attraction. It does not matter as much as the food value in a long-term bait. It does not make much difference to

me if the vindaloo is meat, chicken, fish or potato: can't cope with it, don't want to know about it. But I must have tried it at some time to know I can't cope with it, and that is the thinking behind the design of the attractor bait. It reeks of food. It smells so good and carries such a promise of food that it provokes the carp into picking it up. The fewer free offerings you give the fish, the more effective the bait is likely to be. Give them free offerings and they can assess the promised food value without picking up the hookbait. You are trying to make them pick up the hookbait, not through overconfidence and familiarity, but by compulsion.

I look on instant baits as very short-term baits, but I'll qualify that. I've watched anglers using baits in which I'm sure the attractor levels are too high for effective long-term use. You can see the signs on long sessions and even over a weekend: fish showing over the baits, first night a result then a tailing off in each session. I'll emphasize that this happens each session because it is useful to know. Next session the same thing happens with the same bait. The attraction works over again because the fish have forgotten the after-effects, or there are different fish in front of the angler. It has been more difficult to assess the long- and short-term effects of an overloaded bait. Use them on one nighters, and on weekends when Saturday night is going to be less productive than Friday night anyway, but if you go on a week's session, understand that you need a back-up bait, or you need to move swims after the initial flurry of success. And restrict your free offerings. For two reasons. You don't want to let too many fish assess the suitability of the bait, and you don't want to saturate the water with attractors, which is when you get the heavy rolling and no action.

When I go for a week's session to a water I do not know and I am not in a position to prebait, I go for the best of both bait extremes – the nutritional attractor bait. I want the food source to be valid for the week; I want the attractors to provoke quicker action than I can expect on a long-term baiting campaign. The attractors have to be modified slightly, or you lean towards those which you ascertain the carp will tolerate at high levels (of the type Rod Hutchinson recommends in Chapter 5) or which any other bait dealer worth his salt will explain to you. When you moderate the attractors somewhat you are not expecting instant action. Moderate attractors, moderate amounts of bait. You are trying to capture the attention of the carp within a day or two and hold it for a week.

You are walking a tightrope with this type of bait. You want the attractors as high as possible without achieving the 'vindaloo' effect. Very often you are fishing blind and you can only assess the effectiveness of the bait from the movement of the indicators. The bait is ideal for one-off weeks at distant day-ticket waters, or sessions at far-away syndicate waters that you can only visit every month or so. You need to think hard in the design of the bait, and you need to assess its effectiveness as you go along. What you are aiming at is a nutritional ready-made. Most ready-mades are high on attractors and moderate to low on food value. The packet tells you what the bait is based on (the flavour) and I will give you an example of the thinking behind the bait I used to win the first Horseshoe match in 1991, and I don't think I've revealed this before.

Bob Baker of Richworth had a couple of teams in the match, Bob being one of the anglers. Rightly or wrongly I guessed they would fish Richworth Tutti Fruttis as at least one of their baits. Tutti Fruttis are considered by many to be one of the most instant baits available. So I went and got a bottle of Richworth Double Strength Tutti Frutti flavour, made up a special attractor blend which included it, added it to a nutritional base, and included a taste additive. I figured most of the anglers fishing would consider ready-mades to be ideal for a two-day match, which they proved to be. Tuttis caught throughout the weekend, as did my bait. I don't know how significant the nutritional base of my bait was, but I caught a higher individual weight than any of the other teams.

After the match, I substituted the Nutrabaits Tutti-Frutti for the Richworth one and gave the recipe to Bill Cottam and Richard Skidmore of Nutrabaits. The mix is now their very successful Fruit Special. The principle outlined above holds good for any bait and any water. You can improve the effectiveness and life of a ready made by putting the attractor named on the label on a more nutritional base and coming up with your own version. Do not worry too much that most ready-mades taste incredibly sweet. As a rule, that is part of the preservative system in the bait. The principle of imitating a ready-made's attractor value on a more nutritional base holds good for any ready-made where the company sells the flavour used in the ready-made. Rod Hutchinson in Chapter 5 spells out the principle behind instant attraction.

I will detail some of my experiences with long-term food baits. I fished the Mangrove well, I thought, for two summers with the Big Fish Mix/Garlic Mint bait. In that time, I caught over ninety fish on the bait. By the second autumn, I felt it was starting to lose its effectiveness. I figured that the life of the bait was being shortened by the number of captures, their knock-on effect (other carp being spooked by captures), and the fact that fishmeals had been successful on the water for five seasons. In terms of the life of the bait, I did not help my own cause by not prebaiting during the close season prior to the second season's fishing, which was down to shortage of time rather than a decision not to.

I chose to fish the bait for two seasons because I wanted to see if it would start turning up fish that did not usually fall to bait. Had I persevered with the bait it might well have done so, and there were signs that this was happening. Two of the last few fish I had on the bait were big twenty pound commons that were unfamiliar to

This Mangrove common, in excess of 26lb, came on a bait I had been using for fifteen months on the water at a time when I thought the bait was starting to lose its effectiveness.

me. On the other hand, the bait only accounted for Scaley of the known big fish in the water. This was disappointing, but may have been because of swim choice and levels of baiting rather than the carp's dietary choice.

For a bait to last two seasons or more it has to be a good food bait, and it helps if it is introduced regularly as a prebait. Baits only used in a pressured angling situation will eventually shorten their own lives because ultimately they always represent danger to the fish. In addition, the angler should recognize that some flavours only attract at a level that is unacceptable to the fish over a long term. I prefer essential oils and/or food additives as the identifying attractors in a long-term food bait, although some of

the comments Rod Hutchinson makes have modified my thinking somewhat on this aspect.

At the time my Big Fish Mix bait started to lose its effectiveness on the Mangrove, I changed the bait completely. I felt sure that the carp were starting to get nervous of fishmeals, although looking back in the light of the experiences of others on the water since I now think it was the attractors in the bait that were identifying it as a source of danger to the fish. Fishmeals have continued to catch on the water.

Since changing, I have been fishing the Grange Mix with Corn Steep Liquor. The bait has been catching on numerous waters for over four years now without losing its effectiveness. I fish the bait without flavours or essentials oils. I use the base plus Corn Steep Liquor. I mention this because I think the fact that this is a bait that is best used without a flavour is significant in lengthening its life. It smells like food, it tastes like food and apparently there are no side effects.

I am now of the opinion that a high food-value base has an indefinite life on a water, provided it is prebaited regularly and the attractors do not upset the carp's system. Where attractors are used the source of attraction will, eventually, become a source of alarm. I think that's what happened with my bait on the Mangrove. The base was still all right; the attractors had accounted for too many fish and started to act as a signal of danger. When I think of the longevity of a bait I think of Alan Smith on Darenth Tip Lake in the early 1980s. Alan used the same bait and source of attraction for a number of seasons with outstanding results. Prebaiting was as much a part of his ongoing tactics as was prebaiting in the close season. The first time I saw him fish I had no idea who he was. I saw this bloke arrive early evening, set up his rods, fire out baits for about an hour – then next time I looked, he'd gone! I wasn't at all impressed by his patience level. A couple of days later he was back. 'Oh no,' I thought. 'Here we go again.' He put out half a dozen baits, then put his bivvy up and fished for a couple of days. He explained later that the evening trip had been to keep the baiting programme going. When he came to fish, he didn't want to give them too many alternatives to the hookbaits. He had total confidence in his food source bait and had outstanding results on it. These are high food level/low attraction level tactics.

The only other point I would make about the type of bait and attractors is that there is a theme that different baits and flavours turn up different fish. I have watched carp over baits many times. I am quite sure the initial attraction is by smell. Prebaiting is to instil confidence in the carp's feeding. Some carp are just as likely to pick up a bait on its first application to the water as its hundredth, but, all things being equal, a cautiously feeding carp is more likely to get caught on the hundredth application. But different smells provoke different initial reactions. What percentage of the carp in your water are getting caught? What percentage are feeding on bait? Obviously only those picking up baits are catchable, but by no means all of these will get caught. The only way to catch one of the carp that is not feeding on bait is to change the attractors, or keep applying the same bait until the message finally gets across, 'Here is food.' I know it happens that a bait which smells like food to some of the carp does nothing at all for some of the others, even though they watch their companions feeding on it. These fish are the real challenge; those who still seek to come up with better baits are all too well aware of their existence and work hard at trying to develop a bait to lower the defences of every carp that swims.

It is important that you understand the principles outlined above and apply them as best you can to the bait you need for your type of fishing. Decide on the type of bait most suited to your needs, then refine it to your individual needs. A ready-made straight out of the packet may be all you need, but if you go on a week's holiday with a bait that has brought you short-session success, understand why it may stop working after two or three days. There is a rule of thumb that the more instant the attractors, the shorter the life of the bait in any one session. The lower the food value, the shorter the life of the bait may be in any one season. The more you fish the more important the food value of the bait becomes. You want it to become an habitual food source for the fish, as familiar to them as a bed of bloodworms, which they have been eating for thousands of years without a flavour, sweetener or taste additive in sight!

7 THE PRESSURE CYCLE

Why is there no definitive work on carp fishing? Is there no one book that will answer all our problems and become the standard reference work for those wishing to catch carp? There are excellent technical/practical carp books, but no definitive volume exists because carp learn by their mistakes or unpleasant experiences, i.e. getting caught or being present when other carp get caught. In time, they learn to avoid smells, baits, situations, areas and presentations which their minds come to associate with danger. Captures can equate to pressure, and the way in which carp react to pressure makes their vulnerability to methods and baits difficult to categorize. No writer can safely predict that any one bait or method will catch carp on a water with which he or she is not familiar.

The changing reactions of carp to pressure are known as the pressure cycle and represent one of the more fascinating aspects of carp fishing. The angler has to keep at least one thought ahead of the carp to keep catching them, and those who are best at thinking their way round the carp's thinking are the most consistently successful. Experienced anglers understand the effects of pressure and adapt accordingly. Those who are not familiar with this spoilsport reaction on the part of the carp should have some idea of the variables which are most subject to change. Bait we have dealt with in Chapters 3 to 6, but there are certain areas of bait lore still to be considered, and there are a number of aspects of pressure we will briefly look at here.

The main areas to consider are:

1. The nature of bait.
2. Smells.
3. Areas of the lake.
4. Presentation.
5. Temporary and early-season pressure.

The Nature of Bait

There are some great contradictions and fascinating anomalies when it comes to carp and baiting situations. I'll detail a few of them, without trying to rationalize them too deeply, and leave the reader to consider them in the light of his or her own carp fishing. The important thing to realize is that most baiting situations which catch carp gradually become recognized as danger situations by the carp. That is not to say they do not continue to feed in those situations, although they may start to avoid them altogether in extreme circumstances, but rather that they feed with increased caution in a situation which they have come to associate with danger.

There is an obvious anomaly in the use of particles and boilies. 'Boilies over particle' is a familiar carp-fishing situation which has been used a great deal in the north-west Midlands, and in many other areas too, no doubt. Initially, the situation is productive and the carp are catchable. When the method begins to dry up, alternatives are used and boilies in their own right become popular again. When this happened on the water we know as Erewhon, the anglers trying boilies only started catching well, while those still fishing over particles struggled. What was really interesting though was that the fish caught in the boilie situations excreted particles into the sacks! In other words, the carp were still eating the particles, but were avoiding hookbaits in what had, through the pressure of captures, become a danger situation.

This manifestation of pressure starts to become a part of a pressure cycle when beds of boilies come to represent pressure and increased awareness is shown in the carp's feeding in boilie situations. Understanding where to go from there is to start to come to terms with the pressure cycle. Back to particles? Have all the popular particles been reacted against? These days 'particles' tends to mean tiger nuts, which rather ignores the massive potential of maples, black-eyed beans, chopped Brazil nuts and numerous other baits worth trying in a bid to come up with something different. Test the reaction to seeds, pellets, etc.

In terms of pressure, 'boilies' is too generalized a term, however, and boilies *per se* form part of a pressure cycle of their own. The initial reaction will be against those boilies which are most readily identifiable and least coveted in the carp's feeding. There may be a reaction against baits that are overflavoured, of low food value, are brightly coloured or are even of a size which the carp associates with danger. Smaller baits will often succeed where results have started to slow up on bigger baits. Overflavoured baits may continue working where a change to a new 'irresistible' (different) flavour is tried. Changing from a bright colour to a darker colour may bring success with the same bait, while the addition of some milk protein or fishmeal to a low food-value bait may recycle the bait and renew the carp's interest in it.

Most of these points apply to individual baits, but the question of colour is a serious one which can often only be overcome by resorting to darker baits or darker colours. There comes a time when carp will actually flee from the sight of a bed of brightly coloured baits, be they particles or boilies. Once this happens, I am not sure that there is evidence that the pressure cycle reinstates baits of this type at a later date. Most of the carp's food recognition is by smell and you will be safer with a bait which they first become aware of by smell before they actually see it.

How valid sight aspects are in some of the murky waters we fish, particularly those which fish at night, I do not honestly know, but if you are having bait problems, be aware that brightly coloured baits could be the cause.

Smells

The phenomenon of the deterrent effect of the human scent on fish is well documented. It is a problem we all have to live with, and my theory is that the scent of some humans is more acceptable to fish than that of others. I think that carp like the smell of the likes of Rod Hutchinson, Geoff Rendell, Andy Little, Terry Hearn and so on, anglers who catch fish with monotonous (for us) regularity wherever they fish. It might simply be that some people have little or no scent, whereas others have a distinctive one, but whatever the reason, there does seem to be have been an uneven distribution of wealth when it comes to carp anglers' natural attractiveness to carp.

But I wonder how many carp anglers stop and wonder if their natural smell is a carp deterrent? When I used to smoke I always washed my hands in the lake before handling bait. Although I no longer smoke, I take this precaution even further now and frequently rub my hands on a damp sack or weigh sling to remove alien smells before handling baits. Because of this fear of smells I will not have anything to do with petrol stoves when carp fishing. Contrary to popular belief, the 5kg gas bottles work perfectly well in sharp frosts, and you can quote me all the arguments you want in favour of the handling of petrol and its attractions for carp, I don't want any of it.

I used carp fishing as an excuse to give up decorating, which bores me witless anyway, but if I were a decorator I would be very nervous of handling baits without some sort of protection for my hands. Similarly, I will not fill up with petrol or check the oil on the way to a carp session, and if I were a mechanic I would be neurotic about the effect my livelihood was having on my carp fishing.

Most of you will have heard the expression 'soaping a swim'. It is based on the reality that carp have an adverse reaction to the presence of soap and will vacate an area of water that has been 'soaped'. I am neurotic about the scent of soap on my hands after I have washed, and you should be too. I can imagine this aspect applying particularly to these anglers who combine carping with holidays and come to the lake fresh from civilization each day. The more hygienic you are, the more care you have to take to ensure that you have removed as much trace of civilization as possible from your hands prior to handling your baits.

The same considerations apply to the making of bait. Do not take the risk of introducing alien smells to the actual bait mix or you will give yourself a problem you will not know about and you cannot erase.

These are just examples. The point is that we go to a great deal of trouble to arrive at a bait which we think will be irresistible to carp, then we get careless about the effects of tainting that bait with alien smells. At the first few times of asking petrol may well be a carp attractor, but if everyone fishing a carp water is refilling their petrol stoves then handling bait, sooner or later the smell of petrol is going to become a deterrent.

If you handle substances which may be carp deterrents, check out your past results in terms of the possible effects of your non-carp fishing activities. You may be exerting an unrecognized pressure on the fish.

Areas of the Lake

Most of us will have experienced the phenomenon whereby one season a certain swim is the one to be in, the next season you can't get a take from it, and that's the way it stays for a couple of seasons. When carp start to associate an area with danger, their first reaction is to feed there with caution; their second is to avoid it all together.

This is more true of unnatural feeding areas than natural ones. Margin spots, snag areas, gaps in bars and pressured spots on bars themselves are features which become popular because they are obvious casting targets and are visited by the carp regularly in their travels.

My wife Mary's favourite swim, but you have to be aware that spots like this become less productive as the pressure builds up after a number of fish have been caught in the area.

They tend to become pressured more quickly than feeding areas they visit naturally.

Many years ago, at Harlesthorpe Dam in Clowne, there was a very popular swim which was at the junction of two channels. The water was gin-clear and the hot spot only seven or eight yards out and two or three feet deep. Over a period of two years the carp went from being very catchable in this spot to hurrying through it as though in fear of their lives, which I suppose they were. Pressure will be having similar effects on some productive spots and areas of your lake. Recognize this and do not plug away at hot spots simply because they have produced in the past. The pressure cycle may have cooled them down for a while, but as other spots become pressured and the carp forget past experiences, bear in mind that they may have their day again.

Mary with one of three fish in excess of 25lb, caught on the first day of the season from under the rod tips in her little swim. That was the end of action in the spot for the week's session.

Presentation

The implications of pressure affecting presentation are covered in greater depth in Chapters 7, 9 and 10, but there are one or two rough guidelines to look at here. I guess the obvious example of a presentation blowing through pressure is the use of pop-ups. To start with, the fact that the bait is stuck up off the bottom makes it more accessible, the carp has not learned to fear it and the method works well. In time, the lesson is learned that baits stuck up off the bottom are a possible source of danger and their effectiveness is greatly reduced.

On the other hand, when pop-ups of 2–4in (5–10cm) start to lose their effectiveness and the carp are very cautious with hookbaits fished on the bottom, pop-ups fished well off the bottom can come into their own. A bait 2–4ft (60–120cm) off the bottom seems very unnatural to us and certainly to be feared, but the point about pressure is that the adverse experience has to be experienced for the method to be feared: until there is a record of captures and a build up of pressure on a new method, it is worth trying because there is a chance it will work. The carp of Birch Grove can be very cagey, but on one particular session when they just wouldn't take a bait, I had two good fish in an hour on a double 18mm bait fished 2ft straight up off the lead. The presentation felt so unnatural that it wasn't a ploy I tried regularly, but whenever I was really desperate and put it out, it worked.

On waters where surface baits have ceased to work and the going is tough on the bottom, anglers have had a great deal of success fishing anchored baits a foot or so under the surface.

I have no definite example to relate to but I have heard it said that carp in a water can become nervous of one particular brand of line. No one can prove that happens, but when carp start falling to set-ups incorporating lines other than the most popular one on the water, the presumption is that the popular line has become recognized in some way and has started to pressure the fish.

There is a popular concept that pinning tackle to the bottom may go some way to allaying the fears of the carp. Is pinned-down tubing less likely to spook fish than tubing which may be lifting up off the bottom? If you are using a hooklink material which floats, should you pin it down in case it spooks the fish? For a number of seasons I was nervous of tubing after I'd seen the effect end tackle could have on the carp of Birch Grove. When I abandoned helicopter rigs in favour of running set-ups again I found I wasn't happy

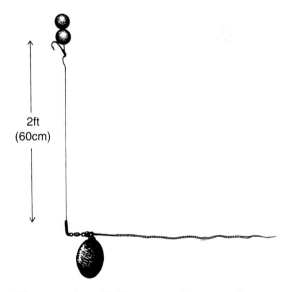

2ft
(60cm)

Why on earth would this set-up catch a pressured carp? I don't know but it has been known to happen.

Pinning down by adding Kryston's 'Drop 'em' to an otherwise buoyant hooklink.

using braided hooklinks without tubing, which I've now used again for the last two or three years. I weight the back end of the tubing to pin it to the bottom, but I don't pin braids down. On the other hand, I have seen anglers having success with pinned-down braids. Whatever you feel happiest with, but bear in mind that carp could start to spook off tubing, leads, looped hooklinks, line or any other aspect of your tackle which they encounter enough times in a danger situation to start to associate it with danger.

Presentation pressure relates to a predictable, frequently encountered source of danger. Move the goalposts slightly and the recognition of danger diminishes, certainly not to the point where the carp are going to throw themselves on the bank, but rather to a situation where the angler is in with a chance at a time when the carp were ignoring all the known, familiar presentation pressure situations.

Temporary and Early-season Pressure

I have included this category just to make the point that carp tend to forget. A bait which stops working on one session may well be working again at the start of the next one. There is certainly a period at the start of each season where the lessons of the previous seasons seem to have been forgotten, and baits and methods which have long since blown have a brief rebirth until the pressure refreshes the carp's memory buds and the revived method or bait suddenly dies a death. This particular phenomenon can be a pain when you are trying to catch with a carefully designed, conscientiously prebaited, apparently readily accepted bait, and someone who has no idea what they are doing (allegedly) comes along with a ready-made that the carp have been fleeing from for seasons and catches the biggest fish in the lake! It happens. It's been done to me. When it does happen, recognize it as a temporary one-off, find out what make of ready-mades was being used (in case it's a two-

off), and try them on a rod until your own bait starts to work.

The problem about anticipating the effects of pressure is that you have to have a good idea of what has gone before on a water to know what the carp are most likely to react against. A tendency to follow fashion means that it is nearly always possible to make an inspired guess as to where any water lies in the pressure cycle, but the more familiar you are with the fish and the water, the clearer your picture should be of what will and what will not work at any given time, subject to the odd unpredictable lapse of memory on the part of the carp.

Pressure point. The Gap Swim on Darenth Tip Lake. A series of captures in the gap through the island resulted in the fish becoming increasingly wary of the spot.

8 PRESENTATION: THE LAST YARD

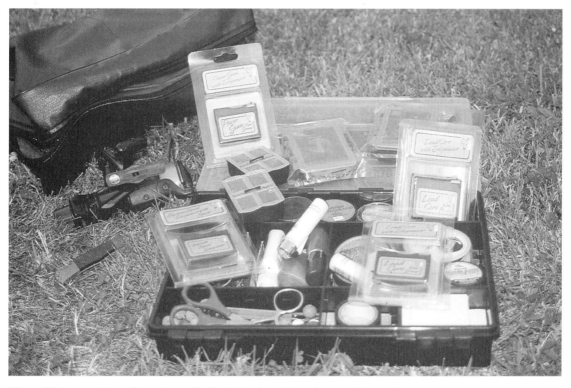

The tackle box and rig wallet – always by the bedchair ready to ring any changes that may be necessary if I do not think I am getting the best out of a situation.

For now, forget the hooklength. I will deal with that in some detail in Chapter 9. Kevin Nash has covered it in Chapter 10, and I have also asked the contributors to the book to specify their favourite hooking arrangement for the circumstances in which they usually fish. This chapter looks at the alternative terminal tackle arrangements up to the addition of the hooklength, and some popular terminal arrangements will be discussed here.

Running Rigs with Tubing

There are two main areas of thought here. Does the line want to run through the tubing with the lead semi-fixed, or are you better with the tubing running through the lead for increased sensitivity? When I reverted to running lead set-ups a few years back I decided I was not happy with the line running through the tubing. This did not strike me as a true running set-up. I opted for the increased sensitivity of the lead running on the tubing, and for the most part that is how I have fished since.

I reverted to running rigs in the first place because the waters I fish had been fished with fixed lead set-ups for a number of years. For real effectiveness, fixed lead means heavy lead, and I was becoming convinced that the fish were learning to pick up the bait, straighten the hooklink and 'feel' for the danger of the set-up without giving an indication. Fixed leads were still accounting for fish, but how many was I missing out on?

I designed a running rig set-up aimed at detecting the attentions of fish which were merely straightening the hooklink and feeling for danger. I did not think that the line running through the tubing would achieve this. I looked at dispensing with the tubing, but because I use braids nearly all the time I was not happy about the increased chances of tangles, even when using PVA stringers.

I have shown the set-up I came up with for running rig fishing. I have used and refined this arrangement over the last few years and I am convinced it has produced a number of fish I would not have caught on a heavy fixed lead set-up. Before I started using it, I struggled with the concept. It was the heavy lead in the previous set-up that was hooking the fish; I would miss out on fish through changing to running leads where the chances of the fish irrevocably hooking itself were reduced. Bearing in mind that I am convinced that the buzzer sounds more often with running set-ups, I have been amazed at the buzzer sounding/fish hooked ratio. In fact, I can think of just one indication which did not result in a hooked fish, and as that was a drop back, it could have been a bream.

On the other hand, the number of indications which were not full-blooded takes which have resulted in good fish have been numerous. When I was struggling with myself over the change, what I could not rationalize is the length of time it takes a fish to get rid of the hook even when it is not what I have just termed 'irrevocably hooked'. When I fish the Mangrove, I am often further back from the rods than I care to be because of the nature of the platforms, but once that buzzer sounds on this set-up then the fish is certainly on the end long enough for the angler to complete the job of setting the hook. Takes have ranged from full-blooded runs, down through half-runs, stop and start takes and cautious tightenings of the line resulting in three or four bleeps. The sensitivity of the end tackle confuses the fish and it gives an involuntary indication, even where it is in control of itself and has no intention of committing itself to a convenient run. I have found this set-up particularly useful in winter where feeding caution prevails and full-blooded runs can be difficult to induce.

I will cover the tubing aspect. I avoided tubing for some seasons while I was using fixed leads, preferring the 'difference' of lead core fly line for the bottom length, and went back to

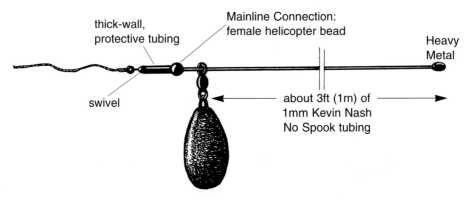

The set-up I use for running lead fishing.

tubing with some reservations. However, I prefer some material other than mono in the immediate area of the hookbait and decided on tubing. I suspect that, other than in exceptional circumstances, carp are always aware of the presence of end tackle, which is why I see the subterfuge involved in getting the carp to pick up a hookbait as a battle of wits.

Having stated my preference for tubing or lead core line to mono at the baited spot, I will make the point that I fish both tubing and lead core in longer lengths than I see many other anglers doing. Tubing is there for two reasons. One is to minimize the chances of tangles. The other is to mask the presence of the mono leader or line. So my tubing is much longer than the minimum length required to prevent tangles, usually as long as three or four feet.

I have a preference for Kevin Nash's No Spook tubing because of its dull matt green appearance. My imagination tells me that this tubing will be less obvious to the carp than some of the shiny materials available, but I have no statistical or observational evidence that one tubing is any better than any other.

When fishing this set-up, I will emphasize that the sensitivity comes from the freedom of movement of the tubing through the lead attachment. You need a generous size of swivel or a John Roberts leger bead to maximize this freedom of movement. When the carp tightens the hooklink testing for danger, there needs to be a minimum of resistance through the lead attachment point.

When the end tackle is lying on the bottom of the lake, I do not honestly think that the difference between 0.5mm and 1.00mm tubing is

For running rigs, use a generous size lead swivel or add a John Roberts leger bead to increase sensitivity.

Running rig with the line running through the tubing; this is popular, but nothing like as sensitive as having the tubing running through the lead swivel or leger bead.

Popular in-line lead 'running' set-up. But just how sensitive is this as a running rig?

Using the Nash safety bead in a non-tubing set-up.

going to increase the chances of a take. Having convinced myself of this fact, I do not torture myself by threading line through 0.5mm tubing. Threading 1.00mm can be difficult enough at times: if it becomes a nightmare, start again with a fresh length of tubing.

Set-ups with the line running through the tubing are much easier to design than those where the tubing runs through the lead attachment. The Kevin Nash leger bead is popular for these set-ups, and I have shown a couple of typical terminal arrangements for this type of rig. To me, this type of set-up is a compromise between fixed leads and true running rigs. They are convenient to fish but nothing like as sensitive as the arrangements described above. However, if you can improvise a very sensitive set-up of this type, then it is worth some thought.

Running Rigs without Tubing

I know that many anglers are happier without tubing, and if you are fishing stiff links or mono hook lengths, tubing can almost certainly be dispensed with. Having said this, I have watched Rob Hughes and Simon Crow fishing an excellent non-tangle running set-up with braided hooklinks. I have included drawings of practical set-ups of this type, the important point being that you have to avoid the hooklink and main line tangling together on the drop, which the Nash safety leger bead is designed to do.

Fixed and Semi-fixed Lead Rigs

These are also commonly known as helicopter rigs. Since this set-up was popularized in the mid-1980s, it seems to have become accepted as the be-all and end-all of terminal tackle arrangements, whereas in reality it is of fairly limited application. Let us just clarify the point that there should be no such thing as a fixed lead rig. That is the effect the rig is seeking to apply. The set-up must be a semi-fixed lead for safety purposes, to allow the hooklink to separate from the rig in the event of a carp being hooked on a broken-off length of line. I will come back to the safety aspect.

Semi-fixed lead helicopter rigs have three major points going for them. They are non-tangle, they are simple to use and they are freely available in tackle shops – so no great thought has to be given to the design aspect of the terminal arrangement. In a carp world where pressure dictates the evolution of bait and tackle arrangements, I cannot think of much else these overused set-ups have going for them.

A fixed lead set-up is designed to hook – or partially hook – the carp at the moment of the line being straightened. This gives rise to two lines of thought. One is that the lead is heavy enough to ensure that the hook penetrates to the extent that the fish cannot shake it out. That is a very simple concept and one which is understandably popular with a great many carp anglers. The down side of the very heavy lead syndrome is that if the carp is not irrevocably hooked, then it may manage to shake the hook out without the angler knowing about it. The very weight of the lead reduces the chance of the buzzer sounding in these circumstances.

A semi-fixed set-up with a lighter lead is a bit of a contradiction in terms. The chances of the carp being irrevocably hooked are lower, but the chances of some sort of indication being given are increased. I will be honest, I can envisage no situation in which a fixed lead set-up with a lighter lead has any credibility. You may as well go straight onto a running lead set-up, which will give you the best of both worlds.

To me, fixed lead set-ups mean leads of at least 3oz, preferably heavier.

Most helicopter set-ups available from the shops are of limited application because the hooklink is locked in position next to the lead. This makes the set-up unsuitable for use on silty bottoms, and means that the lead is always lying next to the bait on hard bottoms. I like using camouflaged leads, but I do not think for one moment that they fool the carp. On hard bottoms, the fish

are always aware of the end tackle, and while you may argue that no carp is ever going to associate a lead with danger, that can only be a matter of opinion. If fish do come to make such an association, then you are reducing your chances of success before you even cast out.

The other point of major importance when the hooklink is locked next to the lead is that the fish has to move the lead to give any sort of indication. To me this is a major design fault in this set-up, a point I will explore further under 'Silt Rigs'.

Helicopter rigs are, however, in universal use, and are extremely popular, so I have illustrated a couple of such arrangements, with emphasis on the semi-fixed aspect for safety reasons.

One of the major pluses of helicopter rigs is that they are so anti-tangle that tubing is not absolutely necessary. This is a set-up which I tend to use in conjunction with lead core fly line, for two reasons. One is to pin the end length of line firmly to the bottom, and the second is just so there is a different material to mono or tubing in the immediate area of the hooklink and bait.

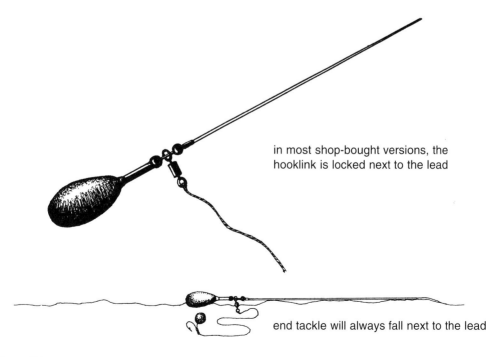

in most shop-bought versions, the hooklink is locked next to the lead

end tackle will always fall next to the lead

The Helicopter Rig.

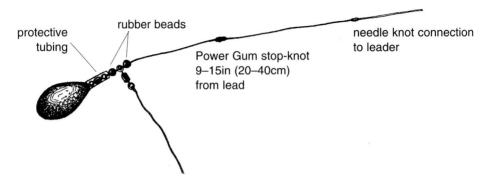

protective tubing

rubber beads

Power Gum stop-knot
9–15in (20–40cm)
from lead

needle knot connection
to leader

An alternative set-up for the lead core fly line.

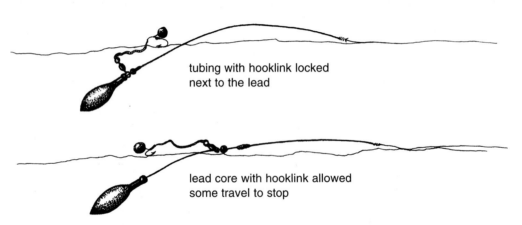

tubing with hooklink locked
next to the lead

lead core with hooklink allowed
some travel to stop

The different end results of alternative helicopter set-ups when fishing over silt.

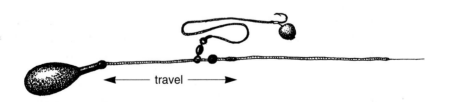

← travel →

The fact that the hooklink is not locked next to the lead allows the carp to give some indication as it straightens the hooklink, but it does not move the lead.

Silt Rigs

How do you fish over silt? This is a question I get asked a great deal. Well, the answer is that for reasons I will explain, all my helicopter rigs are silt rigs. A silt rig is simply a variation on the helicopter rig theme, although that should be the other way round, because the lead on the end of the line silt rigs were in use on the heavily silted north-west waters long before the helicopter rig was popularized by the writing of Zenon Bojko. (Zen never claimed that the set-up he advocated was original; it was his renaming of the arrangement that caught on and stuck.)

As I have already mentioned, I am happier with a heavy lead on a fixed lead set-up. This causes problems over heavy silt because the lead will drag the hooklink down into the silt. Pulling the lead back out will aggravate the problem because it can cause an immediate tangle with braided lines and bury the hooklink in the groove made by the dragging back of the lead. The simple safeguard against both problems is to allow some freedom of movement of the hooklink upwards from the lead to a stop at a suitable distance up the tubing, lead core line or leader. The hooklink rests on the lead knot protective tubing prior to the cast and flies up the line to the stop on the cast, staying there throughout the cast until the lead hits the bottom. When you tighten down, the hooklink is clear of the lead, either sitting on top of the silt or the predetermined distance away on a hard bottom.

I know that the immediate reaction of some anglers is to argue that, because the hooklink can travel, this reduces the deadliness of the fixed lead effect. It doesn't. If you still want the set-up to be fully fixed, pull the line as tight as possible and jam the line in a strong clip. However, when you spend a lot of time fishing this set-up over silt, you learn that allowing a little slack in the line gives sufficient movement at the other end for the carp to give an indication you would not have got with the hooklink locked tight to the lead. This consideration applies equally to fishing over silty and hard bottoms and is a definite edge over a helicopter set-up where the fish has

to move the lead to give any sort of indication. I do not hit single bleeps on running lead arrangements, but I do on this set-up.

Lead Core Set-ups

I like lead core fly line in conjunction with the silt rig described above, particularly over silty bottoms. The lead core lies hard on the bottom and will soon be covered by silt when you have fish feeding in the swim. With the lead in the silt and the lead core becoming covered, the presence of tackle in the baited area really does become minimal. When we are fishing waters where you can bait up from a boat it pays to have the end tackle in position before ground bait is applied to increase the chances of the end tackle being covered. (This is only applicable if you are fishing with someone else. I am not suggesting that you leave your tackle unattended.)

When you are fishing at range, you need a very heavy version of lead core line (30lb breaking strain upwards), and again I use at least a yard of lead core to keep the mono leader as far from the hook length and bait as possible. To avoid creating a captive set-up, the lead core should be connected to the leader by means of a needle knot. I have illustrated the needle knot I use with lead core, but bear in mind that using this set-up necessitates carrying a needle with an eye big enough to allow the threading of the mono leader line.

The lead inner should be stripped from the lead core for a few inches at each end to allow the tying of the bomb knot and the needle knot. Stripping a limited length of line can be awkward with some lead cores. If the entire lead inner starts to pull, overcome this by clipping your forceps on the lead core while you strip the required length out at each end.

I have tried lead core with running lead set-ups but I find it too tangly. I limit its use to extreme range fishing on waters where I do not think the carp's thinking has started to overcome the fixed lead situation.

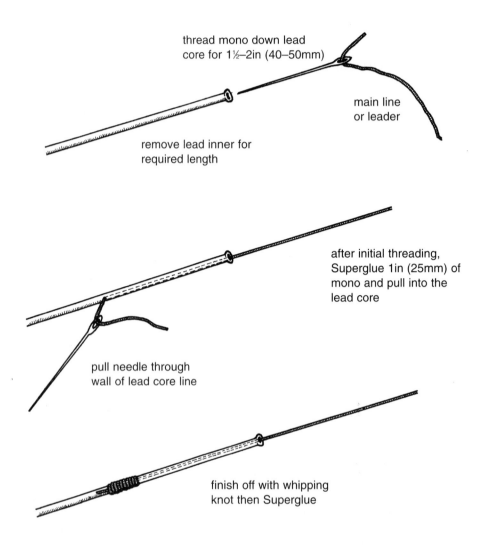

thread mono down lead
core for 1½–2in (40–50mm)

main line
or leader

remove lead inner for
required length

after initial threading,
Superglue 1in (25mm) of
mono and pull into the
lead core

pull needle through
wall of lead core line

finish off with whipping
knot then Superglue

Needle knot for connecting mono to lead core fly line

Pendant Leads

There are two basic design of leads, pendant and in-line. Because I want a free-running set-up with the tubing running through the lead attachment, most of my fishing is done with pendant leads. There are a number of points to look out for when you are selecting a pendant lead. These centre round shape, finish and the

means of attachment to the set-up. I will look at the categories in turn.

Shape
There are a number of factors which determine the ideal shape of lead for the situation in which you are fishing. The dumpier the lead (including round leads which were the fashion a few seasons back) the greater the concentration of

weight. There are those who argue that this concentration of weight is essential for making the most of a fixed lead set-up when the hook has to make optimum penetration at the moment the hooklink tightens to the lead.

On the other hand, dumpy and round leads do not cast as well as longer leads, so lead selection has to take casting distance into account too. I have found the best casting leads to be the Birmingham Angling Centre casting leads, closely followed by the Zipp-shape. These leads are an ideal compromise between weight concentration and casting performance. In theory, longer leads may cast even better, but they have two drawbacks. Firstly the concentration of weight is too spread out, and secondly the length of these leads (which allows speed through the water as well as speed through the air) causes them to penetrate silt bottoms too deeply. Greg Fletcher and I experimented with these leads at Roman Lakes in the early 1980s, and while they undoubtedly flew a long way, we had to hand-line them out of the silt to retrieve them! In extreme cases, this can lead to actually losing the end tackle.

Finish

I like coated leads. I do not know if they give any sort of angling edge in the camouflage sense, but the smooth coat achieved with this finish is a reassuring protection against possible line damage, particularly on waters where gravel and stones frequently damage the leads. If you prefer a straight-lead finish, watch out for damage and carry a file, or use your hook sharpener to smooth down any cuts. Otherwise, you will find yourself changing leads frequently.

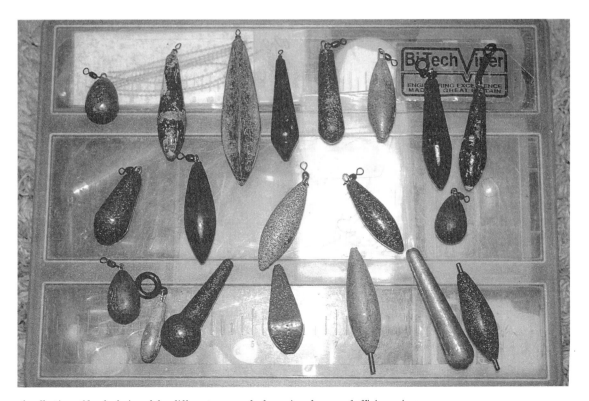

A collection of leads designed for different uses and of varying degrees of efficiency in a variety of carp fishing situations. I carry all sorts of leads with me, and after one clear out of the tackle bag I discovered I had been carrying 14lb of leads round with me!

Means of Attachment

Most pendant leads are now sold with some sort of swivel attachment which is added to the wire of the lead during the manufacturing process. This is usually in the form of a diamond swivel or an orthodox swivel. Diamond swivels are bad news on two counts. One is that the process of forming the diamond causes damage, which can in turn damage line tied to the swivel. (The damage is in the form of creases with sharp edges which will gradually damage and cut through line tied in the point of the V of the diamond.) This potential for damaging line was brought home to us when Mary lost a good fish on a helicopter rig incorporating a diamond swivel at the start of a season on

Dumpy or round leads give a better concentration of weight for self-hooking rigs.

BAC   Zipp-type   casting lead

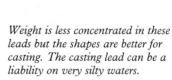

Weight is less concentrated in these leads but the shapes are better for casting. The casting lead can be a liability on very silty waters.

Check for cuts on uncoated leads. Change the lead or smooth it down with a file or hook sharpener.

Be careful if you use diamond-eye swivels. There are sometimes sharp edges in the 'V' of the diamond, which can damage line.

Birch. The other adverse feature of the diamonds is that they do not allow a smooth passage of line or tubing on a running rig set-up. I use a snap link and orthodox swivel in conjunction with these leads when I use them for extreme range fishing.

I prefer orthodox swivel attachments. I also prefer the bigger size of swivel which comes with some of these leads. This gives a freer moving set-up with the running tubing arrangement that I favour. Increasing use of running set-ups has emphasized the importance of the need for a free-running point of attachment and in some situations I now use the John Roberts plastic leger bead for added sensitivity, adding it to the set-up by means of a snap swivel.

In-line Leads

There are some situations in which I always use in-line leads. Again, I look for a lead which allows a free passage of the tubing so I can fish my running tubing rig. The best casting leads are not always the best running leads, and some of them have to be adapted to your own needs.

I always fish in-line leads in weedy waters, on the edge of lily pads, and in margin spots where there is a troublesome chance of the fish getting snagged. The in-line effect reduces the chances of the lead getting snagged.

The two in-line leads I favour are the free-running Birmingham Angling Centre design in weights up to 2oz, and Mike Willmott's Essential Products Comet leads for weights in excess of 2oz. Mike's are better casting leads but the BAC design adapts better to my running set-up.

The longest casting in-line lead I have encountered is the MCF design, which is dumpier than the BAC and Essential Products Comet leads. It therefore flies further, but buries itself in silt bottoms. The MCF and Essential Products Comet leads are very well finished and have simple and efficient semi-fixed lead fittings which can be modified to free-

A. Essential Products'
Comet lead

B. Birmingham Angling Centre
in-line lead

C. MCF Products' in-line lead

Three different types of in-line leads. I use A and B for close- to medium-range fishing and C for long-range work. All my fishing near snags, in weed or near pads is done with in-line lead set-ups.

running set-ups.

I have not much to add on in-line leads. All the angling and design considerations of your bottom yard of line are as outlined earlier in the chapter. I know some anglers favour in-lines for long range work but I prefer the freedom of movement of the tubing through the swivel – or Roberts bead – attachment to a pendant lead.

Other Leads

Advances in tackle design and manufacture have resulted in the emergence of a number of different types of leads for a range of specialized angling situations: flat leads, terrapin leads, rounds leads, flighted leads. If you are fishing a situation where you do not think any of the leads you have available to you are quite right for the job, then check out the adverts in the carp press and you may find the solution to your problem has already been invented and is freely available!

All these alternatives may seem very compli-cated to anyone in their formative carp-fishing years. Carp-fishing experience removes the complications because you learn to discard the alternatives that do not suit your type of fish-ing. Currently I am very confident fishing my running set-ups in conjunction with my braid-ed hook lengths and carp confusing PVA set-ups, but I will emphasize the point that they are all part of the overall end-tackle picture to me. Beyond eighty or ninety yards, I have to think it out again because running set-ups become less effective the further out you go. If I were fishing the huge French reservoirs and rowing my baits out to a couple of hundred yards, I would be using a very heavy lead on a fixed lead set-up. Takes in those circum-stances are all or nothing.

As in any other area of carp fishing, thought has to be given to the set-up best suited to your type of fishing, which is why the alternatives always have to be explored and considered. Design the last yard of your tackle to suit the fishing you are doing, and keep rethinking it on

This lovely autumn mid-twenty common fell to a cautious four-bleep indication on a sensitive running rig set-up.

9 PRESENTATION: THE HOOKLINK

A range of hooklink materials taken straight out of the rig wallet for this shot. I have a favourite hooklink set-up, but I am always ready to put out alternatives if the situation demands it.

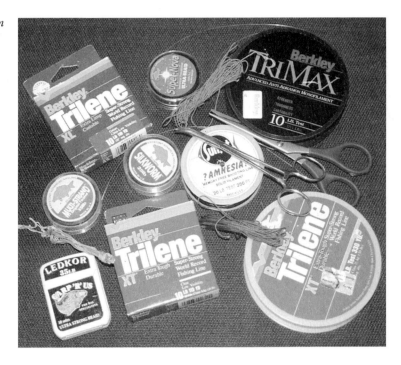

The problem with taking any single aspect of carp fishing and dealing with it in isolation is that its overall significance in the scheme of things can become distorted or exaggerated. The importance of the hooklink cannot be exaggerated, but it can be distorted. My hooklink is designed to do the job I want of it in the circumstances in which I fish, and each component is part of the whole. In other words, over many years I have eliminated the negative to arrive at the positive, an oft-overlooked aspect I will try to deal with as we go along. I will give an example to illustrate the point I am making there.

We have all had hooks open out on us. The reaction from inexperience, or lack of thought, is that the hook was a bad one, the fish was a monster which no hook could hold, the hook was too small, or the angler was unlucky. A partially opened hook happens to me on average once a season. My immediate reaction is that the feeding situation was not quite right, that the hook hit a bony part of the carp's mouth, that the hook was too big, or that the hooklink was not long enough. Short hooklinks, particularly on helicopter rigs, are particularly prone to causing opened-out hooks, because of the change of angle from the initial penetration to the angler setting the hook then exerting increasing pressure. Understand that a hook usually opens out simply because it has not

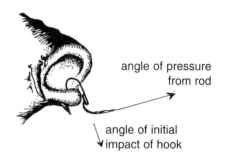

angle of pressure
from rod

angle of initial
impact of hook

Partially opened hook. Lost monster or a poor hooking arrangement?

Hook opening out situation.

penetrated to the bend and you will understand why a strong small hook may be preferable to a larger hook in the same pattern, and why a micro barb, or no barb, is preferable to a barb which impedes penetration.

There is no single right answer when it comes to the design and practice of putting together and using successful hooklinks. However there are guiding principles to work along, and we will examine these principles and the practicalities in some detail. The last foot or two of your set-up is crucial to the success of all your other hard work and thinking, and for me, I want a hooklink to do three things.

- The first is that it must give as little discouragement as possible to the carp when it comes to pick up the hookbait. That sounds negative, but a hooklink will never actively encourage a carp to pick up a bait; the best we can hope for is that it discourages the carp as little as possible, and certainly does not prevent it from taking the hookbait.
- The second point is that when the carp does pick up the bait, the design of the hook and hooklink gives an optimum chance for the hook to actually prick and hook the carp. Estimates of the ratio of pick-ups to takes varies from angler to angler, but if you achieve a take for every two pick-ups, then you are working to a high ratio.
- The third point is that when you do set the hook in a carp, the hook and the hooklink must do the job they are designed to do and help you put the carp on the bank. In other

words, the hook does not break or open out, the hookhold does not give way, the hooklink material does not break, and the knots at the hook and the swivel do not give way.

Let us examine these three points in greater detail.

The hooklink should give as little discouragement as possible. There are three main points to consider here: hooklink material, length of hooklink and the actual presentation, whether to fish a bottom bait or a pop-up. As for hooklink material, there are three main alternatives: braids, monos and stiff links. The categories are a bit too vague to be scientific, so I will talk specifics within my own terms of reference and personal experiences.

Over the last four years, I have caught a great many carp in this country and at Fishabil in France. Throughout that period, I have been experimenting with hooklink materials and the length of the hooklink, concentrating on the three principles mentioned above. I will not pretend that my tests have been exhaustive, and I certainly have not carried out detailed comparisons of different types of materials within each category. In other words, I have found what I have felt to be the most consistently successful material within a category – through personal experience and the observation of other people's results – and experimented with the categories rather than a range of different products within each category. In order of preference I fish Kryston's 25lb Silkworm, the stiff link in 18–20lb bs mono (Berkley Trimax or Amnesia), Multistrand in the form of the combi-link (two-thirds heavy braid or mono and one-third Multi-strand), with lighter mono (Trimax or Berkley Extra Limp in 8–10lb breaking strain) coming out fourth choice.

My switch to 25lb Silkworm is well enough documented, and I changed to that material because I had seen Dave Treasure of South Wales, and others, have consistent success on it. I could not rationalize it, I changed with great reluctance, but the evidence was there and I could not ignore it. Since I changed to the Silkworm I have told myself on a number of occasions that there must be something better, and have fished it against the alternatives and some of the new materials that hit the scene each season. 25lb Silkworm has come out best each time, be it on the Mangrove, Birch Grove or at Fishabil in France.

25lb Silkworm may work best for me because of my style of fishing. Because I spend so much time fishing over silt, I do not pull back after the cast. Because I spend so much time fishing with stringers, a braid may work better than other materials because of the way the end tackles falls and lies – although I rarely fish stringers at Fishabil and the Silkworm still comes out tops in comparisons there.

I will emphasize the point I made earlier about the hooklink not discouraging the fish from picking up the bait here. It is noticeable that certain braids, including Silkworm, have a better success rate than monos during the hours of daylight. Bearing in mind that I do not straighten out the hooklink, and I do not pin it down either, I have come to the conclusion that my first choice of hooklink apparently does not alarm the fish visually. At first glance, that may seem a small point, but when negative thoughts start to invade your thinking the fact that your hooklink does not actively spook the carp is a basis for confidence. I will emphasize that, on occasions, mono users alongside me at Fishabil have scored well at night, but have had noticeably poorer results in daylight.

I have no blind adherence to 25lb Silkworm. A number of my best friends in carp fishing use mono links or stiff links almost exclusively. They are very successful carp anglers, and because their end-tackle choice is at variance with mine, I have included drawings of a number of their favoured set-ups in Chapter 11. I have no wish for this section to give too narrow a view of a subject as vital as end tackle.

I fished 17lb bs Berkley Trimax as a mono stiff link on one rod through a couple of Fishabil sessions. Trimax is a soft mono with a low memory. I had fewer takes on the mono than on the Silkworm, but all my bigger fish fell to that rod. Exponents of low memory hooklinks reckon that they form an anti-eject rig. The carp has trouble blowing the bait out because the hooklink does not bend. I was a bit intrigued by the fact that the supposed anti-eject rig accounted for the bigger fish, but results were so slow on the set-up during the second session when I was experimenting that I abandoned it and tried something else.

I will mention one other statistic from Fishabil. On one session I fished next to young Roddy Porter, briefly one time holder of the carp record. I knew before the session that Roddy prefers to fish mono, so I was surprised to see him using 25lb Silkworm on one rod. He was doing so because I'd gone on about the material so much in print that he just had to try it on one rod. It finished up on two rods out of his three and gave consistently better results than his 10lb breaking strain mono.

Stiff link of heavy mono. Its claimed effectiveness is that it is not supple enough to bend when the carp tries to eject the bait.

I can draw no firm conclusion on hooklink materials. My own experience has narrowed my choice down to 25lb Silkworm. Others have arrived at Multistrand, mono, or stiff links. All I can suggest is that, if your results are not all you think they should be, you keep your mind open on the subject and try fishing different materials against each other to compare results. This is not always satisfactory, but I started out with some scepticism with the Silkworm on one rod and, despite flirtations with other materials, I now use it almost all the time.

Length of Hooklink

One of the defining moments in my own carp fishing was when I managed to rationalize what actually happens when a carp pricks itself and gives an indication. Up to that time, I had a confused notion about the fish pricking itself when it straightened up with the bait, which meant I was messing around with short/medium hooklinks of 4–9in (10–22.5cm). I still see this 'straightening up' theory offered in print, and I totally disagree with it.

I think that the majority of carp are hooked when they pick up the bait, then move far enough to straighten the hooklink. Rationalize this. If they pick up the bait they are either not alarmed by, or have overcome their alarm of, the end tackle and the hooklink material. Before the hair, we used to get twitches from carp. Because the hook was buried in the bait they could straighten the hooklink without getting caught. They were either chancing the hooklink or were not aware of it. Their detection of the danger came from straightening the hooklink.

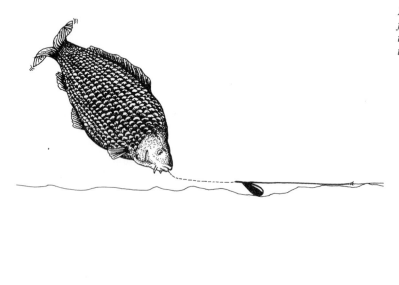

Is your only chance of hooking this feeding carp when it straightens up to a horizontal position? I do not think so!

The moment of truth when the carp straightens the hooklink. This is how the majority of carp are pricked, partially hooked or hooked.

Bare hooks have added an extra degree or two of caution in carp's feeding, but given that they are going to have to pick up the hookbait to test it for danger, their limited thought processes will function best within what they recognize as the danger radius. Within that radius, they will move with extra caution so they can stop and shake the hook out if they get pricked. You rarely see a match angler fish an end trail of less than 2 or 3ft (60 or 90cm). You rarely see a carp angler fish a hooklink of more than 9in (22.5cm).

I have had most success with hooklinks of 15–18in (38–45cm). Beyond that length, I think you have too much material in the area of the hookbait, particularly if you do not straighten out. Short of that length, I think you make the detection of danger too easy for the fish.

I have experimented mightily with hooklink lengths. The season after the *From the Bivvy* season, I spent the summer fishing the silt rig on the Mangrove, using hooklinks of 3–4in (7.5–10cm). My catch rate was similar to the previous season, but I caught fewer big fish. When I reverted to my 15in (45cm) hooklinks in the autumn, I had a run of bigger fish. Inconclusive, I know, but that summer strongly influenced me on hooklink length.

I have experimented with this aspect at Fishabil in France. This Brittany lake can hardly be described as difficult, but when it comes to comparisons, that does not matter. I got takes on shorter hooklinks, but lost more fish. I got the impression that the Fishabil carp liked to roll the hookbait around a bit while they were testing it for danger. Once a carp starts to test a hookbait, flexibility and length of hooklink become of paramount importance. The better the bait application, the less chance there is of the carp pausing in its feeding to assess the danger, but when it does, you need to have done all you can to make identification of the danger bait difficult for the carp.

I think it is a fact of life that more fish are lost on short hooklinks. There are two reasons for this. The first is that the bait is not taken far enough into the carp's mouth. This can lead to hooking around the edge of the lips, a position

from which the hook is under too much pressure and can work out too easily. The second is the point I have mentioned earlier. The initial pricking motion is downwards, because the lead is on the bottom. The fish is lightly hooked – at best – and usually runs because of the pull of the lead, not because it has been pricked. (If anyone ever argues that fish feel pain, try standing them in a pond in the middle of winter – then ask them how they'd like to live in those conditions!)

Now, it is not difficult to figure out what happens to the angle of pull of the hook when you start exerting an upwards pressure. If it has not penetrated to the bend, you will actually be exerting a strong force across the line of the point, which will increase the chances of the hook springing open. Some hooks open out slightly under pressure, then return to their original shape after they have 'sprung', leaving the angler bemoaning his 'luck' at another lost fish.

When I am fishing with boilies, the only circumstances in which I compromise on the length of the hooklink is when I need an extra few yards on the cast and have to shorten the hooklink to allow for the backswing. Even then, I will rarely go shorter than 9 or 10in (22.5 or 25cm). I will emphasize that this comment is about fishing boilies. There will be situations when seeds or particles are being fished when it may be necessary to limit the length of the hooklink to avoid bite-offs, but overpreoccupation on the part of the carp is a lovely sort of problem which rarely seems to occur these days!

Pop-up or Bottom Bait?

Strictly speaking, this is a tactical consideration, but I am covering it in this section because I think pop-ups are vastly overrated and can cost carp anglers more carp than they actually account for. I will qualify that. While they are still valid, pop-ups can be deadly, but there are waters on which they never work, others where they work patchily and other waters where they have been fished out and the carp have become scared to death of them.

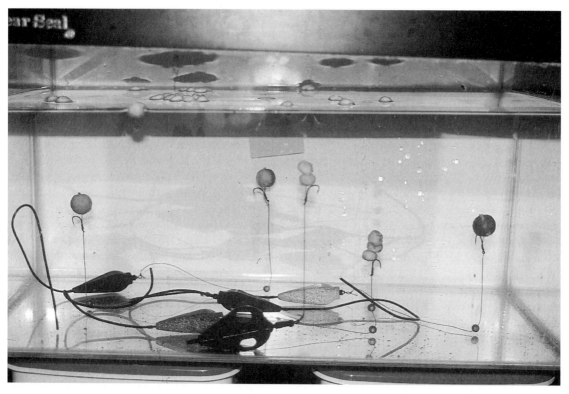

Pop-ups. Sometimes they work, sometimes they do not. On some waters they tend to lose their effectiveness when the pressure is on. Don't be a slave to them if they do not seem to be working. I catch about 5 per cent of my carp on pop-ups.

If in doubt, why risk it?

Over the last few years I would guess that, at the very outside, 5 per cent of my carp have been caught on pop-ups. On waters where they do not work, have ceased to work or work indifferently, you will be limiting your chances and undoing a great deal of hard work by fishing them. Where you are limited to two rods, one on pop-up may be halving your chances. If in doubt, why risk it?

We know that carp feed in and on the bottom. We know that the carp we want to catch eat the free offerings of the bait we are offering them, from the bottom. If we are fishing a prebaited food bait, they may well have eaten as many as a hundred, or even a thousand, baits before they encounter your hookbait. Why risk alarming them by sticking the very one you want them to take up off the bottom? Albert Romp makes an amusing joke of this aspect of presentation in his hilarious slide show. He says he stopped using pop-ups when he found a pea hovering 6in (15cm) above his plate while he was eating dinner one night!

Almost all my fishing is done with bottom baits which have sufficient buoyancy to counteract the weight of the hook and hooklink. In certain circumstances, I use what are referred to as 'critically balanced hookbaits' – usually in winter – but for the most part, I am happiest with baits that are not buoyant enough to cause alarm, but are buoyant enough to come up off the bottom at least as easily as the free offerings.

There are circumstances in which pop-ups may be advisable, or even necessary, but I want to alert you to the possibility that pop-ups may be a waste of time, while some form of bottom bait always has the potential to be taken.

Hooks

Hooks are a minefield if ever there was one. You see more different hooks recommended in print than the number that existed ten years ago! Again, I can only make my own recommendations and assure the reader that they are based on no commercial considerations whatever. When it comes to using a carp hook it must do at least four things.

1. Firstly, the hook should be small enough and light enough to be sucked into the carp's mouth with a minimum chance of detection, but be strong enough to do the job of landing your fish when you have hooked it. There is a variable here in that choice of hook may vary depending on the circumstances in which you are fishing.
2. Secondly, the hook must be sharp enough and of such a design that it gives the maximum possibility of the point taking hold of the carp's flesh when the hook is in the carp's mouth. I am not talking about hooking the carp here. I am talking about the stage of the

Partridge Ritchie McDonald Z13.

This is the best hook I know for grabbing hold of your finger when you do not want it to. Do flatten the barb on this type of hook.

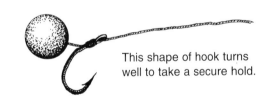

This shape of hook turns well to take a secure hold.

Pull your finished hooklink over your finger to check the turning motion of the hook – preferably with hair and boilie attached.

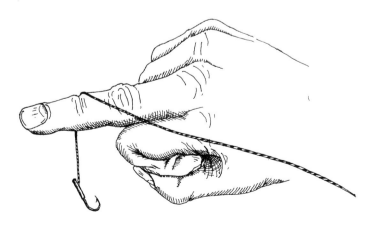

Jim Gibbinson's line aligner. An excellent hooking arrangement.

Knotless knot (see instructions for tying on page 72). This set-up turns most hooks well, but check to see that it works alright with your combination of hook and hooklink material.

take when the fish has taken the bait and hook into its mouth but has not straightened the hooklink. There are some hooks which grab your finger when you reach into the hook box for one and are difficult to shake off. I like the thought of that happening in the carp's mouth. Such a state of affairs may induce a moment's panic and a straightening of the hooklink in a situation where the carp was well in control of its feeding and had no intentions of bolting off with the bait.

3. Thirdly, the hook must turn to give the best possible hookhold when the carp straightens the hooklink. This is achieved through the design of the hook, or the way in which is it tied up. There are three ways of achieving this turning motion. One is through using a shape of hook which turns when the hooklink straightens. The second is by means of Jim Gibbinson's Line Aligner set-up. The third is by means of the knotless knot. The knotless knot is illustrated here and achieves the necessary turning motion with most patterns of hook, but not all. Where it does not achieve the necessary turn or the correct angle of penetration, use the Line Aligner set-up, which is also illustrated here.

4. Fourthly, the hook must land the fish you have hooked. This is not just down to the design of the hook. The hook pattern and size are the starting point. The points mentioned above, the length of the hooklink, and the state of mind of the carp in its feeding are all relevant when it comes to achieving an infallible hookhold.

I have carp fished successfully with a number of hooks, including Drennan Super Specialists size 4 and size 6, Mustad 34021s size 6, Gold Label Penetrator 2 size 6, Mainline Connection Pattern Two size 6 and size 8 and Partridge Ritchie McDonald Z13s size 8.

Over the last year or so I have narrowed the field down to the Mainline size 8s, fished with the knotless knot in braid and the Line Aligner in mono, and the Z13s. The barb on the Z13s is inconsistent and awful and I flatten it completely. I would

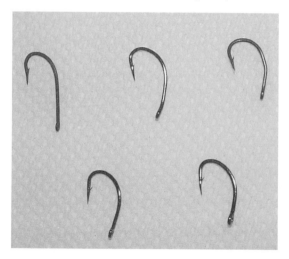

A few of my favourite hooks referred to in the text. Top row left to right: Mustad 34021, size 6; Gold Label Penetrator 2, size 6; Partridge Z13, size 8. Bottom row; Mainline Connection Carp 2, size 8; Owner Cutting Point, size 8. There are now dozens of quality hook patterns available, and the range is growing.

always flatten the barb completely on a hook of this pattern to facilitate unhooking the carp without causing unnecessary damage. The Z13s are the best hooks I have encountered for the 'preliminary grab' syndrome, which is why I use them whenever I possibly can. I do not use them all the time because I have a minor reservation about their strength.

The Mainline Connection Carp Two hooks are the strongest and sharpest I have encountered for their size and weight. They are a similar pattern to the Owner Cutting Point hooks, but in a slightly finer wire (without loss of strength) and a less elaborate point. The one drawback with these hooks is that their needle point is so fine and sharp that the hook almost invariably needs changing after each fish. Usually I change the hook when it no longer brings the tears to my eyes when I stick it in the ball of my thumb, or I can't re-hone it to that necessary degree of sharpness.

I will emphasize that there are many marvellous hooks available to carp anglers now. If in doubt it may pay the reader to study the pages of *Carp-Talk* and check out the types of hooks which are occurring most frequently in the capture reports. The relevant principles outlined above will apply to all the hooks available. It is not just a question of choosing a pattern of hook; it becomes a question of finding out how to fish it to its optimum effectiveness.

Practical Application

The individual components of a hooklink have to be successfully tied together to arrive at the end product, and the hooklink then has to be used to its optimum effectiveness. My hooklinks never let me down, so I will explain how I tie them up, and mention one or two practical considerations about their use.

The knotless knot has made tying braided hooklinks simpler than it was. I use the braid as the 'hair', leaving the length of the hooklink and the length of the hair to be determined at the water. In other words, I tie the knotless knot and leave a generous allowance of line for the finished hair and

Comparison of Owner Cutting Point and Mainline Connection size 6 hooks.

the completed hooklink. The knotless whipping I Superglue, and I also Superglue the line where it leaves the front of the eye. For two reasons. One is to add to the Line Aligner effect. The other is to fix the line in the position on the eye that I want it.

When I am at the water, I tie the loop of the hair to the required length (depending on the size and number of hookbaits) leaving a ½in (13mm) hinge to (hopefully) add to the problems the carp's got when it takes the baited hook into its mouth. The hooklink itself is then tied to the swivel to the required length. I leave a 1in (25mm) trail when I trim the swivel knot. The swivel knot is Superglued, and the trail to the first inch of line. I then Superglue 4 or 5in (10 or 12cm) of the line from the swivel. That is the set-up I use for almost all my carp fishing. It will be a major disappointment to those of you who love to mess around with rigs, but my rig is the carp's confidence in the bait, and the confusion of the PVA set-up.

Stiff links are usually tied up with Amnesia or some other low-memory mono. I tie the mono to the hook with a five turn blood knot. If using the Z13s I do not need a Line Aligner and simply add a dental floss or fine line hair. I fish the stiff link at about a foot. The swivel end is unique in hooklink set-ups in that it consists of an overhand or shoe-lace knot. Take the line through the swivel, double it back down the line, form a loop, then pass both the hook and the loose end back through the loop. Ease this down tight so the loop knot is about ½in from the swivel, trim off allowing a good ¼in (6mm) for the loose end, then Superglue the finished knot. The idea of the loop is that it acts as a hinge, allowing the carp to take the bait into its mouth. The stiffness of the hooklink material makes ejection of the bait difficult.

Knotless knot.

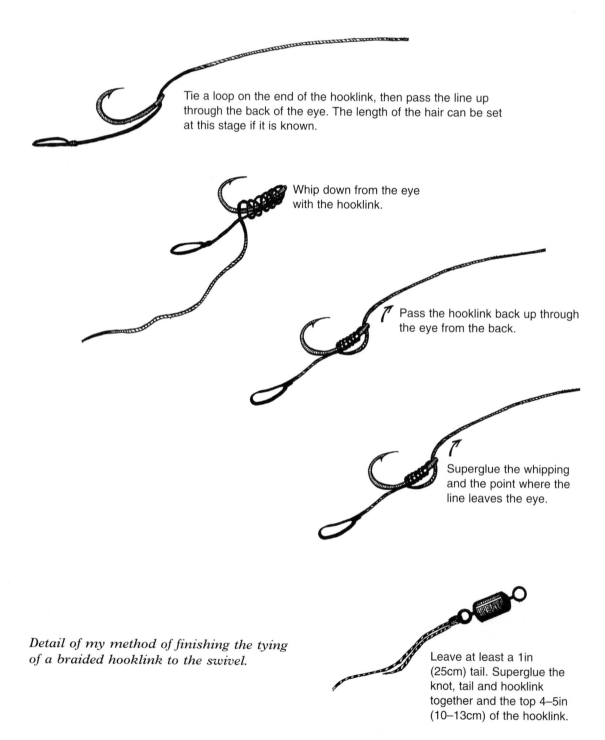

Tie a loop on the end of the hooklink, then pass the line up through the back of the eye. The length of the hair can be set at this stage if it is known.

Whip down from the eye with the hooklink.

Pass the hooklink back up through the eye from the back.

Superglue the whipping and the point where the line leaves the eye.

Detail of my method of finishing the tying of a braided hooklink to the swivel.

Leave at least a 1in (25cm) tail. Superglue the knot, tail and hooklink together and the top 4–5in (10–13cm) of the hooklink.

Stiff link hinge knot.

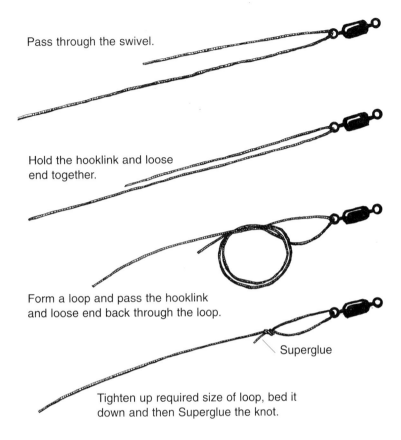

Pass through the swivel.

Hold the hooklink and loose end together.

Form a loop and pass the hooklink and loose end back through the loop.

Superglue

Tighten up required size of loop, bed it down and then Superglue the knot.

I find this set-up works when I am struggling to get takes on the Silkworm, then it suddenly stops working and the Silkworm is working again. I tend to use it as an alternative to Silkworm in the baited area on the 'if the right hand don't get you then the left hand will' basis. On one of the Fishabil trips last season, I was having a difficult day and added the stiff link to the repertoire in the baited area. During the afternoon I lost one good fish and landed my biggest fish of the trip at 28lb 12oz – both these takes coming on the stiff link set-up. I decided the stiff link was where it was at, changed all three end tackles to the set-up, then didn't get another take till I reverted to Silkworm!

The fact that I differentiate between mono links and stiff links may confuse some of you. Well quite simply, I do not consider a mono link of 6–10lb to be a stiff link. I think the differing

definition is accepted by most and that most mono users are talking about hooklinks in the lighter strains. Mono hooklinks are tied up on the basis of the stiff link or with the knotless knot, depending on the suppleness of the mono.

Mono in the lighter strains is difficult to use for hooklinks and will lead to the odd breakage, which I find unacceptable unless the material is giving me a vastly increased number of takes. We are in an era of high-quality abrasion-resistant monos, but still hooklink breakages occur. I have tried the principle at Fishabil and discarded it on the basis of the slowness of the results and the fact that I had a breakage.

Multistrand is understandably one of the favoured hooklink materials. There is a twisted and an untwisted version, both of which are very fine for their strength. The twisted one is

Pass the line twice through the eye.

Clinch Knot.
Ideal for braids and
multistrand but 'crinkly'
with mono.

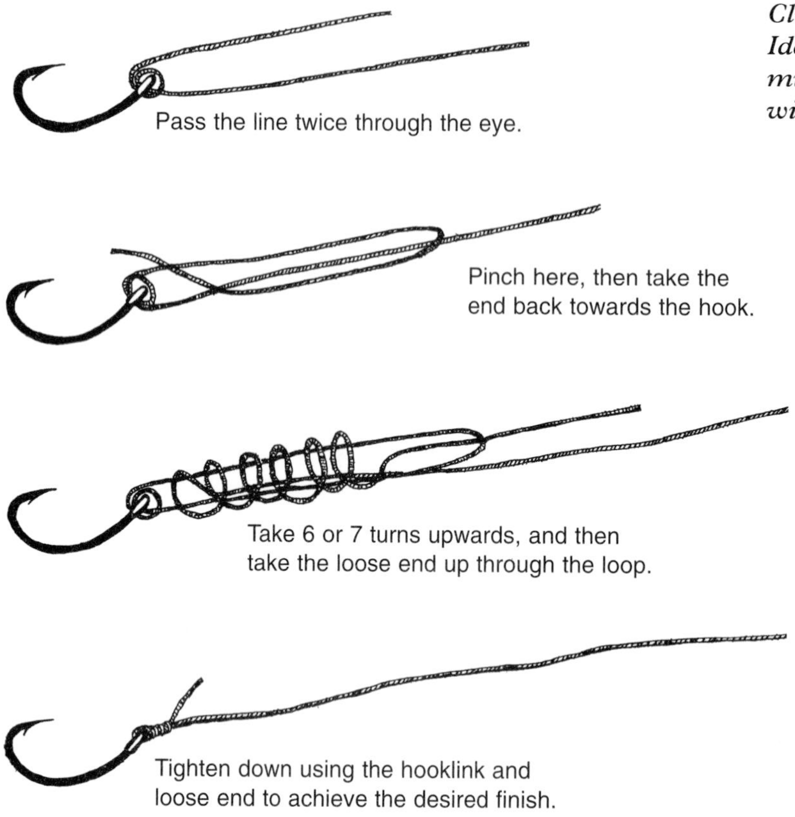

Pinch here, then take the
end back towards the hook.

Take 6 or 7 turns upwards, and then
take the loose end up through the loop.

Tighten down using the hooklink and
loose end to achieve the desired finish.

Blood knot for Amnesia
and heavy mono.

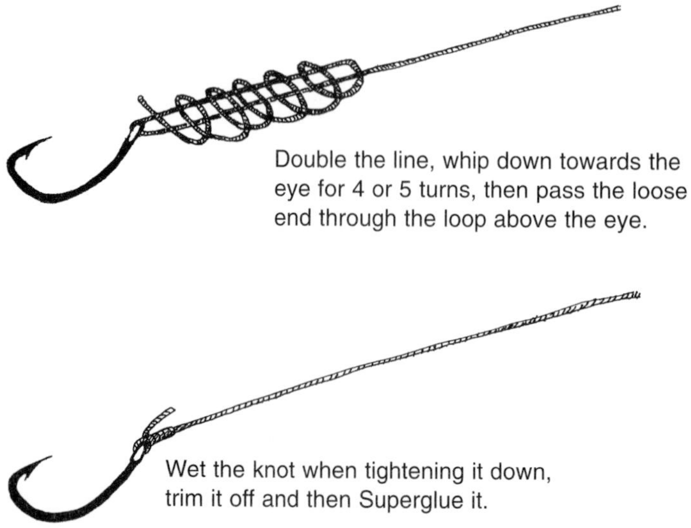

Double the line, whip down towards the
eye for 4 or 5 turns, then pass the loose
end through the loop above the eye.

Wet the knot when tightening it down,
trim it off and then Superglue it.

Whipping knot for hair using light mono, dental floss or hair braid.

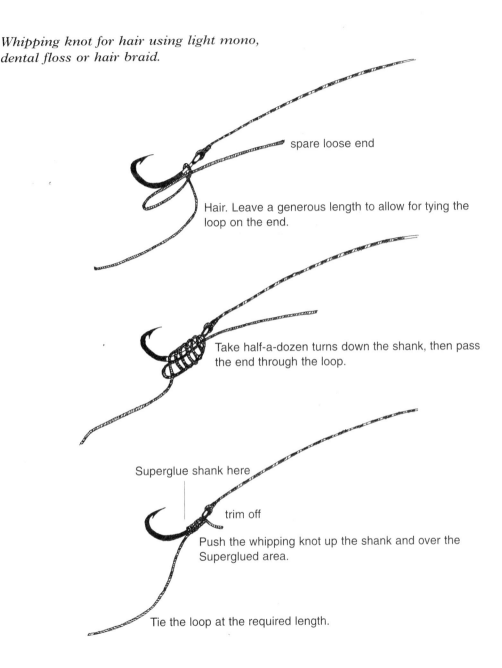

spare loose end

Hair. Leave a generous length to allow for tying the loop on the end.

Take half-a-dozen turns down the shank, then pass the end through the loop.

Superglue shank here

trim off

Push the whipping knot up the shank and over the Superglued area.

Tie the loop at the required length.

favoured by most Multistrand users. It is more user friendly in the sense that it is easier to handle, and gives a simpler presentation under water because the strands do not separate as widely and therefore do not finish up getting clogged up with debris. In the 15lb bs version, it is extremely fine and very abrasion resistant.

The original versions of Multistrand were untwisted versions, and where bottom conditions allow, this is the most effective type, the separation of the strands making the line harder to detect visibly and by touch.

Multistrand is ideal for the knotless knot set-up with the material itself making an ideal fine hair.

Because it is perceived to be tangly, it is usually fished as a combi-link, with the upper two-thirds of the hooklink in the form of a heavy mono or braid, and the bottom third (or even the final inch or two) being formed by the Multistrand. The Multistrand is connected to the other material by means of a water knot or a double grinner, which is then strengthened by a dab of Superglue.

I used the combi-link throughout the *From the Bivvy* season with consistent results and just one breakage, on a bionic snagged fish.

There are a number of hooklink materials in the form of coated Multistrand where the combi-link is formed by the removal of the coating from the required length of Multistrand. The Tackle Box sell some braided versions of such a line, and the famous Kryston Snakeskin is a coated Multistrand which permits a number of alternative hooklink arrangements in the form of stiff links, hinged stiff links, or combi-links.

Kryston have a couple of products which make the use of braids and Multistrand easier

Adjusting the length of the hair.

A

Finished hair. Tie this over-length, then adjust by means of the required number of hitches at point A.

Take the looped hitch, then snug down to determine the finished length. This is useful when you are varying the number of baits on the hair.

Combi-link. One-third multistrand, two-thirds heavy braid, mono or Amnesia. Tie the lines together with the water knot, which is then Superglued. Some anglers prefer to use a small ring for the connections.

for those who have difficulty with them. No Tangle and Super Stiff are gels which are applied to the line to reduce the tangle properties. They are also useful for applying to Multistrand when you are having a rig-tying session. Most anglers have rough hands to which the Multistrand tends to cling, which can be a frustration at the tying-up stage. Simply apply one of the gels to enough of the line for a few hooklinks and the Multistrand is no more difficult to tie than any other line.

If you use braids or Multistrand but cannot be bothered to use the gels, then dip the line in the water's edge before casting. This makes the line heavier and less tangly. If you are using stringers, add the stringer after you have dipped the line in the water.

To straighten out or not after casting? I straighten out stiff links and mono links but leave braids and Multistrand. If you are using critically balanced baits without stringers, there is no need to straighten out the stiffer links because the slowly settling bait will achieve that end result for you (pointed out by Dave Chilton of Kryston).

Dave Chilton of Kryston is single-minded about end tackles and thoroughly understands the mechanics and theory of his business.

Conclusions

I think it is dangerous to draw any conclusions or try to lay down hard-and-fast guidelines about presentation and rigs. I have seen some very complex set-ups illustrated in print, and some anglers will think that the presentation principles I have discussed here are very naive. But the odd thing is that I have observed a great many very successful carp anglers in action and, without exception, their hooklinks have been very simple: a bait attached to a hook on the end of a length of line.

It is in the type of hook and the hook-length material that I find the greatest variation from angler to angler. Only a percentage of my friends share my preference for braids. Some stick with mono; others swear by the stiff link. I do not try to influence them one way or the other (nor they me) and none of us claims that the method we are using is the best. We are confident in it because it seems to be the best for each of us. Do not be too influenced by what appears in print when it comes down to the final choice of bait, hooklink material and hook. These three crucial items are the basis of your confidence. You are the one who has to sit there with them on the other end of your line. Consider the alternatives, make your choices, then fish them with belief and confidence. Only if things do not work out as well as you think they should be doing do you need to go back to the drawing board and think it out again.

The notes in these last two chapters are designed to help if things do not seem to be going according to plan and you are having to think it out again.

10 PRESENTATION: MY WAY WITH RIGS – KEVIN NASH

Kevin Nash needs no introduction. He runs his own international tackle and bait company which is located at Rayleigh in Essex. He has been carp fishing for almost thirty years, has had outstanding success at home and abroad, and has an impressive list of big fish, including a number of forties, to his name. The basis for this chapter was an impressive slide show presentation I watched Kevin give to a fascinated audience at a Carp Society conference. It struck me that his ideas on presentation should reach a far wider audience, and I am delighted Kev has taken the time out from his hectic schedule to put his common-sense ideas on record here.

Tim Paisley

I find the subject of rigs totally absorbing. Indeed, I am never happier than when I am on a highly pressured water where the carp know all the tricks, especially if it is a situation where you can observe the reactions of the carp. I promise you, you would be shocked at how adept the carp are at sussing out our methods. It often surprises me that we catch anything at all!

In the limited space available I will briefly try and explain my approach to rigs in the hope it will give you some further insight into understanding your own rigs. If you understand how something works, you will hopefully understand what is happening when it stops working.

As I write, I bet that at this very moment a carp is feeding over someone's baits. He moves and sucks in a boilie. He then turns his head and moves off to seek out the next boilie he has smelt nearby. It is this movement of the carp after it has sucked in your hook-bait that is critical to your success. Unless the carp moves while he has your bait and hook in his mouth, you will be lucky to catch him.

Your success will be governed to a large degree by three elements in your presentation, your hook, hooklink and lead, and thus you need to understand how to achieve the best from these three elements.

- Your hook needs to be as sharp as possible: the sharper the hook, the better the chance it will catch in the carp's mouth.
- The way you tie your hooklink to the hook is very important, especially with bottom baits. Once the hooklink has tightened, the desired effect is for the hook to turn, which will maximize the chances of pricking and taking hold.

  The way the bait is mounted on the hair may aid the turning/pricking ability of the hook; conversely it may act against it and render the hooking arrangement ineffectual.

  Hooklink length is also a factor. Too short, and the carp may 'miss' the boilie on the suck, i.e. there may not be sufficient movement in the hooklink for the carp to suck the bait in properly. A longer hooklink may not necessarily be long enough, in that the carp may still figure out that the bait is tethered to the hooklink and lead. Conversely, too long a hooklink may result in a bite-off where the carp feeds so confidently that it takes your bait right back beyond its throat (pharyngeal) teeth.
- The third factor is the lead. It is the lead, when it is offering some resistance, that completes the triangle, and hopefully brings about the desired success.

  The mass of the lead offering resistance at one end of the hooklink ensures that, when the carp sucks in the bait and then moves off, the hooklink will straighten. When the slack is removed from the hooklink, then the resistance offered by the lead comes directly into play with the hook:

Fish sucks in bait
↓
Fish moves
↓
Fish tightens hooklink against lead
↓
Hook moves as hooklink is tightened
↓
Hook turns and pricks carp

This is what should happen. Now let us look at making it happen. Back to the beginning and to your hook.

The Hook and Bait Mounting

I will re-emphasize that the hook needs to be very sharp. Personally I do not believe you can buy hooks sharp enough. I have yet to find a pattern of hooks as sharp as those in my own Top Rod range, but I believe my hooks can still be improved.

I check every hook carefully. This is to ensure that the point is perfectly formed, long, thin and tempered hard. In fact, I prefer it so hard it is brittle.

Before casting out, I rub a diamond lap along two sides of the hook point. One or two strokes is all that is required. The objective is to remove the hook's coating, which can dull the edge slightly when it is applied and which I therefore prefer to remove. However, once you have exposed the steel you leave the hook open to corrosion. Few people seem to realize the effect the lake bed can have on their hooks. The corrosion effect of silt/water varies from water to water, presumably reliant on the acidity of the lake/river. On some waters I have fished, it is possible to bring your rig back after a night and find the hook is as sharp as when you cast it out. Conversely, on another water, the hook comes back noticeably blunter after only a

couple of hours in the water. This is why I smear my hook points with Vaseline before I cast out. The Vaseline protects the hook point from the ongoing corrosive elements in the lake, ensuring that your hook is fishing at peak sharpness at all times.

I have made mention of hook brittleness. Because the hook-point diameter of hook points is so fine, and hooks are produced by the million, the temper will vary between individual hooks, batches and makes. You may find the following advice a little strange, but seek out the makes where the hooks are brittle, whereby when under stress, the hook will snap rather than bend. The harder the steel, the better it will take a point and the longer it will keep that point. A hook you can straighten with pliers will have an inferior edge to the hook you can snap with pliers.

Within reason, do not overconcern yourself if the hook has a fine, brittle point for this is your edge in having the sharpest 'pricking device' possible. It is my opinion that it is a fallacy that the hook is at fault if you break it in the region of the point while playing a fish. It simply means that you were playing the fish on the point of the hook, and that a poor hook hold had been achieved, maybe because of bad luck, maybe because of a poorly designed rig. The main purpose of the point of the hook is to gain an initial hold for the hook. It is the bend of the hook that should take the strain of the fight.

Finally, the shape of the hook. You must find the best design of hook for your chosen rig. For instance, with bottom baits I think longer shank hooks are more effective – patterns like Top Rod Pattern 2, Twister and Fang hooks. Of course, shorter shanked patterns are effective when they are tied up utilizing an extended line aligner set-up.

The angle at which the hooklink exits the hook is very important. Therefore all hooks should be tied to the hooklink incorporating a line aligner, or tied in such a way that the mechanics are identical. Achieve this and the hook will turn when the hooklink straightens against the resistance offered by the lead.

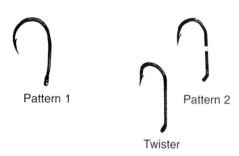

Pattern 1

Pattern 2

Twister

Kevin Nash hooks. I prefer the longer shank patterns for bottom baits – Pattern 2 and Twister. I rarely use tubing to form my aligner, preferring to whip the hooklink to the shank. With longish shanked hooks and down-turned eyes you achieve a hook that turns easily.

The final point I will mention with regard to hooks is the bait mounting. This is probably the least understood element of a rig, and yet a real all-or-nothing element. I am sure that a large number of carp anglers – possibly the majority – fish with the bait tight to (or very close to) the shank. I am not entirely sure what the reason for this is. Presumably it is in the belief that the carp will not pick up the bait and hook unless the two are very close together.

There is a problem here. If the bait is too tight to the hook, it will have an adverse effect on the ability of the hook to turn and prick the carp. My hair length is a minimum of 10mm from the hook shank to the back of the boilie, and I have no problem in my mind in dramatically increasing this distance if I believe the situation dictates such a course of action.

There is a preferred characteristic of what many would consider to be a long hair – not a preference I share. It is that, in tying the hair, it should emerge from an imaginary line through the centre

of the bend, or thereabouts. Achieve this and invariably your hook will turn. Bringing the anchor point of the hair further up the shank to the top of the bend also helps the hook to turn. I am sure this preference is the reason anglers have success with multi-hair bait rigs. It is not the fact that they are using multi-bait hairs that is bringing the success; rather that the longer hair is, for once, ensuring that their rig is working efficiently.

I see many anglers testing the hooking efficiency of their rigs using the finger test which Rob Maylin illustrated in his book *Tiger Bay*, in the chapter describing the bent hook rig. My bottom-bait rigs all pass the finger test; even rigs I know will be ineffectual hookers. It was for this reason that I devised the palm test. Other writers have written describing the palm test and it may well be that you are familiar with the theory. For those of you not familiar with the concept it is important that you use the palm test to check all your rigs prior to casting. Therefore please forgive me for repeating an extract from my book *Top Rig Secrets*:

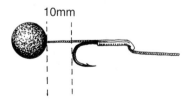

10mm

I fish with a minimum distance of 10mm between the bend of the hook and the back of the boilie.

If the hair is long enough to dissect the bend, this guarantees the hook will turn – if the rest of the hooking arrangement is right.

The palm test.

The palm test is a method I came up with several years ago to test my bottom rigs. I emphasize that I am talking about bottom rigs as opposed to pop-up rigs with which different mechanics come into play. It is a crude test to mimic the way in which the hook-link straightens against the lead and moves the hook inside the carp's mouth.

Rig 1

The hooklink is pulled across the palm of my hand. I am looking for the hook to turn and dig into my hand well before it falls over the edge of my hand (the edge of my hand representing the carp's lips).

1. Tie the rig shown above and pull it across your hand. You will note that nine times out of ten it falls over the edge of your hand without catching.

2. Now tie the second rig featured below, with the one subtle difference of the hooklink exiting through the underside wall of the tube. It catches every time! Your palm is the bottom of the carp's mouth.

With rig 1:
The carp takes in your bait, tightens the hooklink, feels the resistance of the lead, and as the hook probably has not turned and lodged in the mouth the carp easily ejects the bait and rig – without even knowing it happened!

Rig 2

With rig 2:
The carp takes in the bait and hook. As the hooklink straightens against the weight of the lead the hook moves and turns. The point tips over and catches in the carp's mouth. Now he's got a problem!

I mentioned the importance of the bait mounting – the length of the hair between bait and hook. The palm test will illustrate this. If you tie two rigs, one with the bait tight to the hook shank and one with the hair long enough to form a centre-line through the hook bend, you will see what I mean. The boilie tied tight to the hook shank will prevent the hook turning and pricking your hand, thus limiting the rig's effectiveness. I mention this point because I recently saw an article illustrating the palm test. The author portrays rigs without baits mounted. Unless you intend to fish without baits, surely it is best to test what you are about to cast out? When palm testing rigs, test with the baits mounted. (How many thousands of anglers are taken in by the rig writers rather than listening to the rig users!)

Hooklinks

As we have already seen, the length of the hooklink can be critical, although if you read the various carp magazines you may be forgiven for thinking it cannot be that critical. In the last few months alone I have seen authors recommend hooklink lengths from 8–15in (20–40cm)! The

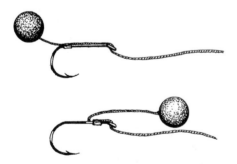

My 'blow-out' line aligner rig. The hooklink is whipped to the shank to create the desired effect of a hook that will turn. The forward position of the hair anchor point also aids the hook's ability to turn and prick the carp. The anchor point must be movable so that when the carp is pricked and blows against the bait the anchor point slides back, pushing the boilie behind the eye.

wide variance is probably because the authors have found the length that works for them on their particular water. Although it may appear contradictory the large degree of variation actually indicates how critical the hooklink length must be.

I think that in the majority of instances the point is being missed. It is not the length of the hooklink that is critical, but rather the way in which we place the hooklink in our swim.

Carp are conditioned by carp anglers. We teach them to be aware of various dangers by catching them. Which is why we change our baits, for example. After a period of time, which equates to approximately 50 per cent of the carp population being caught on a given bait, the bait's effectiveness begins to wane.

This conditioning to danger applies to every fishing element we apply that the carp comes into contact with, including hooklinks. To my mind, the most critical factor with hooklinks is how people approach the water. I will explain.

As an example, let us pick a weedy water with the odd clear spot. The angler has located a clear spot amongst the weed and casts to it. Nice cast, spot on, the angler is confident in his positioning. What is the last thing he should do, which he is not going to do? Pull back in case he snags his hook on the weed. The same would apply when casting tight under overhanging branches on an island. At the thirty-ninth attempt, the angler gets the bait tight in the hole between the bushes. The last thing he is then going to do is pull back to feel the bottom and pull his bait out of the hole.

Therefore, in the examples given, the hooklink will fall loosely around the lead. As most carp anglers fish with supple hooklinks of say 12in (30cm) that will give us an average amount of slack hooklink to be taken up of say 6in (15cm). This is how carp become conditioned. In the examples quoted, the carp come to learn that they can safely pick up a bait and move a limited distance. If they do not feel the lead's resistance they think they have got away with it, that the bait was a freebie. Therefore you require a hooklink with a minimum slack before the effect of the lead comes into effect, or

Kevin with a big December common. Cold weather sorts out the effective rigs from the less effective ones. The less inclined a fish is to feed, the less likelihood there is that it will make a mistake.

alternatively a large amount of slack. If you are going longer, it is my experience that you need at least treble the amount the carp have become conditioned to expect, say 18in (45cm) of slack and thus a hooklink of 24in (60cm).

How you achieve that does not necessarily mean you need a very short or very long hooklink. In the above situation, my standard bottom bait hook length is 10in (25cm). Think about it!

Of course, the opposite may apply on a smooth-bottomed lake fishing in open water, particularly lakes with nice sandy and gravel patches. After all, everyone pulls back, don't they(!), straightening out the hooklink in the process?

Therefore, the conditioned moment of danger for the carp is when it sucks in the bait. A bait that does not come up freely is probably tethered. In this instance, do not pull back or produce a rig where the hooklink has a large

amount of movement if it is appropriate to fish that option.

If a variety of hooklink materials, lengths of hooklinks and lead arrangements are being applied to your water, then your edge is to fish like a matchman and ring the changes.

The Lead

I have tried various lead arrangements from 5oz square fixed leads to the opposite extreme of running leads. In the case of fixed leads, I think it is important that the maximum mass of the lead must quickly come into the optimum effect. Therefore the shape of the lead and the method of fixing the lead to the line are important.

I will explain that. Take, for example, in-line fixed leads. As opposed to off-line or helicopter

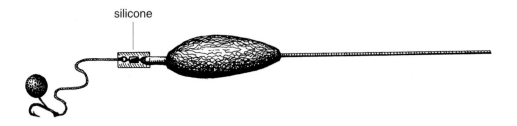

An inefficient in-line arrangement. The 'bolt' effect is diluted by the swivel being away from the lead, and the shape of the lead.

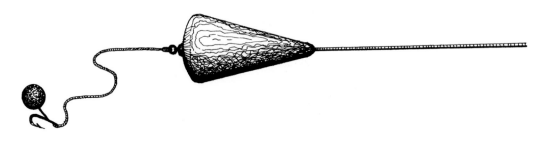

A preferable in-line arrangement. Instant maximum 'bolt' effect is achieved with the hooklink swivel being in the nose of the lead. The lead shape maximizes the bolt effect.

arrangements the main mass of the weight needs to be at the front of the lead (the hooklink end). Also the hooklink swivel needs to be as near to the lead as possible, preferably in it; this way, the objective of instant maximum mass is achieved.

We rely on the carp straightening the hooklink a little too quickly, and pricking itself. It is hence logical to maximize on that 'bolt' effect, with the hope that the carp in its enthusiasm to feed moves a little too quickly and is deeply pricked.

The same theory applies to helicopter and off-line lead arrangements. With the helicopter rig, the hooklink swivel needs to be as near the lead as possible, and that distance between the lead and the hooklink swivel needs to be locked up to eliminate pivoting, which will dilute the hooking effect.

The off-line lead's hooking efficiency is once again improved when the hooklink swivel is as near the lead as possible. This was the basis of my thoughts when I designed my safety bolt bead. For this type of lead arrangement, the safety bolt bead provides the required instant maximum mass.

The weight of the lead is critical. It must be heavy enough to pull the hook in, pricking the

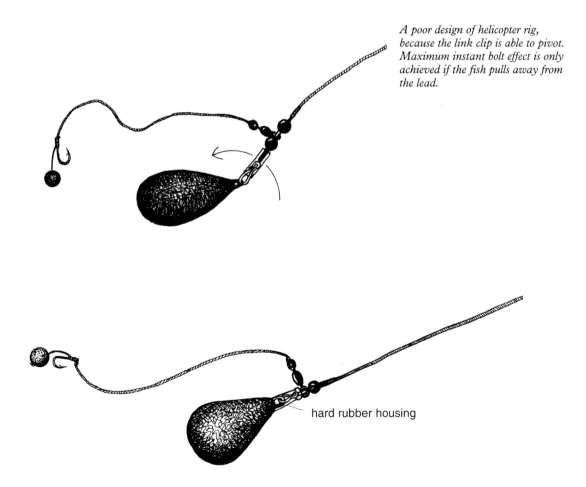

A poor design of helicopter rig, because the link clip is able to pivot. Maximum instant bolt effect is only achieved if the fish pulls away from the lead.

hard rubber housing

My design of the Top Rod helicopter rig. The rubber housing eliminates all pivotal movement as it locks the lead and link clip together.

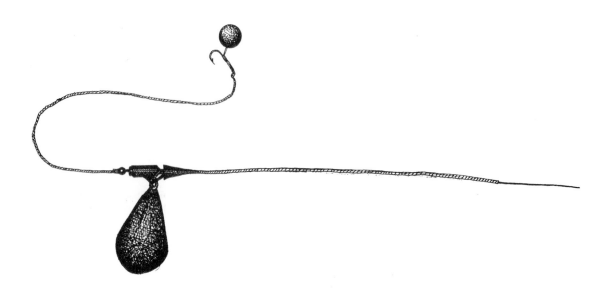

The safety bolt bead ensures that the lead is close to the hooklink swivel. Whichever way the carp moves, the maximum mass of the lead comes into play.

carp when the carp tightens the hooklink and the mass of the lead comes into play. Conversely, if the weight is too heavy, the carp may prick itself against the mass of the lead, but then sit tight, sucking and blowing until it rids itself of the rig. This situation is one of the worst possible scenarios. Because of the overweighted lead, the carp may not move the lead sufficiently for the angler to see an indication, and the angler is therefore oblivious to the fact that he has caught a carp!

Nowadays, I balance my lead to the hook, which means I use the smallest weight that I believe will cause the carp to be pricked by the hook. In other words, the larger the hook the heavier the weight and vice versa.

I have had a great deal of success on a number of waters in the last three seasons using running leads. Without any misgivings, I would recommend the angler try them if your water has not seen anglers using running rigs for many years and/or you take into account what I have written about hooklinks.

If you do have the opportunity to find a situation that responds to running rigs, then hammer it for all it is worth. You may enjoy great success, but I can promise you as sure as light is day, it won't last. Which just about sums up the whole absorbing subject of carp fishing – nothing is for ever. You condition the carp; don't condition yourself.

Stay ahead of the game.

11 PRESENTATION: RIG COMPILATION – FRANK WARWICK

The two previous chapters on presentation have a common theme: refine the components but keep it simple. I believe in that philosophy, but there have been occasions when I have felt I needed something a bit different, and at times the difference has worked very well. I have found that in certain situations Roger Smith's D rig can be very effective; as can extending rigs, as can … Well, nowadays when I think of rig advancement I think of Frank Warwick. Frank has an inventor's mind, and loves designing and experimenting with rigs. In the pages that follow, Frank has detailed enough variations on the rig theme to keep the most adventurous of our rig-oriented readers happy, and we have also added drawings of the rigs the contributors use for most of their carp fishing.

The only point I would make about these various presentations is that using them to their optimum effectiveness is dependent on the angler having a clear understanding of how the carp are feeding on his baits, and how they are addressing the hook-bait. Are they sucking and blowing? Mouthing the bait? Picking it up in their lips? Feeding overconfidently? Over-pressured? Hard bottom or silt? A rig is designed to do a job in a certain set of circumstances. Rig selection still comes down to the angler exercising his judgement, based on facts that are only available to him or her. The rig is just another part of the formula for success, but some can be more effective than others, so thanks to Frank and the contributors for making their hard won secrets available to us all.

Tim Paisley

Frank Warwick's pop-up anchor rig.

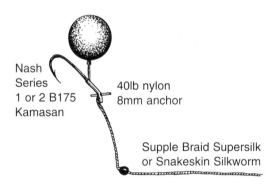

Nash Series 1 or 2 B175 Kamasan

40lb nylon 8mm anchor

Supple Braid Supersilk or Snakeskin Silkworm

Frank Warwick's pop-up 'D' rig.

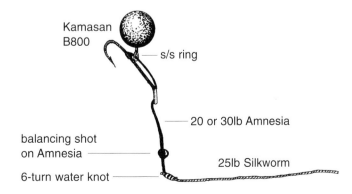

Kamasan B800

s/s ring

20 or 30lb Amnesia

balancing shot on Amnesia

25lb Silkworm

6-turn water knot

Frank Warwick's revolving hook pop-up rig.

Frank emphasizes that if you use this rig, it must be designed in such a way that if the boilie collapses when the fish is hooked, the stop at point A prevents the hook coming clear of the line. In this rig, the hair is just an extension of the hooklink.

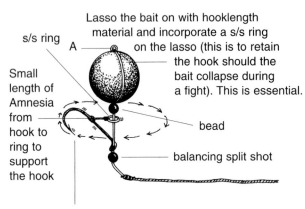

Lasso the bait on with hooklength material and incorporate a s/s ring on the lasso (this is to retain the hook should the bait collapse during a fight). This is essential.

s/s ring

A

Small length of Amnesia from hook to ring to support the hook

bead

balancing split shot

The hook revolves around the hooklength under the bait. It is not tied on but merely threaded on the line.

Frank Warwick's nylon bristle anti-eject rig.

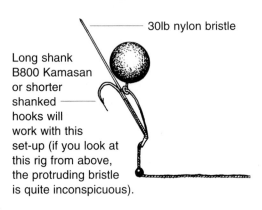

30lb nylon bristle

Long shank B800 Kamasan or shorter shanked hooks will work with this set-up (if you look at this rig from above, the protruding bristle is quite inconspicuous).

Rod Hutchinson's version of the stiff rig.

NB: Brent is much stiffer than Amnesia. Nail varnish on the last 3in creates hook extension.

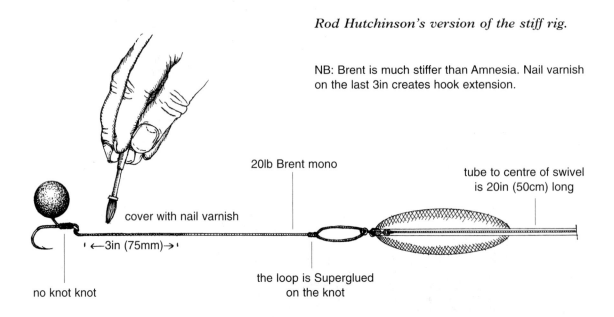

20lb Brent mono

tube to centre of swivel is 20in (50cm) long

cover with nail varnish

|←—3in (75mm)→|

no knot knot

the loop is Superglued on the knot

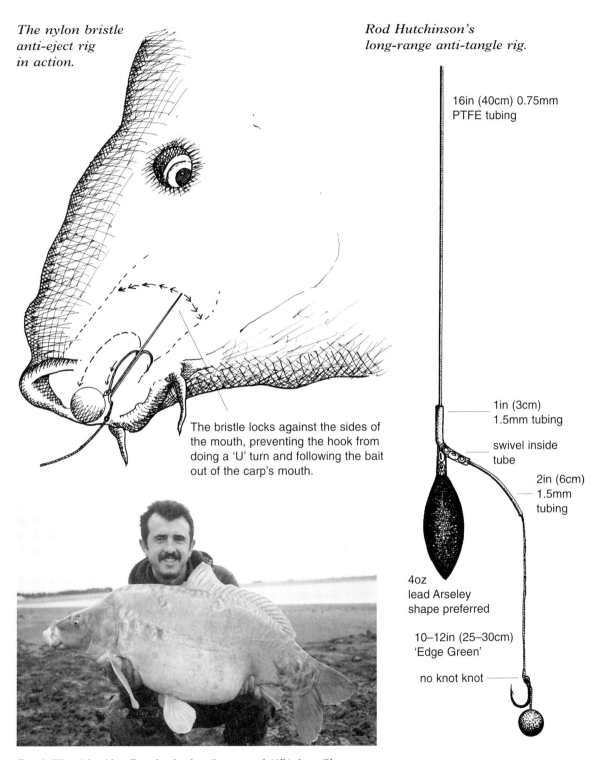

The nylon bristle anti-eject rig in action.

Rod Hutchinson's long-range anti-tangle rig.

16in (40cm) 0.75mm PTFE tubing

The bristle locks against the sides of the mouth, preventing the hook from doing a 'U' turn and following the bait out of the carp's mouth.

1in (3cm) 1.5mm tubing

swivel inside tube

2in (6cm) 1.5mm tubing

4oz lead Arseley shape preferred

10–12in (25–30cm) 'Edge Green'

no knot knot

Frank Warwick with a French whacker (in excess of 40lb) from Chantecoq.

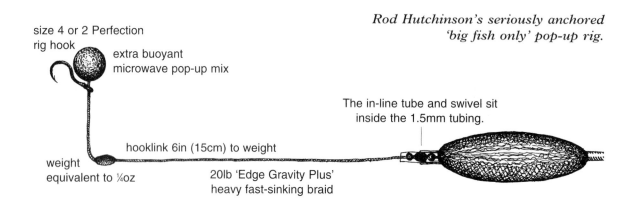

Rod Hutchinson's seriously anchored 'big fish only' pop-up rig.

size 4 or 2 Perfection rig hook

extra buoyant microwave pop-up mix

The in-line tube and swivel sit inside the 1.5mm tubing.

hooklink 6in (15cm) to weight

weight equivalent to ¼oz

20lb 'Edge Gravity Plus' heavy fast-sinking braid

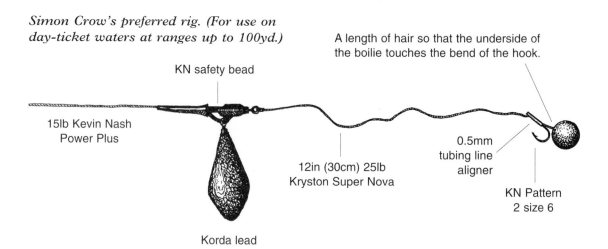

Simon Crow's preferred rig. (For use on day-ticket waters at ranges up to 100yd.)

KN safety bead

A length of hair so that the underside of the boilie touches the bend of the hook.

15lb Kevin Nash Power Plus

12in (30cm) 25lb Kryston Super Nova

0.5mm tubing line aligner

KN Pattern 2 size 6

Korda lead

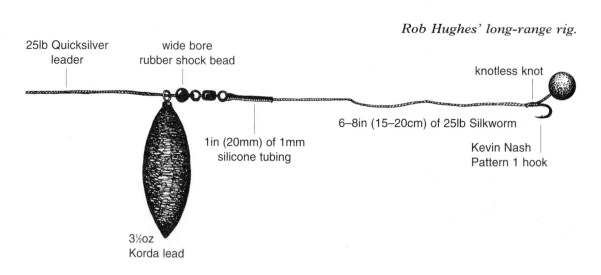

Rob Hughes' long-range rig.

25lb Quicksilver leader

wide bore rubber shock bead

knotless knot

1in (20mm) of 1mm silicone tubing

6–8in (15–20cm) of 25lb Silkworm

Kevin Nash Pattern 1 hook

3½oz Korda lead

Rob Hughes' preferred short- to mid-range rig.

2oz Korda in-line lead

A Kevin Nash swivel is pushed into the tubing to create the bolt effect.

Kevin Nash Pattern 1 hook – knotless knot

12in (30cm) Super Nova 15lb bs

1mm silicone tubing over the eye of the swivel

Rob Hughes and Simon Crow in action during their World Carp Cup victory at Fishabil in Brittany. Their simple but effective rigs worked well with these increasingly pressured French fish.

Rod Hutchinson's variations of the 'D' rig.
(Both are excellent for bottom baits.)

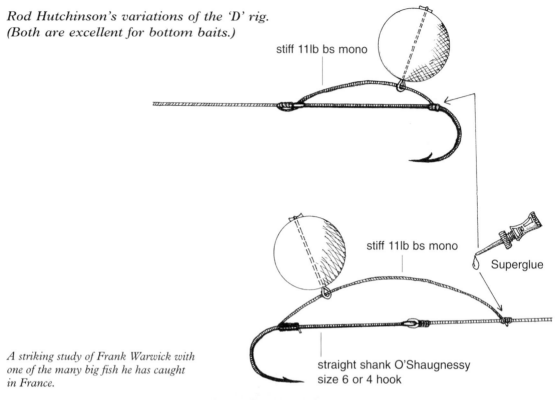

stiff 11lb bs mono

stiff 11lb bs mono

Superglue

straight shank O'Shaugnessy
size 6 or 4 hook

A striking study of Frank Warwick with
one of the many big fish he has caught
in France.

Paddy Webb's standard rig. (The one he uses most of the time.)

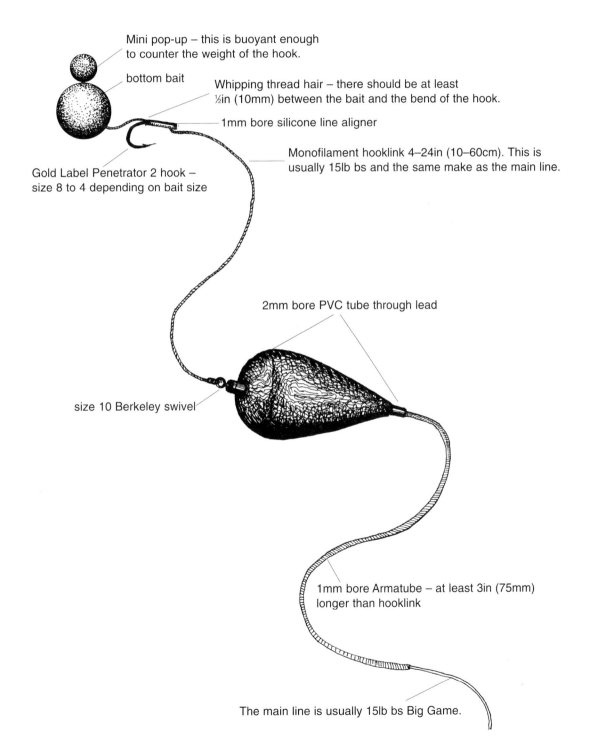

Mini pop-up – this is buoyant enough to counter the weight of the hook.

bottom bait

Whipping thread hair – there should be at least ½in (10mm) between the bait and the bend of the hook.

1mm bore silicone line aligner

Monofilament hooklink 4–24in (10–60cm). This is usually 15lb bs and the same make as the main line.

Gold Label Penetrator 2 hook – size 8 to 4 depending on bait size

2mm bore PVC tube through lead

size 10 Berkeley swivel

1mm bore Armatube – at least 3in (75mm) longer than hooklink

The main line is usually 15lb bs Big Game.

12 PVA: THE CONFUSER OF CARP

As is the case with anyone who is supposedly a carp expert (as the saying goes, 'you can fool some of the people some of the time'). I get asked a great many questions about carp fishing. I remember one such questioner particularly well. He was fishing a water where he found the fish extremely difficult to catch. I didn't know the water, or the difficulty of the carp, and one of the questions I asked him was if he'd tried PVA. 'No, the carp in that water couldn't be caught using PVA,' he assured me. I gave up and we went our separate ways. He'd wanted an all conquering rig-and-bait combination and couldn't be bothered to fish with PVA.

What is PVA? The letters stand for polyvinyl alcohol. PVA is a temporary solid which dissolves in water. There are a number of useful products made from PVA, our greatest interest centring on PVA string, bags and tape. A number of companies make PVA products. My favourites are Kevin Nash PVA bags and Kryston PVA string (Meltdown). I use these for variations on a theme of multiple baiting situations.

I have two principal requirements of any PVA product: that it doesn't fall to pieces while I am setting up the baiting trap or on the cast, and that it dissolves within the designated time span once it is on the water. In other words, that it is practical to use and reliable in terms of dissolving to order.

I very rarely cast out without some sort of PVA enhancement of the end tackle. I possibly use it much more than any other anglers I fish with, but it gives me confidence, and it helps create a better angling situation for four reasons. The first three are practical. A multiple baiting situation cuts down on possible casting tangles, increases the source of attraction in the area of the hookbait and creates a small feeding spot in that same area. In theory that increases the chances of preoccupation of the carp when it is having a feed, but because of the alternatives made possible by using PVA, I look on the end tackle trap as being a chance of increasing the carp's confusion in addition to any possible preoccupation. With the help of PVA, I try to create a state of confused preoccupation in the carp's feeding.

I will deal with that aspect first. I have included a drawing of one of my typical end-tackle set-ups.

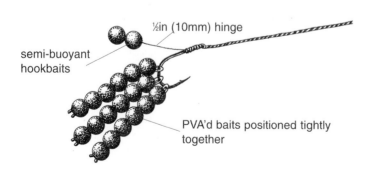

½in (10mm) hinge

semi-buoyant hookbaits

PVA'd baits positioned tightly together

The PVA part of the set-up is designed to divert suspicion from the hookbaits.

The mechanics of the rig I have dealt with elsewhere; it is the mechanics of the use of the PVA we are looking at here, and when I cover this aspect in slide shows, I can tell that a high percentage of the audience is fascinated with the concept.

This set-up presumes that the carp will be suspicious in its feeding on baits. If it is not, the set-up will score anyway because the carp will gulp the lot in and move slowly on looking for more. That is how carp feed, as Richard Walker pointed out in *Still-Water Angling* in the early 1950s. The fish takes a mouthful of bait, then moves off to eat it. When I first started using this multiple bait set-up with tiny baits I was nervous that it would lead to bite-offs, but its use has not resulted in a single one. If the carp is feeding strongly and without suspicion the set-up results in preoccupation, which makes the carp very catchable. If it is not preoccupied, then I try to confuse it.

The set-up is designed to take account of preoccupation and nervousness. The two or three bait hookbait has a degree of buoyancy to counteract the weight of the hook and line. I do not think the degree of buoyancy is critical as long as the hookbait is as likely as – or more likely than – the free offerings to enter the carp's mouth when the fish sucks at the baited situation.

When you are creating this carp confusion set-up, it is essential to bear in mind that the PVA has to be exposed to water to dissolve. In the set-up I use, some is intended to dissolve; some is not. The PVA looped over the hook must dissolve. The PVA within the two six-baits strings of baits must not – or need not. I have got the carp feeding in a small bait situation where it is having to move about to find food. The wider scattering of small baits does not create suspicion. We're presuming here that the hookbait/stringer group is viewed with some suspicion. Hopefully, the two six-bait strings that do not separate will create more suspicion in the carp's little mind than the hookbaits. The idea of the set-up is to focus the carp's attention on the baited trap, then to divert the carp's suspicions from the most dangerous baits in the trap.

The variations on this theme are endless and all I have shown you here is a set-up I have had consistent success with – summer and winter – for three seasons now. At times, I vary this to five three-bait baits, four non-dissolvers and one hookbait. The intention is the same, to divert the carp's attention from the dangers of the hookbait by confusing it in what it may well perceive to be a danger situation.

The quantity of bait in the trap has to be monitored with the seasons. I am not a believer in the stringer/hookbait-only syndrome (without free offerings) in winter: I think that presumes that only one carp in the water will be feeding, and that

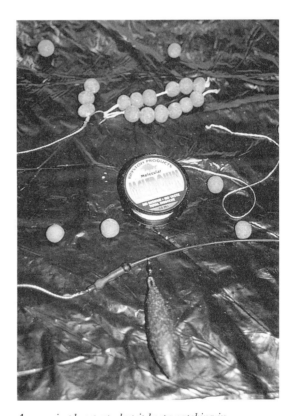

A very simple set-up, but it keeps catching in difficult conditions. The PVA'd free offerings are grouped tight together to discourage the PVA from dissolving, with a view to diverting the carp's suspicions away from the hookbaits. Normally I have the bait hinge longer than shown here, where I look to have crammed three little baits on a two-bait hair.

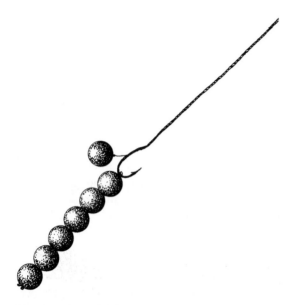

Six 18mm baits PVA'd tight to the bend of the hook. This is a popular set-up which can end up as a seven-bait hookbait!

carp has a reasonable appetite on it at the time it encounters the baited trap. I like to stick with the scattering of bait and the disappearing food source to increase the relief at finding the little feed situation, but I then have to make sure I do not overface the carp when it encounters the trap. How many baits represent a reasonable little feed in the colder months? I do not know, but in really adverse feeding conditions I scale down the number of free offerings in the stringers.

That is not to say that only the first carp to encounter that baited trap is likely to get caught, but I think the trap diminishes in effectiveness if the first carp in finishes up with the free offerings and the hook bait – or part of the trap – is left *in situ*. That is why I prefer the tiny bait trap in winter and why I have reservations about a stringer consisting of six 18mm boilies and a hookbait, particularly when these stringers are often cast out with the baits tight together and PVA'd tight to the hook. In that situation you are asking the carp to take a seven 18mm bait hookbait! I think such a trap has limited application at any time of the year, and certainly will operate against you in winter when you are trying to encourage a handful of

carp to compete with each other for the little feed you hope they will have.

While I'm referring to winter-feeding situations, I will emphasize the need to make sure your PVA dissolves at the required rate in cold-water conditions. Monitor the effectiveness of your PVA at all times of year, but be aware that the dissolve rate slows down dramatically in cold-water conditions. Some PVAs that do the job in the summer take much longer or, worse, do not dissolve at all in the winter. In addition, tests carried out in the dropping temperatures of November need to be repeated in the icy water temperatures of January. Temperature is critical and there is an inverse graph here of dropping water temperatures and increasing PVA dissolving rates.

Some seasons ago I carried out a series of tests in varying water temperatures, and settled for Kryston's Meltdown PVA string. That is not to say that there are not other PVAs which do the job admirably at all times of the year, but I have total confidence in Meltdown, which for me has three big pluses going for it. The first is that it is strong and allows some margin of error during end-tackle preparation in the rain, in damp conditions and on the cast. Secondly its dissolving rate is predictable in the coldest of cold water conditions. Thirdly, and very importantly, its packaging is excellent. It comes in a small container which will house the PVA in waterproof conditions after the original packaging has been opened. I am amazed how many PVA manufacturers (or marketers, because a number of them probably use the same PVA) overlook this somewhat vital detail. When you need the PVA permanently to hand during a session, you need to keep it waterproof, and the Kryston packaging allows for this. Bear this point in mind because the most effective of PVAs (Meltdown included) can become non-soluble over a period of time if they are allowed to get damp, and are then stored away again over a close season or longer period. Never take the effectiveness of your PVA for granted, and never use a spool from one season to the next unless you have retested it for effectiveness. I test mine by reeling straight in after the first cast with PVA from a new spool.

There should be no residue by the time I have reeled the end tackle back from fifty or sixty yards; if there is any I make further tests.

I emphasize that I never knot PVA. It may seem extravagant but I thread the PVA double through the baits, then loop the doubled end over the hook, and leave at least three-quarters of an inch between the top bait in the string and the hook. I am not bothered about the baits in the string separating, but I do not want the stringer itself to stay attached to the hookbait because that would negate the whole ploy. I accept that there may come a time on your water when the carp become so accustomed to picking up strings of baits that they will feel quite relaxed about sucking in a six-bait hookbait, but that is just an extension of the battle of wits between the angler and the carp to be experimented with when the time seems right.

I use PVA bags when I am fishing in weed or lily pads. Bags have an obvious edge over string or tape in that you can create a more effective baiting situation with each cast. Many of the modern pellets are ideal for this type of fishing and I have included a picture of a typical baiting trap created with the use of two types of pellets, Micromass and boilies. Obviously, the baits you put in the bag have to be dry, and you have to be aware of the limitations on casting distance because of the unwieldy nature of the baited bag. This set-up casts easier with the lead in or below the bag, but even then I find forty to fifty yards to be a practical maximum for accurate casting.

Once you have put the end tackle and the baiting situation in the bag, seal it by twisting it around the main line – or tubing – and damp it

The baited trap created when a PVA bags dissolves. In this situation, the fish will be suspicious of the obvious-looking boilies, but will have difficulty controlling their 'suck' at the tiny pellets and Micromass baits. Two tiny semi-buoyant hookbaits in the middle of that lot is a difficult trap for the carp to come to terms with.

to seal the twists. Alternatively, always carry a box of staples and a staple gun with you, and simply staple the twists together. I find this device particularly handy when I am using PVA bags in conjunction with floaters and speed is of the essence in ambushing a visible fish. I suspect one or two of you may frown on the use of staples on conservation grounds, but I have no reservations about their use, and I am sure they represent no source of danger to the carp. I do know that this is the cleanest and easiest way of sealing PVA bags!

PVA bags cut in half are very handy for casting longer distances and for casting a hookbait,

Never knot PVA. For the most part PVA knots do not dissolve.

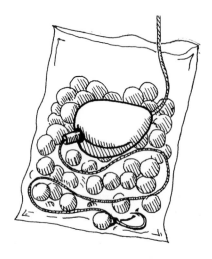

Loading a PVA bag. Push the hook through the wall of the bag, then load the free offerings and the lead on top.

or a hookbait and a handful of free offerings, into holes in the weed. Simply cut the bag down the middle then roll it round the hookbait and seal it up by licking along the edge and folding over as you would a cigarette paper. (No, I don't use cigarette papers either, but I've seen friends use them often enough to know how they work.)

There are a number of excellent PVA bags products on the market, with different size bags, mesh bags, and tape in addition to the string I have already described. I have used a number of bags and checked their strength and dissolving rates, and I am happiest with the Kevin Nash bags, again for a number of reasons. I guess the main one is that these bags are thicker than most on the market, which gives them an advantage at the end-tackle preparation stage and at the positioning stage after the cast. Because of their

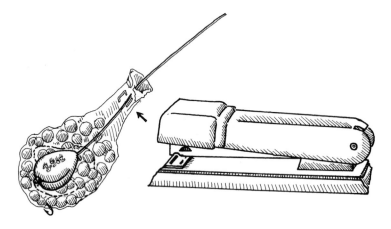

Carry a stapler with you for securing the PVA bags prior to casting

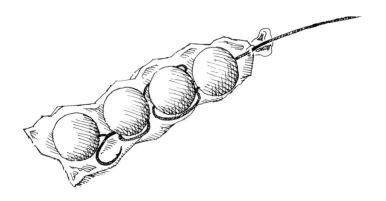

A useful set-up for casting into holes in weed is to cut the PVA bags in half and roll them around the hookbait and a few free offerings.

When fishing at range, any free offerings are better than none. This one free offering set-up can confuse the carp where double hookbaits are in regular use.

bulk and because I tend to use them in holes in the weed, I rarely get a PVA bag in exactly the right position first cast. The thicker bags give a slight margin of error on an overcast, in that you can pull back a foot or two (but that is about as far as they allow). They are also easier to use when the cast has to be repeated and your hands, the end tackle and the hookbait have to be dried off before you can resume the rebaiting procedure. It is just a failing of human nature that we always start into a repeat bag too soon after the previous cast before everything is quite dry enough for comfort.

When I am using bags, I put the baited hook into the bag first, pushing the hook point through the side of the bag to strengthen the end tackle/PVA bag unit, then add the free offerings, pellets, or whatever other additions I wish to make to the baited area before twisting the bag round the line and sealing it. If you want to use particles in a PVA bag, you will have to dry the free offerings out prior to introducing them into the bag.

The further out you are fishing, the more limiting the use of PVA becomes, and on long casts I may have to cut down to two or three free offerings on occasions. I do think that any free offerings with the hookbait are better than none and likely to create an element of preoccupation or confusion in the carp's feeding. If you were casting out a couple of maggots or casters to sixty yards, you would not consider doing so without the use of a swim feeder. Why would you use one? Because of the need to create a feeding spot with a view to preoccupying or confusing the carp. Look on PVA as the carp angler's swim feeder and make it work to your advantage in trying to take the carp's mind off the dangers of the hookbait. For me, the use of PVA is an edge which I would not be without, and the carp in the waters I fish are still falling to the same old confusing PVA traps three years after I started using them, and many more years than that since PVA was first used on the waters.

13 MECHANICS OF BAIT APPLICATION

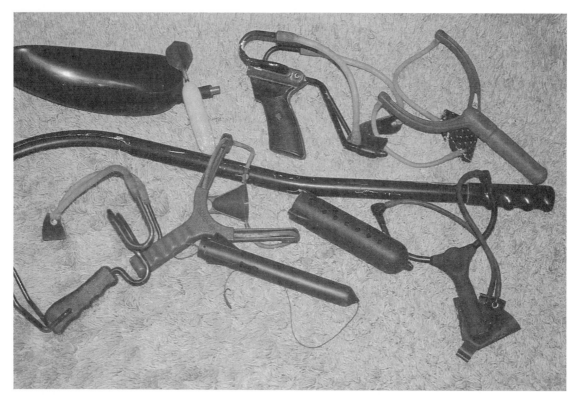

Tools of the bait application trade. I do not carry all these with me but I did have them all to hand in the garage when I wanted to take this shot. I have always got a range of them with me at the water to meet any changes in plan needed in applying bait. In shot: Cobra Throwing Stick, Drennan Feederpult, Fox Swing Head Catapult, unidentified pouch catapult (John McCarthy?), Black Widow Slingshot, Barnett Diablo Slingshot, Cobra Groundbaiter, Gardner Bait Spod, Angling Workshop Bait Missile and a Kevin Nash Marker Float.

I think it is fair to say that before anglers take to carp fishing, most of their bait application is done with specially designed catapults or by hand. The distances often involved in carp fishing lead to a baiting application lore peculiar to carpers: my observation is that many anglers are reluctant to make the change over, and therefore limit their carp-fishing abilities. It is not as though they do not understand the need to create a baited area, or that they do not want to. Put them on a water with a boat and they are out there applying bait by the bucketful. Take away

100

the boat and their efforts are restricted to the use of inappropriate tools of limited application. What follows is a brief look at the alternative baiting tools you may need with you when you go carp fishing, particularly on waters where you do not know the angling situations which will face you in advance.

If you are serious about your carp fishing – as most carp anglers tend to be – applying bait at distances of one hundred yards (or more) should not be beyond you. Not having current command of any baiting-up method is no excuse for not making an effort to come to terms with it if you know your baiting abilities will not enable you to cope with a carping situation facing you. We have all used a throwing stick, a spod or a bait rocket for the first time. No one is born with that ability, just as no one is born with the ability to cast one hundred yards, or to tie an end tackle. You learn to tie rigs because they are essential to catching carp: applying free offerings at distances in excess of your current capabilities may be just as essential an ingredient to success.

The main baiting-up tools are boats, remote-control boats, slingshot catapults, pouch catapults, groundbaiting sticks, throwing sticks, bait rockets and spods. I will cover their usages, the circumstances in which each tool is most likely to be used and the methods of using them.

Boats

There have been a number of tragic drownings involving the use of boats for baiting-up, particularly on the huge reservoir inland seas in France. Some boats are inadequate for baiting. If you use one, make sure it is adequate for the job, then use a lifejacket at all times when you are out on the water.

There is a strong temptation to stand up when you are baiting-up from a boat. In theory, it makes the bait application far easier; in practice all it does is make it quicker, and more dangerous. Remain seated and take an extra turn or two around the baited area to achieve the spread of bait you are trying to achieve by standing up.

It can be awkward achieving the desired spread of seeds and particles by hand or with a scoop. Try a frying pan. This gives a better spread, and you finish up with far less bait in the boat than is the case with other methods.

There is a temptation to overbait when you use a boat, particularly if you take the full container of baits out with you. Allocate a premeditated amount of bait to a separate container, and only take out with you what you really intend to apply.

It is a fact of life that on waters where boats are used, far more free offerings go in than when a boat is not allowed, which either indicates overbaiting, or a reluctance to use alternative methods where no boat is in use.

Where the rowing out of hookbaits is allowed, give some thought to the method to be used before doing the rowing out. I have watched anglers take the rod out with them when they are rowing out a hookbait! That's daft! Ideally, you want a companion on the bank to make sure the line runs off the spool smoothly to the distance you require. If you are on your own try running it off along the bank to remove any sticking points where the line may have become bedded down before going out in the boat, particularly when you are rowing to extreme ranges. When everything is ready for rowing out, find some method of clipping or fixing the end tackle (or end tackles) on the back of the boat, or under your feet, with the rods solid in the rests and the bail arm(s) open. Then start rowing, lining yourself up on two very visual bankside markers. Do not let the boat spin or you will get in an awful tangle. Drop the end tackle(s) in the designated area, then row back to the bank and wind down to the end tackles. The further you row out, the heavier the end tackle needs to be to make tightening down to the end tackle possible without moving it.

Look on rowing out hookbaits as a desperation measure to be used when weed makes bait-placement impossible, or the carp are definitely out of range of more orthodox carp-fishing methods. Applying bait from a boat and rowing out end tackles increases the pressure on the carp and makes orthodox methods at moderate ranges difficult to achieve results on. Short-term results may improve through using boats, but in the long term, the carp will become much harder to catch.

Make certain that the use of boats is within the rules before planning to use one.

Remote Control Boats

I have never used one, but I have seen them in use. There are waters where boats are not allowed but remote-control boats are, and on other waters anglers who are nervous about going out on the water may find the use of remote-control boats preferable.

Remotes tend to be expensive, but they are very useful. They make provision for the end tackle and free offerings and are operated by means of a control panel. They will obey all the commands necessary to take the baits out to the designated dropping area, 'park', drop the end tackles and free offerings, then return to the angler.

Remotes are not readily available from tackle shops so you will have to look for an advert for them in the carp press if you want to buy one.

Only a limited number of waters permit the use of remote-control boats, so ensure that they are within the rules for your water(s) before you embark on the major expense of buying such a baiting aid.

Groundbaiting Sticks

This is a device like a small shovel which screws into the end of a six-foot pole. It is used for applying balls of groundbait to distances up to sixty yards, or particles in the margins up to a distance of thirty to forty yards (depending on the nature of the particle). This tool is growing in popularity with the growth of methods of groundbaiting for carp. These groundbaiters are not freely available but they are stocked by some shops. If you are having trouble obtaining one,

get in touch with Cobra, the manufacturers and distributors, and they will advise you of the nearest stockist.

Catapults

Slingshot Catapults

These are actually hunting or pest-control catapults. When boilies first became popular they were fired out by means of the Black Widow slingshot, or the American model, the Barnett Diablo. They differ from pouch catapults in that they employ powerful surgical rubber elastics, and are built on a frame which fits over the wrist for added power and accuracy. The 'pouch' is actually a strip of leather which is ideal for firing out individual boilies but has few other bait application uses.

They are very accurate, and will fire an average 18mm boilie seventy to eighty yards, depending on the conditions, the angler and the density of the boilie. I recall that when I was fishing the Tilery (*Carp Season*) I stepped up the size of my baits so I could fire the free offerings out to one hundred yards to reach a particular feature. (The make-up of the boilie is an important aspect of achieving distance with catapults and throwing sticks, size, weight and roundness being the essential features.)

The slingshots are accurate and fire further than most pouch catapults, but they do have their drawbacks. You need a supply of spare elastics with you because they wear and their mortality rate is high. Slingshot elastics are actually at their best after a couple of breakages, in that the elastics are not replaced immediately; both arms are trimmed to the length of the break and the elastics are used until they become too short to give the required power. In addition, slingshots tend to be hard on the hands when you are striving for distance, the elastic occasionally (or frequently, depending on the user) painfully slapping the catapult-holding hand on the follow-through and recoil. When I was putting in a lot of bait with slingshots, I carried a glove for my gripping hand to limit the damage!

Slingshots were immensely popular during the early to mid-1980s but their use declined with the arrival of the throwing sticks and you rarely see them in use nowadays. If much of your fishing is done with boilies at sixty to eighty yards and you do not get on with throwing sticks, then slingshots may be the answer. From memory, the Barnett Diablo was ten to fifteen yards stronger than the Black Widow.

If you cannot track one down in an angling shop, try a gun shop.

Pouch Catapults

I describe them thus to distinguish them from the slingshots which do not have a pouch but a strip of leather ideal for firing boilies.

My current baiting-up armoury consists of two pouch catapults, a throwing stick and two or three bait rockets. The pouch catapults are useful for applying floaters, and other small baits, to the margins out to distances of up to fifty yards. I use a pouch which will take four or five 14mm boilies rather than the individual boilie pouch.

Features to look for are the strength of the elastic, the size and feel of the pouch (most are leather) and the nature of the frame. I have tried a number of different models and favour the Fox Swinghead and the Drennan Feederpult frames. I rarely use the pouch which comes with the pult, usually finding that the ideal frame and elastic does not have the ideal pouch. My finished product tends to be an amalgam of the best features of two or three different catapults.

When using particles, seeds or a multiple of boilies, most catapult users grasp the pouch to avoid loss of bait before firing, rather than pulling back with the finger-hurting tag which is usually sited at the bottom of the pouch.

Whatever your set-up, always make sure you have spare elastics, ties and pouches with you, and have them to hand when you are applying bait. Some elastics have a much longer life than others, and there is a great deal of variation in the power of the various elastics, too. Carrying spare catapults means you can be sure that you always have one ready for use.

Throwing Sticks

Bill Cottam first convinced me of the value of throwing sticks. We were on the Mangrove in the mid-1980s and I was toiling away with the slingshot, knocking hell out of my hands and struggling to make the eighty-yard mark in the prevailing conditions. Bill brought his throwing stick into the swim, picked up a couple of my baits, swung into action, and exceeded my best efforts by a clear twenty yards or more. I was instantly converted to the principle, although I still retained the objection that 'they are difficult to use'.

For me, they were difficult for about half an hour. The first thirty or forty baits either went straight up in the air or hit the water five yards in front of me. But if Cottam could do it... Half an hour in, I'd more or less got it sorted, and I now find throwing sticks absolutely indispensable for certain types of baiting situations.

When you become adept with a throwing stick, you learn that misfires (baits coming out too high or hitting the water in front of you) are just part of the warming-up process: you tend to get a few each time you start applying bait with the stick. When you are a novice and in awe of the stick, a few misfires can shatter your confidence and convince you that you cannot use a throwing stick. Persevere. We all have to go through the learning curve of making fools of ourselves on the route to mastering any new talent.

Depending on the size and density of the baits, throwing sticks are ideal for a range of 50–120yd. With practice you can become very accurate with them. With specially adapted free offerings where the size, weight and shape are right the best throwing stick exponent can achieve accurate baiting at ranges of 120yd (possibly longer in some circumstances) but I would consider 120yd to be a realistic optimum distance for most carpers.

I favour the Cobra range, the metal King Cobra being the most useful in that it will fire long distances and not cause too much fatigue and muscle damage. Bigger baits will fly further than smaller baits of the same design and when you step up to 25mm baits, you will need to come to terms with the Jumbo Cobra, which is not ideal for everyone because of the circumference of its grip and its weight. I would consider 100yd to be the likely maximum for the metal King Cobra (baits up to 22mm) with greater distances being achievable with the Jumbo Cobra (baits up to 28mm).

I have used a number of throwing sticks which have made some fancy claims on distance, but in tests they have been consistently ten or fifteen yards shorter than the most powerful of the Cobras.

How do you learn to use a throwing stick if you cannot already do so? Well, the obvious way is to ask for help from someone who is good with a stick. Failing that, teach yourself. Most throwing-stick novices go wrong because they forget how to throw when they get a stick in their hands, as I did initially. Most throws go wrong in the back swing. Throw with the stick. Note the limit of your backswing when throwing a stone or a ball, then limit your throwing stick backswing to the same distance. On the throw itself, aim over the top of a distant line of trees, or cloud formation. Do not throw at the intended spot on the water. Find a spot above and beyond that spot and aim at that. If you are firing off to the left or right, keep coming back to the throwing position before starting the swing.

Once you have come to terms with throwing sticks you will soon learn that the state of the bait is important for achieving optimum results. Here are a few guidelines on the use of boilies in various states of preservation:

- Frozen baits are best when the outer has thawed but the inner is still frozen. Baits with a tendency to break up are at their best when they are in this state, coming out of freezing. In their frozen state, the stick cannot grip the boilies' surface and the baits tend to fly too high.
- With fully thawed and other baits that tend to break up, you will have to dip the throwing stick in the water to moisten the inside. This cuts down on distance slightly but limits the breaking up tendency.

- Air-dried baits are difficult to throw with a stick. The loss of moisture makes the baits too light, and there is too little grip on the boilies' surface. An air-dried bait will fly twenty yards shorter than the original version.
- Boilies do not have to be perfectly round to perform from a stick, except where you are using baits of a near optimum size for that model of stick. In those circumstances, any distortion means that the baits will jam in the stick.
- Perfectly round, very hard baits fly better than distorted or slightly soft ones.
- If you make your own baits, it is not difficult to modify their make-up and size to cut down on breaking-up or distance problems. The addition of an ounce of Nutragel toughens most baits sufficiently to eliminate breaking up.

One of the beauties of throwing sticks is that you can put out more than one bait at a time. Only at extreme range do I find that this cuts down on distance. If I am baiting at a range up to ninety yards, I know that two baits will fly just as far as one. Three baits will cut down on distance a bit but they are manageable at up to eighty yards, while for distances of less than that you may be able to use up to five or six baits at a time.

Initially, using a throwing stick hurts your arm. One particular autumn, I thought I'd done permanent injury to my right upper arm through an excess of throwing, but it was only temporary. Once you've come to terms with the basic throw, you will find that throwing sticks are very versatile; you can adjust your action slightly to fire baits under the wind, or whack them out higher to take advantage of a following wind.

Bait Spods

For ease of definition I will emphasize a difference between bait rockets and spods. A bait rocket will hold bait and liquid, while the design of a spod allows liquid to drain away. As a rule, though, all baiting implements which are designed to cast out quantities of bait beyond catapult range are usually collectively referred to as 'Spods'.

Most spods I see in use are home-made affairs, although there are a couple of commercially available models. The most easily obtainable of these is the Gardner Bait Spod, which is available from Gardner stockists.

For the most part, the bulkiness of spods limits their casting range, as does the quantity of bait they are designed to take. The Gardner Spod when loaded is just about at the upper range of the weight a 3–3.5lb test curve rod can cast with comfort. When you start trying to cast a bigger load, you have to upgrade the rod to beach caster status, or seek a pike rod in the 4–5lb test-curve range. I think it is fair to say that the heavier the test curve of a rod, the fewer the number of anglers there are who can cast efficiently with it.

The size of a spod is influenced by the load it will carry. Too light a load and the spod just won't fly. Too heavy, and there is a limitation on the number of people who can cast it. Most spods are drilled with holes to give the effect of an aerodynamic miniature colander. Spods which allow the liquid to drain away are dependent on the bait load for casting weight, which is why spods tend to be bigger than bait rockets – because they have to carry more bait to make casting them possible. Some people assess this as an advantage because more bait can be applied with fewer casts. For most of us the further limit of a spod is fifty to seventy yards. I have used spods in the past, but all my long-range baiting and application of smaller baits is now done with a bait rocket.

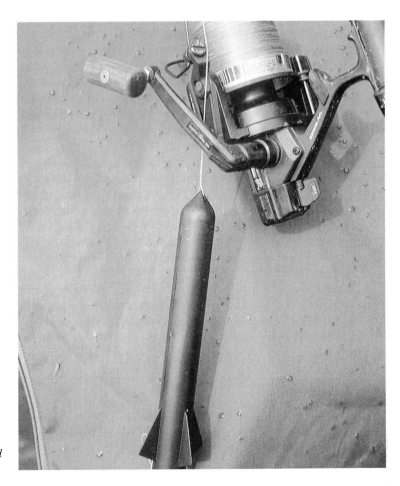

Angling Workshop's Bait Missile. This superb weapon will cast well over 100yd and is invaluable for applying seeds, pellets, particles and boilies.

Bait Rockets

I have actually been using bait rockets for over ten years, although they have only become commercially available in the last three or four years. Others may have played around with them, but for most of us, Tony Baskeyfield from Stoke invented bait rockets. He made them available to others by making them for friends and publishing detailed instructions on how to make them in *Carp Fisher* magazine in the 1980s.

Bait rockets are aerodynamic and easy to use at ranges of a hundred yards or more. The Angling Workshop Bait Missile when loaded will cast in excess of 120yd, possibly as far as 140yd in the right hands.

Most bait rockets (Gardner make one, too) are slimmer than spods, slightly longer and are enclosed to retain liquid. This means that while the rockets carry less bait than a spod, they will cast much further because of the extra load obtained from topping the rocket up with liquid.

I do not find the fact that these weapons will carry less bait than a spod per cast a disadvantage. You are talking about a few extra casts to achieve the same baiting level, and the smaller load per cast results in a better spread of bait in the baited area. For me, the fact that rockets will cast tens of yards further than a spod gives them a massive edge.

The fact also that rockets tend to be less bulky than spods for the reasons described above means that they will cast with standard carping gear, provided the rod is a strong one in the 3–3.5lb test-curve range.

The great edge that rockets have over spods is their ability to put boilies out great distances. You need the extra load obtained from topping up with liquid when you are casting out boilies. 'Liquid' does not have to be water. If you want an additional attractor in the swim, make sure it is a liquid which will sink, otherwise it will drift away on the surface.

I am especially enamoured of the Angling Workshop model because, in addition to its aerodynamic qualities, it does not sink over the baited area or on the retrieve. This means you can actually put out free offerings while the end tackles are in position, which you just cannot do with those spods and rockets which sink and have a propensity for picking up the lines of your angling rods.

I have been using Angling Workshop Bait Missiles for a number of years now, always have a supply with me, and as far as I am concerned they have made Tony Baskeyfield's invention available to all of us at a very reasonable price.

Bait Rocket and/or Spod in Action

I get asked how you use a spod so I will briefly cover the methods I use, although I look on them as fairly standard and based mainly on common sense.

Most of my spodding work is done with pellets, Micromass and small boilies, none of which will cast long distances, or accurately, without the addition of the added load given by the addition of water or some other liquid.

I start by putting out the marker float to give a precise indication of the area to be baited. Even if I am not going to bait 'tight', I prefer to have a visual guide for the baiting. I have the baits to be applied in a bait bucket by my feet. The bait rocket is filled with bait, then topped up with water for extra casting weight. I used to mess around with a bucket or bottle of water to fill the rocket, but I now simply lower the loaded missile into the margin of the lake after I have filled it with boilies and prior to the cast. The Angling Workshop and Gardner bait rockets are of a similar size and will take up to nine 18mm boilies or twelve 14mm boilies.

Cast out to the area of the marker. The first cast will be a range-finder. I will start by baiting at the back of the marker, so when I find that range, I clip the line in the spool-clip for a few casts, which cuts out the need to judge distance accurately. If your spodding reel doesn't have a spool-clip, temporarily fix the line by means of an elastic band.

Do not heap all the bait in one spot; spread it in a line each side of the marker, and chuck the odd load wide of the baited area. After a number of casts and a decent spread of bait at the first fixed distance, take the line out of the spool clip or elastic band, take a few turns back onto the spool, then reclip and repeat the casting pattern slightly closer in, for instance along the line of the marker.

Once you have applied sufficient bait at that range, repeat the reclipping process and put in a good quantity of bait short of the marker. Build up a visual picture of the bed of bait you are

creating, concentrating on a spread of bait to keep the fish moving around in their feeding. Overbaiting one spot can lead to preoccupation, which can lead to angling problems when you are hoping to induce runs, and a target which is difficult to hit on the cast and recast.

To make it easier to hit the baited area in the dark, I create a lane of bait at right angles to the

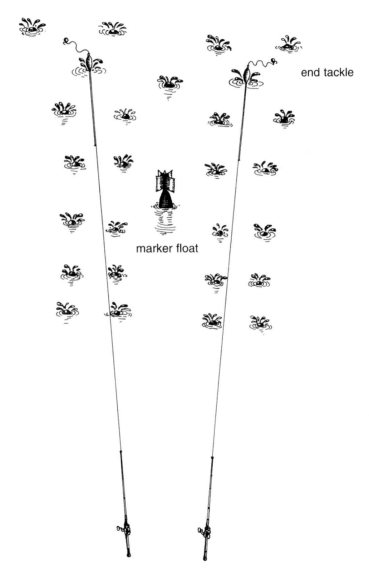

end tackle

marker float

Creating a baited area. Use the marker float as a guide to create a lane of bait and to position the hookbaits towards the back of the baited area.

bank. The end tackles are positioned while the marker rod is still in place with the rods going each side of the marker on the back of the bed of bait. Carp almost always approach beds of floating particles from the rear, which isn't to say that the same applies to beds of bait on the bottom, but I think the carp might be at their most vulnerable on the back edge of the baited area and initially I position the stringer cluster or hookbait accordingly.

I cast a few rocketfuls of bait off the baited area and position one rod accordingly. On a two-rod water, I will position one terminal tackle on the baited area and one off it. If I get feeding action on the bed of baits, then the roving rod is recast onto the baits.

The quantity of bait applied will depend on the number of fish present and their feeding intensity, but someone recently made the point that a rocketful of bait is the equivalent of three or four pouch loads of free offerings. In other words, fifty pouches of bait is the equivalent of twelve to twenty casts with a spod rod. That's no big deal, is it?

Even when I am using standard size boilies in the 18mm range, I always have my spod rod ready. A wind getting up in your face can soon put the baited area out of range of a throwing stick, but I know that I can cast a loaded rocket as far as I can cast my end tackle, which makes topping-up the swim possible at any time in any conditions.

My spodding is carried out with a Spodnik rod, a twelve footer specially made for me for spodding by Alan Young of Liverpool. The rod has withstood all the abuse I have been able to throw at it during three or four years of hard spodding and I am delighted with it.

Deterrent Effect

How big a deterrent is spodding to feeding fish? I will answer that with a question. How big a feeding deterrent is any form of baiting-up to feeding fish? There is a great deal of negative carp lore about the effects of spodding. For instance, the carp will all disappear up the other end of the lake. Well, if everyone spods there are a limited number of other ends they can disappear to, aren't there?

Having said this, I have a certain irrational nervousness about the effects of spodding which have been allayed on a number of occasions in recent seasons. Rationally, carp are attracted by splashing and they eat bait, which means that they should be attracted by spodding! They are more likely to be nervous of the splash of a 4oz lead which can mean danger than the splash of a spod, which carries no direct danger. A number of times I have had takes from bream while I have actually been spodding, but I have always felt that a three- or four-hour time lag was a reasonable guess for the carp to start feeding confidently on the baits after I had finished spodding, and I have baited-up accordingly. I feel that, as a rule, the same sort of time lag is reasonable after I have put a lot of bait out with a catapult or throwing stick.

Last November on the Mangrove, I arrived for a session during the afternoon, put the bivvy up, then spodded my mini Grange baits out from four o'clock till quarter past five. The end tackles then went out, the marker came in, I put the kettle on and started to assemble the brewing up equipment. I was still digging around in the living quarter rucksack when there was a double bleep on one of the marker rods, heralding a two inch drop back. I looked at the rod with a mixture of interest and disappointment. A bream take if ever I saw one; they'd turned up a bit early. I got up, wound down, and gave the rod a bit of a smack in mild annoyance. The rod slammed down and there was a 33lb mirror carp on the end!

I think a take soon after you have just finished baiting is rare no matter what method you use, and in that regard I now look on spodding as no different to any other method of bait application. It is certainly one I have used with a great deal of success for many seasons now and one I have complete confidence in.

It should go without saying that spods and rockets are essential tools for bait application from as close in as thirty yards outwards, and are therefore not just big-water tools. The creation

Conan from the Mangrove at 33lb. Autumn 1996. The take came within twenty minutes of me finishing an hour's spodding!

of baited areas with some of the most attractive carp attractors is limited in range with a catapult. Seeds, Partiblend, pellets, Micromass, and numerous other carp goodies which may well have hit the market by the time this book appears – and during its life – are all popular and effective groundbait materials. The methods described above apply equally to creating baited areas at twenty yards or one hundred and twenty, the only amendment I would make being that with any of these materials used on a small water, you may be advised to try creating a very tight bed of bait, which is easily done with a marker float and a spod. I have seen spods used in circumstances where the angler has actually been flicking it out underarm to a hole in the weed or some other close in feature.

In closing this section, I would emphasize that it is essential that carp anglers accept that the angling situation should be determined by the water and the fish, not the angler's current capabilities. We have all had to come to terms with strange and new abilities to extend our carp-fishing capabilities. To my mind, it is in the areas of casting and bait application that the least imagination and effort is expended by the unsuccessful or inconsistent in trying to increase their carp-catching potential. In a carp era when pellets and similar products are acknowledged carp attractors, and boilies the main carp catchers, it still amazes me how many carp anglers express a dislike for, or even ignorance of spods, rockets and throwing sticks in particular. If your bait application potential is limited, then so is your carp-catching potential.

14 ACCURATE CASTING – PADDY WEBB

While I was writing about casting elsewhere in the book, my mind kept straying to an excellent article by my friend and *Carp-Talk* colleague Paddy Webb which had appeared in *Carpworld* in 1996. In part, it dealt with accurate casting, and the description of the methods involved and the accompanying graphic drawings described the technique clearly and concisely. I asked Paddy to write a chapter putting across the technique of casting accurately – to the required length as well as in the intended direction – and I am grateful to him for coming up with what follows.

Tim Paisley

Accurate casting demands the ability to send the end tackle out in the right direction and to the right distance. This in turn demands both practice and familiarity with the tackle being used. There are no short cuts, although some anglers will find it easier than others due to natural ability. I am not a naturally good caster and I need constant practice to stay on form.

Most of my carp fishing is done at ranges up to eighty yards; in fact it is over ten years since I did any appreciable amount of fishing at ranges over eighty yards. Consequently, I cast with the rod held directly over the top of my head, which allows me to sight down the butt at the target. Although this method of casting is by far the most accurate, it does not give the greatest ranges. More power can be developed and, therefore, longer casts achieved by casting with the rod held over the shoulder; but the over-the-shoulder casting technique is not as accurate as overhead casting. Regardless of preferred casting style, it has to be understood that accuracy tends to diminish as the range fished increases. This is simply because small errors in direction or power are magnified by

distance. Obviously, the more the angler fishes at long range, the more accurate he or she will become.

My usual method is to give the cast a little too much power for the distance required: I watch the end tackle in flight and feather it down into the right spot. 'Feathering' means slowing the passage of line from the spool using the index finger on the spool lip. This is a skill that also requires practice but is well worth mastering. Besides enabling the angler to drop the end tackle on the right spot, it is the best anti-tangle device you can use. The hook-bait will trail behind the lead in flight, but feathering has a braking effect which causes the hookbait to overtake the lead and straightens everything out as the end tackle lands. Feathering also allows you to keep in contact with (and, therefore, control) the end tackle as it sinks to the lake bed. I will come to that aspect later.

I use Dacron stop-knots in conjunction with the spool clip present on most modern reels in order to achieve accuracy in the placing of the end tackle. However, this is not a technique that provides anybody with a miraculous casting ability. It is a technique that requires learning and experience, demonstrating once again the need to invest time and effort into improving your abilities.

The process of clipping and marking your line is easy. You may have read some pieces in which the writers expressed doubt about the wisdom of putting the line in a spool-clip. I have not suffered a single loss due to the line parting at the clip in the six years or so that I have been doing it – and I certainly have not found any line damage caused by the clip. If you have experienced such damage, then I would suggest that your line is not up to the rigours of carp fishing...

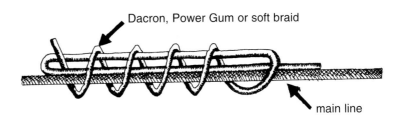

Dacron, Power Gum or soft braid

main line

A simple stop knot for distance working.

When fishing an open-water feature such as a bar or plateau, I mark it with a plumbing float, then pick a casting spot (from which all subsequent casts must be made) and cast an unbaited end tackle next to the float. In deeper water, account has to be taken of the manner in which the end tackle sinks, but again I will deal with that later. It may take several casts before I get it right, but once I do, I place the line straight in the spool-clip. I then tie a Dacron stop-knot (see diagram) a couple of inches beyond the rod tip. Some anglers prefer to place this knot just above the spool. It does not really matter, but I do have my reasons. After catching a fish at night, I need to relocate the spot it came from with a minimum of fuss. I cast out in the general direction of the spot and stop the line as I hear the stop-knot rattle up the rings. I wind in until I hear the knot click through the tip ring, then backwind slowly until it just clicks out again, then clip the line at the spool. The rod is now ready for rebaiting and accurately recasting.

Fishing against an emergent feature, such as an island or the far margin, requires a slightly different approach. I creep up on the spot with a series of range-finding casts, meaning that each cast gets a little closer to the spot. The starting point and number of casts will depend on the difficulty of the cast and how much you can rely on your natural judgement of distance. Once the unbaited end tackle lands within a couple of yards or so of the target spot, I start to use the spool-clip to prevent overcasts and their almost inevitable result, pulling for a break. As each cast lands, I judge how far short it fell and release that amount of extra line from the spool before reclipping. I try to be conservative about the amount of line to be released. Eventually the end tackle will land in the right spot and when this has been achieved, a stop-knot is tied at the tip ring as already described.

The procedure for reclipping the line after a capture from an emergent feature is similar, but the end tackle has to be recast in a direction away from the feature to allow the stop-knot to pass through the rings without risking a cast into a snag, e.g. cast diagonally down the water to avoid hitting the emergent feature being fished. Once the stop-knot has been located at the tip ring, the end tackle can be rebaited and recast to the right spot.

Given time, Dacron stop-knots, or knots made from any other braid for that matter, will loosen and slip. Fortunately, it usually slips down the line so the first thing you know about it is when the clipped-up end tackle lands some way short of the target. I always count the paces when I regularly untwist my line by taking off the end tackle and walking it loose down the bank, so I always know exactly where the stop-knot should be.

Once the line is clipped in the spool, the maximum distance that can be cast is not fixed. Put a fifty-yard length of monofilament line under tension and it stretches to significantly more than 50 yards, although this stretch does vary with the make. This has implications for the accuracy of the cast and allowance must be made. The line can easily be put under tension and stretch if the lead is still flying when the line runs out to the clip during the cast. Be warned: the lead can and will stretch the line enough to allow the rig to end up in the bushes and trees of an emergent feature. The elasticity of the line can also cause the tackle recoil – the bungee effect – so it actually finishes up on the bottom some way short of the splash where it hit the water. Every carp angler has to come to terms with his or her tackle, to know how it feels in use, and to be able to make the end tackle land exactly where you want it to.

If fishing an open-water spot, I cast slightly harder than I need to for the range, then feather the line as it leaves the spool so the line straightens to the clip with minimal force. This prevents any undue stretch, or potential recoil, as the lead hits the water. If fishing close, but not tight, to an emergent feature such as an island, I do much the same apart from holding the rod at 60–70° while the end tackle is in flight, instead of the more usual 45°. When the line pulls taut against the clip, the rod tip will tug forwards – and I let it. I still feather the cast so the lead has lost most of its impetus. The rod tip absorbs the remainder. Allowing the tip to pull forward prevents any tension in the line pulling the lead back and allows it to sink in the right spot (*see* diagram).

For both these types of cast, the lead is launched conventionally, i.e. at 45° to achieve a consistent power to range ratio. The laws of ballistics demonstrate that an object launched at 45° will also land at 45° where no other external forces are applied. For a fixed amount of power, an object launched at 45° will cover more horizontal distance than an object launched at any other angle (*see* diagram).

The angler can only apply external forces to the end tackle via the line. Feathering and allowing the line to tug the rod tip forwards both serve to steepen the end tackle's angle of descent and entry, i.e. to make it more than 45° (*see* diagram). This is no good at all if you wish to position your hookbait under an overhanging bush or branch, which requires an angle of entry of less than 45°. With an angle of entry of 45° the end tackle can be placed no further beneath the overhanging trees than their height above the water: if the branches are three feet above the

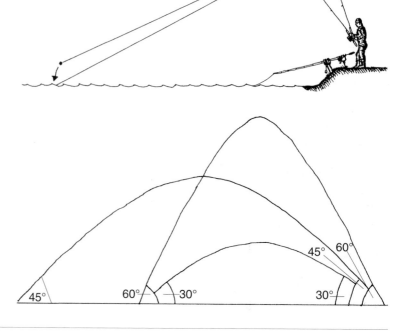

Allowing the lead to tug the rod tip forward absorbs any stretch in the line.

Ballistics. Projectiles launched at 45° have maximum range. Projectiles land at the same angle as launch.

water, then the end tackle can be positioned a maximum of three feet under the overhang.

The laws of ballistics show that the angle of entry mirrors the angle of the launch. If the cast requires an angle of entry of 30° then that is the angle at which it must be launched. Additionally, in order to achieve the intended range, a cast launched at less than 45° requires more power than one launched conventionally, and the required power increases as the angle decreases.

In this situation, the use of the stop-knot and clip will not assist the angler to achieve accuracy;

they serve only to minimize the possibility of having to pull for a break and retackle should the angler decide the cast has been misjudged. In short, a bait cast to a spot under an overhanging branch or bush which requires an angle of entry of less than 45°, has to be cast there. The cast has to be launched with enough power at the required shallow angle of entry is deemed necessary. If the spool clip is to be relied upon in this situation, then the line has to be reclipped on the basis of the original method described earlier.

No matter how well practised, nobody gets it right all the time. If a cast looks or feels grossly

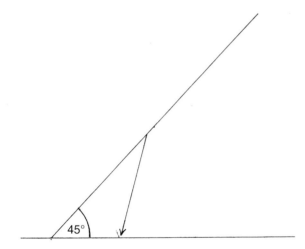

Both feathering and allowing the lead to tug the rod forwards steepen the angle of entry.

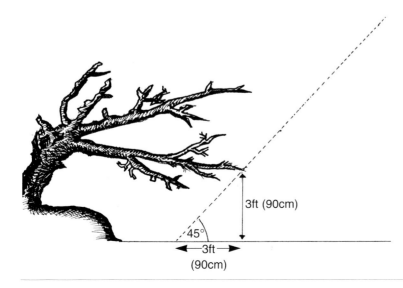

The path of the end tackle.

wrong, stop it straight away to avoid reeling in from a distance. If it looks about right, let it go. Casting like this requires the angler to make a series of judgements in a very short space of time: about three seconds for a fifty-yard cast. I cope with this by only looking for things going wrong and aborting the cast as soon as something negative occurs. I would sooner recast than retackle.

As the end tackle gets closer to its target, the angler is able to make better and better judgements about the likely successful outcome of the cast. Even if it becomes obvious that the end tackle is not going to land in exactly the right place, as long as it is not going to land somewhere which will necessitate a retackle, I let it go. This at least gives me a feel for the range and helps improve subsequent casts.

If a cast has to be aborted at the last instant, whip the rod tip back as far as possible and stop the line. This is where the clip comes in; it will stop the line if your finger is too slow. Getting the rod tip back as far as it will go counteracts the inevitable line stretch as much as possible. No casting method is infallible, but in 1995, I lost only four end tackles to the trees of Selby Three Lakes, and three of these came during one evening when I was totally off form.

It is inevitable that this sort of casting often requires multiple attempts to hit the right spot and a balance has to be achieved between getting it right and spoiling the swim through too much disturbance. I would rather risk spooking the carp if I knew it was a really good spot. I have at times thrashed the water to a foam trying to get it right. I could tell that those observing the

The gap in the tree line that Paddy refers to in the text. A number of fish fell to baits placed accurately in this little hole. The gap is the tiny dark triangle two-thirds of the way along the tree line towards the right of the picture.

performance thought I was a right idiot. Then that hookbait gets picked up within half an hour, and I am not looking like an idiot any more.

Casting under overhangs is the one type of cast where I cannot properly control the behaviour of the end tackle as it sinks. Consequently, this type of cast results in more tangles than any other. Being aware of, and controlling, the sinking tackle is as important as accurate casting in getting the hookbait in the right place. The greater the depth of water being fished, the more critical the correct control of the sinking end tackle becomes.

When fishing a weedy water I am happy that my rig is in a spot where it can work effectively if I feel the lead 'bump' the bottom. You do not get the 'bump' when it lands in thick weed. The only way you can feel the lead hit the bottom is by being in contact with the end tackle as it sinks. You cannot feel it if the end tackle is allowed to sink on a slack line. To remain in contact with the lead, you must stop the line leaving the spool the instant the end tackle touches the surface of the water. Anglers who have learned to feather their casts already have their finger in the correct position to stop the line and can react instantly.

Do not make the mistake of assuming that the end tackle will sink to the bottom exactly beneath the spot at which it touched the surface – in most cases it won't. An end tackle which is allowed to sink on an uncontrolled slack line will travel some distance beyond the splash. The distance it travels will depend on its speed and angle of entry, and upon the depth of the water, and is very difficult to predict. This is why, I believe, so many tangles occur when casting under overhanging trees: feathering is impractical because it can steepen the angle of entry to a point where the end tackle cannot get far enough under the overhang. However, be aware that the lack of feathering does increase the tendency to tangle.

Most of the time, however, the angler will need to control the end tackle as it sinks in order to make it land on the right spot. An end tackle that is stopped dead as it hits the surface will swing-in towards the angler as it sinks. Do not assume that this swing-in towards the angler will be negligible, and centred around a pivot point at the rod tip; that does not take into account the additional pivot point at the surface of the water. This additional pivot point is due to a combination of surface tension and water resistance, and it moves towards the angler as the end tackle sinks. I reckon the swing-in to be about two-thirds the depth of the water (*see* diagram). The implications of this are obvious: if you cast next to a marker in six feet of water and let the end tackle sink on a tight line, it will settle some four feet short of the marker. The deeper the swim, the further away from the marker the end tackle will end up. Bear in mind that this effect can be exaggerated when you have a strong cross-wind blowing.

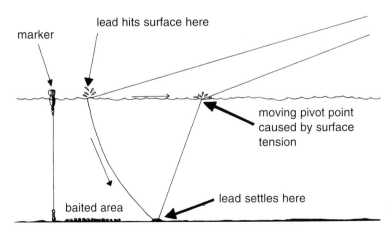

End tackle swinging in on a tight line.

Paddy with the lovely Linear from the Mangrove at 28lb. I have not caught it since 1983; John Lilley's never caught it; it was Paddy's second fish from the water during his second night of fishing the place! Funny things, carp.

*End tackle sinking almost
vertically.*

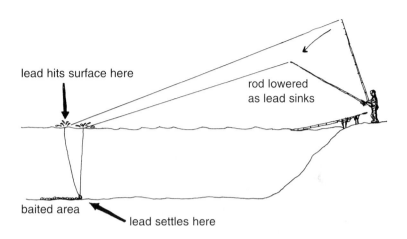

lead hits surface here

rod lowered
as lead sinks

baited area

lead settles here

The obvious answer is to drop the end tackle past the marker by the same distance as the expected swing-in. This is fine in open water, but not if there is surface weed present or you are fishing against an emergent feature. In these situations, the angler obviously needs a method that will allow the end tackle to sink virtually directly under its entry point.

The way to achieve this is to utilize the same surface tension and water resistance that causes a pivot point at the surface. The cast is made to the right point and the end tackle is stopped as it hits the surface. If fishing in six feet of water (or less) the end tackle is stopped with the rod tip raised. As the tackle sinks, the rod tip is lowered so the line just remains taut (see diagram). The surface tension and water resistance now act like a pulley over which the angler feeds line

allowing the end tackle to sink just about vertically. In depths greater than six feet, it is necessary to release line from the spool; lowering the rod tip will not feed out enough line to get the end tackle into the right position. The line can be released from the spool using the index finger in a manner similar to feathering. Alternatively, push the rod forward as far as possible as soon as the lead hits the surface, which will again make more free line available to the sinking end tackle to achieve the desired effect.

Obviously, none of the above is going to be of any relevance to anyone who uses a boat to position their hookbaits. Fortunately, most of the waters in this country do not allow the use of boats, so those anglers who go to the trouble of learning how to place their hookbaits accurately through skilful casting are placed at a distinct advantage.

15 LONG-RANGE CASTING

I include this chapter to cover an ability most carp anglers should have in their armoury, but which most do not because they tend to overestimate the distance they can cast. Aided by modern equipment a cast of 100yd is within the capabilities of most carpers. Some cannot cast this far because they have no need to, and therefore never learn: others cannot because they think 80yd is 100yd and are therefore out of their depth when they are faced with an actual 100yd situation.

I will explain why I think there is a real angling problem with overestimating the distance you can cast compared to the distance it is possible to cast. There may be fish, or obvious target features, in your water, or in waters you visit, which you consider to be out of casting range. If you are actually casting 80yd and falling 20yd short then the feature is not out of range of a 100yd cast. The further you can cast, the more features and 'safe' areas you will be able to reach, which will increase your chances of catching.

Overestimating your casting ability is nothing new. I frequently tell the story of my introduction to long-range fishing at Roman Lakes in the 1970s . It was my first visit to the water. I'd been told to get on the cafe stretch (open to carpers in those days) and cast across to the hedge. I duly got on the cafe stretch and cast across towards the hedge. The end tackle fell 40yd short. I reeled in and tried again. It fell 30yd short. I tried a few more times. Thirty yards short was my maximum, which I presumed to be of the order of 100yd. I moved down the stretch and fished the open water. Half an hour later, a young carper arrived and set up in the spot I'd just abandoned. When he came to cast,

I tried not to watch but was so startled by the frightening sound of the leader knot going through the hard chrome rings that I involuntarily turned my head to watch the end tackle in flight. It touched down a yard from the hedge. I had been casting about 70yd, which is a common enough maximum for those new to long casting. And, it has to be said, gearing up to and achieving 100yd in the mid-1970s was a different proposition to achieving that now quite modest target, made far more attainable by advances in reels, rods and line.

I am not going to detail the equipment needed for long-range fishing. Your local specialist/ carp tackle shop will advise you, although if you really want to do it right, you will have to go to a carp conference or a specialist carp shop. I prefer anglers to take this kind of advice. Advice on equipment may be sound only for a couple of years. I will give the specifications of the tackle I am currently using as this may be of some guidance, but do seek up-to-date expert advice too.

For the range of 80–130yd, my set-up is as follows. Carp Seeker 3lb TC 12ft 6in rods built by Alan Young of Liverpool. They are powerful for casting and flexible enough to play fish on. My reels are big-spooled Shimano Power Aero GT6500s converted to a bait runner facility by the Tackle Box, Dartford, Kent. I think the rods will still be valid ten years from now, but reel technology moves rapidly. The principle of a deep spool will always be valid for long-range work though. On the cast, the line has got to come off the spool as smoothly as possible with a minimum of interference from the spool lip to minimize friction. Minimal friction is also the thinking behind the ringing specification of the rods. Butt ring, four intermediates and a tip ring is the accepted ringing for many long-range rods now. Most rod makers recommend a 30mm butt ring or bigger. There are a number of types of low-friction rings on the market, again an area for advice from a rod maker or tackle specialist.

After the design and spooling of the reel, the resistance caused by the line coming off the spool and flying through the rings is the biggest restraint on the length of cast. My current line preference is Berkley Trimax, which is extremely smooth, tough and long wearing. It is also expensive. There are now a great many brilliant lines on the market, including those sold by Rod Hutchinson, Kevin Nash and Terry Eustace of Gold Label.

Once you have decided on a brand, come to terms with the concept that to achieve a long cast, you need the lowest breaking strain line which will serve you reliably in the angling situations you are about to encounter. If you are fishing an open-water swim you can go as low as 6lb breaking strain. If there are bars and other snags on which you may come to grief, you will have to scale up! 8lb? 10lb? 12lb? You have to assess the situation yourself. The heavier the line, the shorter the potential of the cast will be.

When you are going to cast a long way you will need a heavy lead of up to 4oz or even more

in some situations. Be warned that you cannot cast a 4oz lead with 6lb–12lb breaking strain line. For long-range work, you need a shock leader, a length of line from lead to spool to absorb the stress of the cast putting the lead into orbit. If the leader is solely a casting aid, it need only run from the lead onto the spool for a few turns. If there are marginal snags and other potentially hazardous features, then it is as well to tie a long leader, which will be a shock and snag leader. The heavier the line, the more abrasion resistant it is going to be, which gives added protection if the line rubs against snags. My leaders are always 10–15yd to serve as snag and shock leaders.

You need a good, reliable knot to connect the main line to the leader. I have illustrated three such knots, the Water knot, the Double Grinner and the Frank Warwick knot. I have not illustrated it here but I think the reader should be aware of the Mahin leader knot. The latter is the most widely acclaimed of these knots but I have trouble bedding it down when I am tying mono to mono. Frank Warwick has recently demonstrated his own leader knot to me and I like the look of it. It is simpler to tie than the Mahin knot and extremely strong. If you use the double grinner, keep wetting the line at the bedding-down stage and snug the two halves of the knot together very carefully. Keep wetting

Frank Warwick's leader knot.

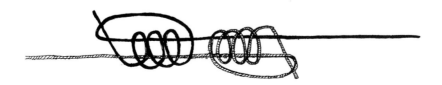

Double grinner.

Water knot.

Andy McDonald showing good casting form at Fishabil. We were fishing a long-range marker here, fishing three rods each on a tight-baited area, requiring consistent accuracy and distance.

the line when you are tying any leader knot: take care in the bedding down stage when you have taken all the necessary turns and are easing the two parts of the knot together, tightening it down to achieve the small, neat end product.

When you have finished the knot, give it a really good pull with your bare hands. If it isn't right, this will be sufficient force to snap it. It usually takes me two or three attempts to get the double grinner right because it is an awkward knot to bed down, but when it's tied right, I find it perfectly reliable. If you can learn to tie the Frank Warwick or the Mahin knot successfully, so much the better. Frank's knot really does look the ideal combination of simplicity, neatness and effectiveness.

For a number of years we ran trips to Fishabil in France, a water at which most of the fishing is at long range. Many of the anglers we took with us were new to range work, and invariably some had actually tackled up for the trip. We can all learn from some of the mistakes they made.

Rods were usually too stiff. For 100yd work or thereabouts, 3lb TC is perfectly adequate. If you cannot bend it on the cast, you will miss out on the action of the rod and lose much of the potential distance. Most anglers spooled up with line that was too heavy for casting long distances. For most open-water fishing, 8lb breaking strain with an 18lb-plus breaking strain shock leader is adequate. Spools not filled to the lip was a common mistake. You must spool to level with the lip then add the leader. Most modern monos are very abrasion resistant and unless you are on a snag-ridden lake like the Madhouse that Martin Clarke writes about in Chapter 23, you will be perfectly well served by a heavy mono leader. Kryston's Quicksilver is a very specialized leader material which tears your hands to pieces on long casts. Only use it where you really need it to avoid cut offs, in which situation it is brilliant.

Most anglers who are new to long casting are scared of subjecting the rod to the stresses necessary to achieve the required range. Modern carbon long-range rods are designed and constructed to withstand far more abuse than you can heap on them. A long-range cast is not a lob, it is a controlled thrash. You work at getting the rod and reel set-up right, then you position yourself in a solid launching spot. I look for a 'launch pad' in the long-range swims I fish, a spot I can get a firm left-foot stance against and a pushing-off point for my right foot. Get yourself set right then build up power, then you whack it as far as you can. The secret is in making the set-up and the casting action reliable enough for the end tackle to fly straight even though your hands have to move fast enough to be out of control at the point of release. You can watch a variety of athletes and sportsmen building up this controlled release: golfers, javelin and hammer throwers, tennis servers. They are flat out at the moment of release, their accuracy coming from a correct set-up and a grooved, well-practised action.

How do you achieve the necessary build up of power to arrive at the correct casting position at the moment of release which will give distance and accuracy? Below are a few of the key points. Bear in mind that the description that follows is of an overhead cast. I am throwing a 4oz lead and baited end tackle 130yd in the picture. I am casting with an overhead cast, using the rod and reel detailed earlier, 10lb breaking strain Trimax main line and a 17lb breaking strain Trimax shock leader (which breaks at about 23lb otherwise I would use a stronger rated leader). At 130yd, you are nearing the maximum for an overhead cast for mere mortals. There are some exceptional casters who would throw further with that set-up, but for most of us 130yd with a 10lb breaking strain main line is a reasonable objective. There is some room for an increase in the length of the cast with a lighter main line.

Most extreme range anglers use a different style of casting than the straight overhead punch, which I have not covered here because I think it is a specialist enough subject for coverage in the carp periodicals.

The description that follows, therefore, is of a powerful overhead cast. You may have to modify the action to over-the-shoulder, or research the technique of the uni-cast, if you need to seek an extra 20 or 30yd in your casting. There are some 150yd casters in the carp world but they are in a very small, talented minority. The British Surf Casters put on a display of extreme range casting at the NEC Angling Exhibition each spring which is well worth watching, and demonstrates just what it is possible to achieve in terms of distance with a rod and line.

A few casting points:
- Most carpers cast with too short a drop to the end tackle. Fish as long a drop as the bankside terrain and vegetation will let you get away with.
- Set your feet properly when arriving at the casting stance. Set the front foot firmly. You want to feel as if you are casting against the resistance of your front leg and getting added power from the push with your back foot. I make a conscious effort to push with the back foot to build up power with a movement of weight from back to front foot.
- When you are setting up hold tight with the left (front) hand and relax the right (back) hand. (Vice versa if you cast the wrong way round.) The first movement in the cast should be an involuntary pull down with the front hand, which helps with accuracy and in the build up of power. If your initial casting movement is with the back hand, it may destroy the timing and throw too much power into the cast too early. There is no need to make a conscious effort to involve your right hand; you will not be able to keep it out of the cast, but the longer its entry into the action is delayed, the greater the build up of power you can achieve.
- If you are casting overhead, you must get your hands up clear of your head to give yourself freedom of movement. You get added power if you

Paul Kerry making a 200yd plus demonstration cast at the NEC Angling Show. This championship style cast is different to the overhead style described here, but the weight transference principle is the same, as Kerry's footwork clearly shows.

give your hands room to travel back a few inches in the build up. If your cast is all wrist action, you are restricting the build up of power.

- My casting improved dramatically when I started making a conscious pause at the end of the backswing. If you start back too quickly,

the build up of power is lost. The pause stops you putting too much power into the cast too soon.

- Once you have taken the bail arm off and are taking up the casting position, make sure you retain the line in such a way that the timing of the release comes naturally as part of the over-all casting movement. I retain the line on the ball of my forefinger, well clear of the rod. Some successful casters trap the line against the rod, but many find this a handicap and an interference with their timing. There are arti-ficial aids which help with the line release, but I do not think these are necessary for the ranges we are talking about here.

- I have heard anglers complain that the bail arm of their reel is prone to closing on the cast, with disastrous consequences. I have heard this said of a number of types of reel, includ-ing the one I currently use for much of my fish-ing, the Shimano 4500GT. Enquiry usually reveals that the angler is casting with the reel set in reverse mode. Always cast with the reel set on anti-reverse to avoid the problem.

- Modern carbon rods are designed to cope with stresses greater than any you can inflict on them! Once you have set yourself up in the casting position, then loosened your muscles for freedom of movement, go slowly back, pause, then hit it as hard as you can. The actual cast is a sort of controlled thrash. The pause will give the control: the better your natural timing the more controlled the actual thrash will be – and the longer the cast.

- Optimum power comes from great hand speed resulting in great rod tip speed. If you are not achieving the sort of results you are seeking, work on the build up of rod tip speed because that is where your power will come from.

- The cast does not end with the launching of the end tackle. It is essential to keep the rod pointing directly up the flowing line when the lead is in flight. Ideally, you do not want the line working against any of the rings in flight, and you certainly do not want it running out at an angle to the tip ring. This is what will happen if you drop the rod tip prematurely, or hold it higher than the line of flight.

The optimum angle for the lead's ascent is 45°. You can get away with a lower angle than that on occasions, but if you go higher you will lose distance. Most new long-range casters tend to

This chunky Fishabil thirty-pounder fell to long-range tactics.

cast too low to start with. Raise your sights a bit if everything feels right and your results are still a disappointment.

I have already mentioned a number of sport-ing disciplines that involve a similar build up of power as the one that goes towards the making of a long cast. None of the actions mentioned is easy to master, and neither is long-range casting. On the other hand, achieving 100yd is by no means impossible either. On the Fishabil trips, anglers who had not tried to cast long distances before tended to struggle at the start of the week. By the end of the week, an average improvement would be of the order of 30yd. Some had improved their casting distance by as much as 50yd. As in any other sport, you need the right tackle, the right stance and some ability. Then you learn to come to terms with putting the the-ory into practice. If all carp fishing was as easy as casting 100yd, we would all be good at it!

16 NATURAL HOT SPOTS

The concept that carp can be caught on the basis of putting out a bed of bait and waiting for them to feed on it only has a certain mileage in carp fishing. It is the way most carp anglers fish at one time or another, and when the carp are feeding on the baits without restraint, there is no need to complicate the situation further than putting out some bait, positioning a couple of hookbaits on the bed, then waiting for action. It is a formula that works, but only some of the time. The rest of the time you have to have alternative concepts in your mind, and the more pressured the carp get, or the more naturally they are feeding, the wider your thinking has to range to cope with alternative baiting situations.

On all waters, there are areas and spots where the carp are more likely to get caught than in others. Some of them are obvious, and will be regular targets for end tackles. Island margins, lake margins, the edge of lily beds, bars, gullies, weed beds, snags. If you fish a swim with any of these features in them, it is likely that you will position at least one of your baits next to the feature.

For many years, my thinking did not go far beyond fishing features, and the majority of my carp came from such areas. Snowberry, Harlesthorpe Dam, Waveney D Lake, Cuttle Mill, Roman Lakes, Darenth Tip Lake, Birch Grove; all these waters offered obvious, visible features to fish to, and the majority of my fish came from targeting such spots. And why not? They have a long life as producing areas, and they don't over-tax one's location instincts. When you walk onto a strange water a long way from home you have to find a short cut to catching, and fishing to snags and features offers such a short cut.

But fishing to such obvious features offers two drawbacks. One is that they are always pressured areas because everyone else who fishes the swim in question fishes the same spots that you do. The other is that while such features are often holding areas, or at least visited regularly by the carp, many of them are not actual feeding areas. I remember reading on this point a long, long time ago, I think in Rod Hutchinson's first book, *Carp Book*. Find the feeding spots. He even drew some diagrams explaining where the feeding spots were likely to be in gravel pits. I liked the concept but was not sure how to go about finding these spots. And to be honest, the vague concept I had in my mind was of an area of indeterminate size. Apart from when I actually saw fish show I struggled to come to terms with fishing anything other than the obvious features I have already listed.

I got by, and I think that it is easier to get by with this type of fishing on bait-orientated waters, which is where much of my fishing took place. But even when fishing to features, it soon became obvious that there were spots which did produce, and others which did not. For instance, gravel bars were always a mystery to me, and it showed in my angling. I could find the bars, plot them, assess the depth and position the baits accurately, but I never felt very confident about just where the bait should be in relation to the bar. On top of it? Half way down it? At the bottom of it? I did an interview with Terry Hearn recently. Now Terry has had some huge fish from gravel pits, and he reassured me by saying that he did not know exactly where to put the bait on the bar either! If you can watch the fish, they will show you the best spots on the bars, but otherwise they are just features which are no more likely to hold hot spots than any other area of the lake. Finding the feature is one thing, knowing exactly how to fish it is another.

Similarly with islands. Almost everyone who fishes to an island has to cast as tight to the margin as possible. On some waters it works regularly, on others it works occasionally, and on others it hardly works at all. Depending on the depth of water, the carp are as likely to move round the island at the bottom of the island shelf as tight to the margin. Just where is the bottom of the shelf? That will depend on how the island was built. The margins of any island need plumbing with a marker float to get a clear picture of exactly how the contours stack up. This is a typical situation where trial and error and a bit of thought are needed in positioning the bait, and where most of us would not bother and settle for casting tight to the bank.

Just as I could never envisage that the top or side of bars was a natural feeding area, I could never think that island margins were either. Yes, carp eat bait, therefore there is a case to be made that areas where they find bait regularly become natural feeding areas. It is not a convincing argument. On most big-carp waters, the fish have grown big by taking advantage of all the food sources available to them, and in many cases this means that much of their diet consists of natural food. My concept of natural food in realistic quantities is that it is either in weed or in the silt. Either way, these food sources will tend to be in unseen pockets rather than covering vast areas or being conveniently positioned next to the most obvious feature in the swim. Some weed beds will hold more food than others. Pockets of bloodworm in silt may be well spread out around the lake but very localized.

The first time I saw Rod Hutchinson fish he was at the Lido, fishing across to the island. As we sat and talked he pointed to a spot half way across the channel. He told me that there was a spot there that the fish visited regularly. They always dipped down there, sometimes to have a little feed; on other occasions, they would just dip down, come back up and carry on their way. Rod was describing a natural feeding spot which

sometimes had a food supply in it, and at other times did not, but at the time the concept did not really register with me.

I read articles by both Rod and Jack Hilton describing the natural feeding habits of the carp in Redmire. The fish would have their little larders which they would visit regularly to check them out for food. Sometimes the larder would be empty; at other times there would be some food there and the fish would have a little snack; just occasionally, there would be a feast in one of these spots which would attract numbers of carp. The point that both Rod and Jack were making was that if you could get your bait in such a spot, then the carp's defences could well be down when they encounter it. The carp are happier feeding in an area they are accustomed to visiting to feed than in one which you ask them to visit to feed.

Looking back, I think I was put off this concept of hot spots by Rod's or Jack's affirmation that the hot spot may be as small as a yard square. There was an element of detective work and precision angling in that philosophy that I did not think I could aspire to at the time. I have since accepted that the hot spots can be as localized as that, and recognize that most of us spend much of our time fishing as precisely as that. When we are fishing to snags or features, the end tackle has to be right on the money for us to be happy with it, and in open-water fishing, a marker float makes pinpoint accuracy of bait placement in known or created feeding spots possible.

I guess I have always accepted the principle of hot spots and natural feeding spots, but it is one thing accepting the situation and quite another grasping the full implications of it and doing something about coming to terms with it. Many of us get by for much of our carp fishing without locating natural hot spots, as I did for many years on heavily featured waters. Then there comes a time when you have to accept that there is an extra dimension at work and that fishing to features is no longer enough. Quite simply, on some waters bait placement is far more critical than on others.

You need to know the contours of the island, and the lake bottom around it, to make an accurate assessment of the distance from the island bank the carp are most likely to patrol or lie up.

Looking out from Lightning Tree on the Mangrove. The bottom consists of 18 acres of apparently featureless silt, but the carp know where their preferred feeding spots are. Tell-tale signs are head and shouldering or swirling at dusk, or swirling at other possible feeding times. The hot spot I came to rely on was 50yd out, on line with the small tree at the left-hand end of the taller tree line.

Prior to and at the start of the season described in 'From the Bivvy' I prebaited the Mangrove heavily with the Big Fish Mix. I concentrated the prebaiting in an area I knew the carp visited in the close season, the idea being to get them confidence in the food source, not to try to concentrate them in any particular area. The carp were already on fishmeals prior to that season, so the prebaiting exercise was a confidence builder in my own version of the bait. By my standards, I put in a lot of bait that close season (of the order of 70lb from memory); I was convinced the fish would be fully confident in the bait by the start of the season. After that, I thought that achieving success would simply be a question of walking into a swim with fish in it, putting out a bed of bait, and waiting for it to happen. It did not quite work out like that on the first session, although I certainly had fish in front of me.

Up to that season, I'd had some success on the Mangrove, but not of a consistent nature. Much of the fishing was to open water and I couldn't put my finger on the reason for me not doing as well as I thought I should be doing. I felt the establishing of a bait would make all the difference and was convinced the fish would come onto beds of bait. They did not on the first session, and for the first couple of nights they did not on the second session. On the second night of the second session, a fish head and shouldered in front of me, eighty yards out and ten yards to the right of the bed of baits. Nice one. They were moving onto the baits and I would get some action. I did not. I was disappointed, and puzzled that the bed of bait hadn't produced when there were clearly fish in the area.

Towards dusk on the following night, a fish head and shouldered again – in the same spot the fish had shown in the previous night. I had been thinking about the possible significance of the fish head and shouldering since the previous evening, and this time I moved one of the carefully positioned hookbaits, and cast it to the spot the fish had shown in. I felt that the carp must have visited the baits the previous night, but they obviously hadn't got caught there. If they had fed on the baits either they were not happy about the fact that they were feeding on a bed of baits, or they were not confident enough about the area to make a mistake with the hookbait.

Why would it show in the same spot two evenings running, not at feeding time and not over bait? Was it making one of a regular series of visits to a known feeding spot? Was it marking a spot it was going to feed in later? Catching time was 1a.m. onwards, and I equate catching time with the strongest feeding time. That is not necessarily right but that is how it works out with floaters when I can see what is happening. When they are feeding on floaters, you can often observe the difference in feeding intensity between catchable and not catchable carp. Was the head and shouldering the equivalent of the fish at the Lido dipping down in the known spot on the look out for food? I stuck a hookbait on the spot and left it there, whereas the previous night I had reeled it back in at dusk and repositioned it on the bed of baits. The moved rod produced three fish before 8.30 a.m. while the bed of baits again failed to produce a run.

That single head popping out of the water two evenings running on the Mangrove spelt out an invaluable lesson, and one which has produced numerous Mangrove carp for me since – most of them from just half a dozen open-water spots the carp have identified for me. Why do I think that carp showing in this way are giving an

indication of a feeding spot? I am guessing, but the fish show there, then consistently turn up at feeding time, and the spots are very consistent at producing takes. In some of the Mangrove swims I have located a couple of such spots, in others one, in others none. Which is not to say that I do not get takes in the other swims, but the action is nothing like as consistent as from those hot spots which I look on as natural feeding spots.

If head and shouldering is a promise of feeding to come, then it is my experience that a swirling carp is a carp feeding in a temporary feeding spot. A swirl over a hookbait usually presages a take. On a couple of occasions casting to swirling fish has led to a series of takes, although fishing to the same spots on subsequent sessions has not suggested that the fish were showing in ongoing natural feeding spots. I am sure that one of the sequence of takes came from fish feeding on fry, but as one of the other multiple take swirls occurred in November, I was not sure what the fish were feeding on.

To recognize feeding activity, it helps if you can recognize carp activity which does not appear to be geared to feeding and feeding spots. Strong activity over a bed of bait with little or no indicator action usually means that the level of your attractors is too high. The carp are responding at the level in the water at which the 'here is food' message provokes a feeding reaction, six or eight feet above the baits. Carp seem to leap for a number of reasons, and I know for a fact that one of the reasons is cleaning themselves out. I have seen the evidence for that on Birch Grove when leaping fish have deposited large quantities of undigested groats. A leaping carp may take a bait that is cast to it, but on the waters I have fished, leaping has never been an indication of current or future feeding activity.

Carp do not head and shoulder on all waters, and they show at different times on different waters. If you watch the water hard enough and learn to understand what it is you are looking for on your water, then I am sure your carp will help you identify unknown natural feeding spots, which will make life much easier for you. There

Paddy Webb with one of a number of Selby Three Lakes big fish which fell to good angling and accurate casting.

Fish spotting at sunset on the Mangrove, for me one of the most important and most enjoyable aspects of carp fishing.

One of Rod Hutchinson's many big French fish caught on baits flavoured with attractors.

(Above) *Some fish do seem to be pop-up oriented. I caught this lovely common, in excess of 27lb, twice in twelve months, both times on the pop-up rod when all my other captures were falling to bottom baits.*

(Right) *Kevin Nash with a stunning Essex mirror, in excess of 45lb, which fell to one of his carefully designed end tackle arrangements.*

Big Bill Cottam of Nutrabaits, bait authority and long-time friend who convinced me of the distances that can be achieved with a throwing stick.

(Above) Casting 130yd at Fishabil in France. I fish few waters where I need to cast this far, but occasionally it will cost me fish if I cannot reach them when they are sitting out at range.

(Left) Frank Warwick returning a hard-earned Oxfordshire big twenty-pounder.

(Above) *Leave the lake as you find it: the legendary Redmire Pool, pictured here, is fished virtually every day of the season, but it is always kept immaculate; a credit to the anglers who fish it, and Les Bamford of the Carp Society, who controls it.*

The magnificent Ashlea Pool leather known as Lucky at 34lb 12oz caught by Mike Willmott back in 1988. This lovely fish has since died. RIP old friend.

(Above) *This 25lb February Birch mirror fell to an attractor bait fished over Micromass. This was the truest winter fish I have had, with freezing north-east winds and light snow flurries prevailing at the time of the take.*

(Above) *Greg Fletcher showing good form in landing a fish at Roman Lakes in the early 1980s. It was in this swim that I learnt the valuable lesson that luck can give a very welcome helping hand at times.*

(Right) *Hull carp angler Eric Hodgetts with a big mirror from the Motorway Pond. The fish weighed 36lb and equalled the Yorkshire record at the time.*

(Above) *Martin Clarke with the big mirror known as the Fat One from 'The Doghouse' at a water record weight of 44lb 4oz. This fish fell twice in a few weeks to Martin's margin fished bait.*

(Below) *Rob Hughes with a lump of a mirror from Fishabil in Brittany.*

(Above left) *18 December 1994, a memorable occasion. Scaley at 38lb 8oz following the capture on the previous evening. John Lilley drove up from Hereford to take the pictures for me, and my wife Mary drove across from Sheffield to see the great fish.*

(Above right) *Chris Ball with a Redmire common in excess of 20lb caught off the top at the famous pool. Chris is one of the most authoritative writers we have on floater fishing, and co-authored the book of the same name with fellow floater freak Brian Skoyles.*

Simon Crow with a big fish from one of his French excursions: a common in excess of 30lb from Fishabil, a day-ticket venue in Brittany.

are obvious feeding signs beyond head and shouldering: bubbling, colouring up, swirling, and vortices from deep swirling fish; all these are signs of feeding activity, and if it is not occurring over your bait, then it may well be natural feeding in a natural hot spot, or identifying a productive feeding spot.

When you discover such a spot mark it by cross-reference from two swims, then fish it when you get the opportunity. Do not alarm the fish by overbaiting a spot it visits to find food, however. Carry the 'little snack' concept in your mind for these spots and bait them accordingly. They are ideal spots for single-bait or stringer fishing. One of the first hot spots I discovered on the Mangrove still produces for me four years on. If I go in the swim called Lightning Tree, I stick a bait in this spot with total confidence, and most nights my confidence is rewarded. That one spot has produced two different 35lb-plus fish for over a three-year period. Other hot spots have dried up over the seasons, either because they are no longer a natural larder, or because a succession of captures have resulted in them being marked as danger areas.

My main concerns on a water I do not know centre round bait placement and feeding times. Carp showing at feeding times may well be feeding carp. Seeing a carp move at feeding time gives you an indication of how they show and where they feed. It is a starting point. If they do not show you have to pin down bait placement by detective work. Sometimes you get lucky and drag some bloodworm in on the hook. Chances are you picked this up as you started to reel in, so your end tackle has been on a feeding spot. Guesswork, experimentation, watching the reaction of the water birds.

You think the last example is a bit extreme? Well I will give you two examples of it happening. At Horseshoe Lake, some of the local anglers insist that the coots are always over the carp. It's certainly true some of the time and on one occasion when I was fishing the boat point I could tell when the carp were in front of me by the presence of a dozen coots. If the coots weren't there, I didn't get action.

A couple of winters ago, there was a small flock of tufties on Birch Grove when Alan Young and I fished the water at the end of the season. I was fishing the caravan swim and Alan the far end of the lake. The tufties were in residence at the far end and kept showing an unhealthy interest in Alan's baits, but never came anywhere near mine. I was well happy with that arrangement. On the second morning, Alan had a run while the tufties were hanging around his baits, and it was from a carp. After that, I watched the tufties each morning. They would start their journey in the snag-holding area where there are always carp, travel sixty yards out into the lake, apparently aimlessly, stop at a known productive winter spot, then move across in front of Alan, back across to the winter spot, then back to the snag holding area. Alan had another fish on the third morning, again when the tufties were over his baits. After that, I didn't feel too smug about the tufties not coming anywhere near my baits, and I had no action at all.

Because of the nature of the waters I fish, most of my location of hot spots comes from observation, but there will be spots you can discover by leading and plumbing. Always have a marker float with you and investigate the bottom of your swim for humps and hollows, patches of silt, hard spots and patches of bottom weed. Locating a feature does not mean you have found a feeding spot, but until you fish the feature, you will not know whether it is a productive spot or not. Do not make the mistake of thinking that the known producing spots are the best spots. Most carp anglers are quite happy to go to school on the efforts of others, and a great deal of carp fishing is by remote control on known spots in favoured swims. If they are known, they already have a pressure history. Finding new unpressured productive hot spots will give you a definite edge until your spot becomes *the* spot and you have to work it out and think it out again. When others start going to school on your efforts, you are starting to crack it, although you may not be overflattered by the attention when it happens.

Rod maker Alan Young, pictured here with a stunning Mangrove common in excess of 36lb. At the end of the season on Birch, the only time he got any action was when the tufties were diving on the baits. We got the impression the small group of tufties was actually following the carp and joining them in feeding on the baits. The tufties never came near my baits, and I had no action from the carp!

You can locate hot spots in weed by observation and by finding the weed with most natural food in it. Even within one weedy water (or one swim) there will be a number of different types of weed. Some types will house more food than others, and carp seem to naturally prefer some types of weed to others. Dragging in weed will help you locate the natural larders; watching the carp will identify the carp's preferred weed types.

There are times when catching a carp is simply a matter of putting out some bait and waiting for them to feed on it, but for the most part there is a great deal more to it than that. There will be spots in every swim where the fish feel more relaxed and are more likely to make a mistake with the hook-bait. Focus your mind on this key area of finding the spots that produce and you will achieve success on a far more consistent basis. Carp feed most days, which means that they visit their natural food stores most days. That knowledge can take a great deal of the hard work out of the difficult location and bait-placement aspects of your carp fishing.

17 THE DISAPPEARING FOOD SOURCE: CREATING A HOT SPOT

I have referred to this method of focusing the feeding of carp in a couple of other chapters, but I am writing about it in more detail here, for two reasons. One is that the method intrigues people when I describe it in slide shows, and the second is that it is a very effective way of catching carp.

Like most good carp-fishing methods, the idea for this one was born accidentally because of a couple of related incidents. It then grew in my mind after I had spent some time watching carp feeding, then developed as a tactic when I began to make a connection between some apparently disconnected experiences and observations and put the obvious conclusion to practical effect. It is really a rationalization of a number of carp-fishing methods coming together and being refined as a carp-catching method.

I think the starting point was the realization that a bed of bait (particles and seeds in particular, but boilies too) can start to take effect long after it is intended to promote feeding activity. We put out some bait; we want the carp to feed on it. We go home at the end of some sessions not sure whether they did or not, and if they did, they didn't let us know about it. With me, there was always the niggling thought, 'Do they eat it eventually?'

When I first started writing and publishing, my work practices changed and I switched to starting my sessions on Sundays. Monday through to Wednesday I would see signs of feeding activity in unusual areas, spots which I soon started to recognize as baited areas from the weekend's fishing. The experience I had on Birch Grove while fishing crumb (which I describe in Chapter 20) was a stark example of a delayed action in the carp feeding confidently in one area (or becoming catchable in an area). To me, results over hemp and particles always tended to be disappointing, and I felt it was because the main feeding occurred later rather than sooner.

The obvious answer was that, to take advantage of this delayed-action feeding, it was necessary to fish long sessions and spend as much time as possible in the one swim. On the bed of bait, chances from day three onwards would possibly be much better than at the start of the session. This was not to suggest that carp were uncatchable at the start of the session, but for the first couple of days anglers would be better concentrating some effort away from the main baited area to avoid sitting twiddling their thumbs for three days.

Theoretically, this tactic was all very well, but it fell down on a number of fronts, the most obvious being that the majority of carp anglers cannot spend four or five days waiting and hoping for the carp to start feeding confidently in front of them. Limited time, time restrictions in one swim, carp remaining in residence in another part of the lake, or moving out of the angler's swim because of changing weather conditions, are other variables that make sitting and waiting a very minority carp-fishing tactic – but a very effective one if time and patience are on your side. In the end, I put the delayed-action feeding syndrome to the back of my mind and got on with the business of making sense of more conventional tactics.

Meanwhile, through the late 1980s and into the early 1990s, the co-founder of Richworth Baits, Clive Diedrich (he and his fellow founder

Malcolm Winkworth left the company in the mid-1980s) was playing around with some original bait concepts and from time to time he would send me the odd sample. From memory, the first concept was the prototype Ball Pellet, which I could not really see the point of at the time (which explains why I don't invent things)! Then in the early 1990s along came a packet of what Clive referred to as Micromass, an artificially created particle-sized boilie. The version I received was black and subtly flavoured, and the baits were of an unusual texture: individually they were not bound together but seemed to have been made by compressing the ingredients. This gave a loose structure which would allow water to act on the small boilies (I think the originals were either 4 or 6mm).

I liked the look of them. Mary and I took them down to Birch during the close season to see if we could assess the carp's reaction to them. That weekend the water was gin-clear – ideal viewing conditions – and there was the odd carp in evidence at the caravan end of the lake. Supply of the Micromass was limited so I scattered a few handfuls in the margins of the caravan swim, went back to working on the caravan and surrounds, returning to the margins to check the baits a bit later.

Now when I say 'Check the baits' I actually mean 'Check the area where the baits went in'. They were small and black and invisible on the bottom, and I knew from tests that they would soften up quickly. The only evidence of their presence in the water was the occasional globule

The intense reaction of these Birch fish feeding on tiny black Micromass baits opened my eyes to the potential of disappearing baits leaving the scent of food. As the numbers of fish and the feeding intensity built up, the water became too cloudy to take any further pictures. I knew there was not enough bait there to occupy them for the two hours they fed, which suggested that they must have been feeding on the smell.

of oil rising to the surface. The carp were well aware of their presence, though; there were a number of fish browsing around over where the baits had gone in and there were some good fish among them.

I had a problem in that the carp knew where the baits were, but I didn't. To make observation easier I introduced some more bait, concentrating it on a little clear silty patch behind a bush. Now, although I couldn't see them, I knew exactly where the baits were, and I could watch and possibly photograph fish feeding on them without spooking them.

There is a good mix of sizes of fish in Birch. This experience was immediately prior to the season in which the water was producing its first thirty-pounders, so the known fish in the water ranged from low doubles to big twenties. The intriguing thing about that day was that as more fish gathered in the swim, it was the big fish in the water which were in evidence. I could easily identify known fish and they included a number of big twenties, including one fish much bigger than the rest which I didn't recognize from captures or pictures.

I took some pictures and watched with more than a passing interest as the feeding intensity built up. Within an hour of the bait being introduced into the square yard of silt, the water was heavily colouring up, there was a scum forming on the surface and when the feeding was at its most intense, there were a dozen tails waving around within the baited square yard. The baited patch received the full and undivided attention of the carp for ages: I honestly cannot remember how long, but at least two hours. The water was becoming increasingly coloured and every time I went back there seemed to be more carp in the area (although twelve tails over the baits was the strongest feeding activity).

I was excited, intrigued and puzzled by the incident. The puzzling aspect was that I just hadn't put enough bait in to promote that level of feeding activity. I had never seen carp preoccupied in the fullest sense of the word before, as these had been and in angling terms I had to wonder how it was possible to provoke a run in

a situation like that. With difficulty. You would have to spread the bait out more. I started to wonder if that was how they fed on hemp, and if that was why it could be difficult to get runs from over hemp. Watching carp feeding as intensely as that actually raised more questions than it answered.

At some stage, it occurred to me that I had been watching natural feeding activity. I was reminded of Rod Hutchinson's and Jack Hilton's concept of the hot spots the carp visit to check them out for food. The feeding frenzy I had witnessed had started with a couple of carp browsing around a baited area, then built up to a group of carp eating a patch of silt which smelled of food, but which can have produced very little by way of physical or nutritional returns. As the baits softened up, the carp wouldn't even have known what it was they were digging for, which is almost certainly what happens in natural bottom feeding.

I was less sure about what to do with the concept once I had analysed it. The plus was that the bait had only drawn bigger fish in to feed, when I had suspected that smaller fish might have been drawn to the small baits. In that respect, this was a confirmation of Rod's Redmire Jelly Tots experiment all those years previously. The bright ones had been taken by the smaller fish and the black ones had laid there uneaten until the bigger fish discovered them. Here we had got a black bait that broke down and had the fish feeding on the smell. On the other hand, the level of preoccupation could be an angling problem. Three-inch hooklinks and heavy leads?

Mind you, the biggest problem of all was that Clive had only sent me a couple of kilos of the stuff and I had used it all up feeding the carp at Birch that day! The process was experimental, the machinery unpredictable and development funds at a premium; supplies were hit and miss, to put it mildly.

That was the close season prior to the *From the Bivvy* season and my prebaiting and ongoing baiting of the Mangrove with Big Fish Mix took precedence over other considerations. The Micromass concept was put on hold till the back

I have long suspected that in natural feeding carp just eat the bottom and leave their system to sort out the nutrients from the rubbish.

end, then delayed further while I waited for Clive to send me fresh supplies.

The concept must have sunk in by the time I started fishing Birch Grove that winter because my baited patches were based on boilies chopped up tiny to create a food scent with as little bait in evidence as possible. In retrospect, I was still struggling with the idea tactically though, and stuck with the idea of putting more chops in each day to maintain the smell level. It was from such a spot that Richard Seal had his remarkable five fish in one night Birch haul. I had pulled off on the Tuesday, Richard had his catch on the Friday night, but the real significance of that didn't occur to me till much later. At the time, I felt Richard's catch was an indication I was getting it wrong, but the fact that he was fishing single hookbaits (almost) over the disappearing food source was confirmation that between us we were getting it right! The mistake I was making was in continuing to top up the baited area during my sessions when I should have been leaving it to mature. In my mind, I was equating the feeding activity I had witnessed in May or June to the cold-water conditions of January and February, when for the

most part, fewer carp would be feeding with far less intensity.

A fresh supply of Micromass arrived early in the year, and I caught my first definite Micromass-induced carp from over a small bed of the stuff fished in the Black Hole on the tree line. As the fish was a 25lb-plus mirror caught in February in bitterly cold conditions laced with the odd snow flurry, it was massive encouragement. The fish fell to a heavily flavoured pop-up fished on the Micromass.

For various reasons – like hit-and-miss supplies of the bait and the birth of *Carp-Talk* – it wasn't till the winter of 1994/95 that I started to get my mind round the disappearing food source concept again. In the meantime, I had caught odd fish over the Micromass, including a December 1993 Mangrove twenty-three-pounder, and a clonking three-fish catch from Birch on the opening night of the 1994 season which included fish of 28lb and 27lb 12oz. But when you're trying to come to terms with a method, it often takes a long time for the real significance of certain aspects of the tactic to assume their true significance. The connection between cause and effect can easily escape you when there are all sorts of other variables to take into account. However hard you analyse what you are trying to do, you never quite know why you have caught a carp.

I think the Mangrove in winter is a fair test of an angling method. I went onto the water in the autumn of 1994 armed with a supply of small (about 6–8mm) Mainline Grange baits, determined to fish through to the end of season. I had a reasonable supply of Micromass and debated with myself over whether to fish it in conjunction with the Grange or rely on the small boilies to do the job on their own. In the end, two considerations decided me to go with a combination of both baits. The memory of the fish with their heads in the silt haunted me. They were feeding on a food source they couldn't see. In natural feeding terms, they would keep coming back to

this spot to check it for food. This concept would allow me to keep the actual food available in the swim to a minimum. After the initial baiting with Micromass and Grange, I would limit fresh supplies to the stringer traps, supplemented by a few miscasts' worth.

It actually took me a couple of sessions to decide that it was a mistake to top up the bait in the swim to any degree or freshen the background food smell, something I began to recognize was a mistake I'd made in previous winter campaigns when action tended to be concentrated early in the session with no follow-up. Once I'd accepted that topping up the free offerings was a mistake (in winter), my chances of catching later in the session definitely increased, and on a couple of occasions I caught on all three nights. In addition, action away from the anticipated feeding times

A lovely winter mirror, in excess of 25lb, from the Mangrove winter when I was coming to terms with the disappearing food source and the tiny bait traps fished over it. Another February fish, this was part of a three-fish evening catch in quite pleasant conditions.

became more regular. I finished the winter period (1 November to 14 March) with thirty-eight fish, nineteen of them being twenties, and two of those thirty-five-pluses.

I have got to be realistic and give credit to the Micromass for opening my eyes to a situation I couldn't visualize, and for making those exceptional winter results possible. But I have also to be fair and point out that there are now a number of products around which will create this disappearing food source for you. The difficult bit is in making it work quickly. The quicker you want it to work, the quicker you must achieve a level of frustration in a carp's feeding. The disappearing food source has got to disappear quickly, and a situation which has the potential for preoccupation must lead to the element of frustration which makes the carp careless. If you walk into the dining room at dinner time hungry and the air is full of the smell of dinner (but it takes you half an hour to find it) when you do eventually find it, you won't spend another half an hour looking for a knife and fork: you'll just launch yourself on it! If there are more than one of you competing for the same dinner...

I think I possibly made a mistake during the Birch *From the Bivvy* winter by using the actual bait to achieve the background smell; ideally you want the attraction from the main food source to be more evident than the background smell. I think the reason for the delayed action in some situations is that the background smell is initially too strong; the baited area does not become effective till the background smell fades and the attraction of the bait overrides it. Some of the pellets and other baits available for creating this type of situation are too strongly flavoured for me. They will be saturating the swim with a source of attraction, which is a mistake. You are trying to create a frustrating natural feeding situation with a subtle smell at or in the bottom to provoke feeding at or in the bottom.

Rod Hutchinson has a new subtle range of breaking-down pellets about to come on the market. Quality Baits have some breaking-down pellets which do not strike me as being too

strongly flavoured. I have seen a startling response to the Mainline Response Pellets. And of course, I have a very soft spot for Micromass, but I feel you should seek out the subtler versions for the best effect.

Tiny seeds can produce a very effective background disappearing food source, Hinders' (Swindon) Partiblend being particularly effective. Again, you are creating a situation where the carp are having to work hard to make inroads into a food source they can scent but have difficulty identifying physically. I emphasize 'tiny seeds' here. Bigger seeds which they can detect physically and are therefore able to target can provoke preoccupation, but not frustration. Sometimes it is possible to get takes on or over hemp and similarly sized seeds but I haven't found them to be as consistently successful as a background food source.

Some of you will have problems with the use of the tiny baits, particularly at range. Spodding is not everyone's cup of tea, and carp aren't always within catapult range of the tiny baits we are discussing here. Well, baits like Ball Pellets and Crumb Ball can be fired out to sixty or seventy yards by catapult or throwing stick. These break down in the swim and can be used to produce a modified version of the situation I have described. The method is fairly immediate, but I do not think it produces as effective a baited area as Micromass, etc. for pressured carp.

The quicker you want this situation to work, the quicker the breakdown you need and the *lower* the smell level. I cannot emphasize that low smell level enough. When a matchman fishes, he wants a groundbait which attracts, but which does not fill the fish up, and does not distract them from the main attraction, the hookbait. All your carp-fishing efforts are directed towards getting the carp to pick up the hookbait. On the good days, the method I have described here will get them to pick it up through preoccupation. On the difficult days, the pick-up will be from frustration. Trouble is that in advance you never know whether it is a good day or a bad day, so this situation is designed to make the best of both worlds.

18 SHORT SESSION FISHING

When I wrote about short session fishing in *Carpworld*, the article received a great response. This suggests that there are either more anglers who fish short sessions than I suspected, or the article struck the right chord in suggesting the best tactics to adopt when embarking on short sessions. I am happy to think that there is some truth in both theories, so this chapter is based around the advice given in that article, subject to some modification and elaboration.

short session fishing here refers to daytime-only waters, or overnighters. I know there is a form of short session fishing which is just an extension of an ongoing campaign on a given water. short session fishing in the sense of establishing a bait and fishing known feeding times (possibly first thing in the morning, during the evening, or even at lunch time) can be very productive, but I think this type of fishing is an individual thing. Your water has to be close at hand, you have to know it intimately, and you have to establish the carp's feeding routine to take advantage of a known feeding spell. I think you have to be really on top of what you are doing to aspire to consistent results in this type of fishing, and the fish have to be reasonably co-operative by being willing to feed at a time which lends itself to short sessions. When your time is really limited, you are often better focusing your talents on floater fishing and stalking to aim for opportunist results, rather than hoping to take advantage of known feeding times in a static angling situation.

I am mindful of the fact that these days my fishing is very different to that which many of you practise, and what will work for me may need adapting, or totally rethinking, if it is to be applied to the angling situation of those of you

whose angling time is restricted. In particular, I have in mind the anglers who fish daytime-only waters, or who only fish one night per week, probably during the pressured weekend period. I rarely go for one night, preferring to miss a week to make additional time available, and my sessions are usually of at least two or three nights duration. Yes, I'm 'lucky'. I spent a traumatic few years rearranging my life to make such a state of affairs possible!

Daytime-only waters and overnight sessions are two very different animals. The big question facing any carp angler, but particularly those fishing short sessions, is 'When do the carp feed?' The answer to this question dictates your whole attitude to tactics and the introduction of bait. Unknowingly, many carp anglers reduce their chances of success to a minimum within minutes of arriving at the water by unthinking bait application. The longer you are at the water, the better your chances are of recovering from early mistakes, but the shorter your stay, the more right you have got to get everything at the first time of asking, which means careful planning, and strict self-discipline in carrying out the planning to the letter.

I have fished a number of daylight-only day-ticket waters, including Cuttle Mill and Roman Lakes. Over a period of time, it became apparent that the feeding reactions of the carp were apparently dictated as much by angler pressure as natural feeding instincts, and I guess this will be true of many daytime-only waters. What do most anglers do at these waters? Get in the swim, fill in with bait, set up and start fishing. That is how one carp fishes, so that's how you go about a day's carp fishing. On waters of this type, the tactic makes very little sense.

Cuttle Mill, a very pleasant day ticket water where the carp's feeding is geared to pressure and bait availability rather than the presence of natural food supplies. Originality and the element of surprise are important angling assets on this water. Even on this pressured lake there are some spots which produce much better than others, for reasons only apparent to the carp!

For the first hour of daylight, some of the carp in front of you will be catchable, a characteristic you may well eradicate by dropping a load of bait on their heads. The first thing you should do is cast out, possibly using a stringer if you can reach the fish with one, using a limited stringer or a single hookbait if range is a restricting consideration. This first cast of the day need not even be with the bait you are going to introduce later. You want a one-off attractor bait which will increase your chances of a pick-up from a bonus fish. You will help yourself considerably by having the rods set up ready when you arrive at the water, preferably with the bait already on, suitably protected by foil and a food bag. Chuck out even before you set up the buzzers and banksticks. Just make a bait available to the carp while you go about your business of setting up stall. If you are fishing close to the fish, hammering

in banksticks does not make a great deal of sense at this stage of the proceedings, so be prepared to fish with a rod pod if it aids ease of setting up and minimizes bankside disturbance. I don't mind the odd bit of hammering when I am setting up for a three-day session, but if I've only got a few hours, I want to take advantage of every minute of them. Carp are hard enough to catch without giving yourself a few hours handicap by scaring them while you are trying to get them to settle down to have a little feed.

Knowledge of the venue will tell you how long the water's 'initial chance' period will last. From memory, it was about an hour at both Roman and Cuttle Mill. What happens next depends to some extent on the prevailing conditions and the number of rods you can fish. That last point may surprise some of you, but it can be important. The number of rods in use dictates the number of alternatives available to you. Here is a fairly typical scenario.

You've gone through that first hour, the bed-chair and brolly are in position, and you've got to decide whether to stick with the attractor baits and look for the odd pick-up, or go for a multiple feeding situation in the hope of bagging up. Multiple captures are red letter days to me and there is a part of me which always wants to aspire to such occasions. On the other hand, experience tells me that on most waters they are very few and far between. However, if I don't set my stall out to make such a result possible by encouraging a number of fish to move in and out of my swim, such a result won't come my way. So I try to aim for the best of both worlds.

An hour in when nothing has happened and conditions aren't looking favourable – and the weather man is decidedly gloomy about your prospects – it is easy to write the day off as a scratching time sort of occasion and design your tactics accordingly. Don't. Always go for it. Carp's feeding reactions are geared to conditions and a slight improvement in feeding conditions can sometimes trigger an unforeseeable feeding binge. In advance, you can have no inkling of the circumstances in which that catch of a lifetime will come.

I always fish a bed of bait, although I do make concessions as to the quantity of bait according to the conditions as I perceive them. On a day-only three-rod limit water I am not very familiar with, I would start by fishing one rod on the bed of bait, one on the edge of it and the third rod away from it, the third rod being fished with a stringer, or as a single hookbait. On a two-rod water, the rod on the edge of the bed of bait would have to go, the one on the bed of bait being essential. This bed of bait rod is the feeding thermometer. On the rare day when they really have it, they will be moving on and off the bed of baits and this rod will produce.

Once it becomes apparent that I have encountered such an occasion, all available rods go into or around the baited area. Sometimes the action is concentrated into one tight spot. At others, the fish seem to be well on the move and action

will come to two rods, or even more (very unusual in my experience). In other words even though the fish are feeding strongly they still have preferred spots where their guard is down and they are more likely to make a mistake.

It is worth emphasizing that while multiple captures are red letter days, if you put all your eggs in one basket in really going for it from the outset they may pass you by. They tend to happen out of the blue as a result of luck, or through careful planning. Even when you are getting it absolutely right, your sessions may result in the capture of one carp, at best, and that capture will come through you stacking the odds in your favour on every session. Start out by giving yourself alternatives, then adjust your tactics according to the reactions of the carp to what you are doing. And always keep your mind open on this point. The bed of bait is a reference point and a handy way of making a quantity of your food source available to the carp. But multiple captures of pressured carp are just as likely to occur on a rod away from the bed of baits as to a rod on it. A bed of bait is an attempt to focus the carp's attention on your feeding ground. Sometimes they just get focused in a spot for reasons that aren't apparent to we mere mortals, a theme we'll cover elsewhere in more depth.

Back at the day-ticket water. We're one hour in and we are going to put some bait in. There is a possible feeding time around lunch time/early afternoon, then the usual last knockings nerve-stretcher to take into account. What are the tactics? Bait quantity will depend on the number of fish you are fishing for, and their size. With three rods, you can put in more bait than you can with two. An open-water baiting situation has to be based on local knowledge, or sightings of carp movement. If you are fishing a new lake, your eyes should be glued to the water during that initial hour's wait. In the absence of any other information, position your bed of bait in the area of any signs of movement. If you're fishing blind, have a plumb around after the hour's up, then introduce a modest quarter to half a pound of bait into a likely spot. Introducing the sort of quantities of bait many writers suggest on a twenty-four hour session – or shorter – may have a disastrous effect on your fishing. Then again, spend your time with your eyes glued to the water.

There are two lines of thought on beds of bait, and you may choose to use one or the other depending on the conditions and the likely carp activity. When you are applying your bait, you can either spread it widely to keep the carp on the move searching for bait, or you can concentrate the baits to help focus the carp's attention towards the hookbait. In most circumstances, I fish one rod on a tight bed. Use the second rod on a roving basis, recasting stringers or singles to likely looking spots, or into areas of fish movement. Carp on pressured waters will often investigate a bait as soon as it is introduced. A hookbait may be tried and marked as dangerous if it does not result in a chance. (I originally wrote 'pick-up', then changed it to 'chance'. On the waters we are discussing here, your hookbait will be picked up a number of times but for the most part you won't know about it!)

The confrontation between the angler and the carp becomes a psychological war of nerves on some venues and you have to think your way into a pick-up much of the time. Here's a couple of examples of ploys which have resulted in pick-ups when I was quite sure the carp were around the baits, the free offerings were probably gone, and the hookbait had a sign indicating it had passed its sell-by date hung on it.

I have had success using stringers of new baits in conjunction with a recast hookbait on pressured waters. New baits are possible sources of danger; baits which have been lying there some time may be more acceptable. So a new bait stringer with a recast hookbait can lead to them nervously avoiding the stringer baits and making a mistake with the 'safe' hookbait. On a bed of bait, I'll use one dangerous hookbait to emphasize the safety of another one fished within a yard or two of it. For instance, a double bait on one rod, with a single hookbait fished close by, the single having one free offering PVA'd to it. Some days they'll prefer the double. On others, they'll play with the double, and be fooled when the alternative presentation turns out not to be a double, but a couple of free offerings. Pop-ups blown? Then fish one with a bottom bait close by. Nervousness about the one hookbait can induce a momentary carelessness about the alternative. On waters of this type, you are not waiting for the carp to feed, you are waiting for them to make a mistake, and with limited time you may have to work hard and use a little imagination to induce that mistake.

The last paragraph spells out the difficulty of assessing the carp's reaction to bait. Are you better leaving the hookbait in position throughout the day to allay the carp's suspicions? Or might it not be better to have an occasional, or frequent, recast in case the hookbait has been investigated and sussed out? Vary the tactics from rod to rod and find out which method brings the best results.

Minor variations on a theme can have a startling effect, as I discovered at Waveney many years ago. I had a terrific session on D lake at Waveney in the early 1980s, and couldn't work out what I'd done right until long after the session. Big beds of bait and double hookbaits had accounted for a great many carp through the summer and autumn. I went at the back end, aware that beds of bait might be a problem, so stringers were to be my main line of attack. Unfortunately, the big winds that week made it impossible for me to cast a multiple-bait stringer out to the producing area, so for much of the week I had to settle for just one freebie PVA'd to the hook and the single hookbait. I had a terrific run of fish, including two of the lake's thirty pounders. I had a good bait, my positioning of the hookbaits was good, but I was following a period of high pressure when boats had been used to position the hookbaits and I really had thought I would struggle for the odd fish that week. The only real explanation I could come up with for the result was that most of the fish had been caught on double baits that season and were nervous of them, so when they found two baits lying together they approached the trap with great caution. The fact that the baits were independent of each other apparently allayed their suspicions and, as a result, the hookbait was

The Leather at 31lb 13oz from D Lake in 1983. A good bait, guesswork and inadvertent trickery led to this pressured carp's downfall.

taken time after time. Too silly for words, really, but it does open your eyes to the tiny margins between success and failure in carp fishing, particularly with nervous, pressured fish.

I recall a charity fish-in at Cuttle Mill. Clive Gibbins was fishing to my left and had a number of fish showing over his baits, but he couldn't get a pick-up. He was actually fishing two beds of bait, with a different type of bait for each bed. When his hair tearing-out mode was at its peak during the afternoon, I suggested he try fishing the hookbait of one type of bait over the bed of the other type; changing the hookbaits over, in other words. He started to get action right away!

I once accidentally reeled in a rig from the snags at Waveney, and recognized the type of hook and the braid. Well, hooks and braided hook lengths, actually. I carried the rig round with me for ages until I finally met the angler I thought they'd belonged to at a meeting. 'This yours?' I asked the somewhat startled star. He knew I wanted some sort of rationale of the set-up. 'Look, when I am using stringers at very pressured waters I prefer to use three hooklinks. They know there's going to be a hook with one of the baits. They may manage to work out that could be a hook with two of the baits, but they'll never figure out that there could be a hook with three of the baits!'

I am not defending it, and I am certainly not suggesting that you fish more than one hooklink. I have quoted the circumstances to demonstrate the battle of wits that goes on between pressured carp and thinking anglers. And I should put on record the fact that I did try a two hooklink set-up in an area where two hooks were (and are) permitted, one with a pop-up and one with a bottom bait. My thinking was that the pop-up would be viewed with some nervousness, which would result in a confident pick up of the bottom bait, which would be viewed as a free offering. That was exactly what happened with a couple of good fish on the only morning I ever tried the tactic.

I became nervous of the ethics of the tactic after that one morning, but the lines of thought quoted above are those which have resulted in me preferring to saturate a baited area with as many hookbaits as possible rather than spread them around. The identification of one source of danger may just mean a relaxation of the carp's danger instincts and make it more at risk with the next trap it encounters.

Single hookbaits may catch through attraction, or frustration, or for any of a number of reasons, but when it comes to fishing beds of bait, you are aiming to achieve that momentary lapse in concentration that is the trigger for a high percentage of carp takes.

Once you have created a bed of bait on a day-time-only water, do not introduce any more bait that day unless you have had action and know that your carp will stand for more bait being introduced while they are in the swim. Just don't. I've done it times many, usually for something to do and because I couldn't visualize what was happening in front of me. I now look on bait as a food source and a bed of bait as a feeding area which has helped my thinking considerably. Feeling you need to be certain you have bait in the swim can lead to confused thinking and poor angling.

Yes, I know, you may be thinking in terms of preoccupation. If a carp has just picked up ten baits it will be at risk from the eleventh. Some days. On others, it just will not pick up ten baits while it is in the swim. It'll pick up one, two or three, then it'll be off on its travels. Then it will come back later for another little feed. It is fully aware of the feeding area and it is coming back for more food. If you have just topped-up, the possibility is that you are reducing your chances. It knows there is bait there, and my own thinking is that when they are revisiting the area, they are at greater risk as the bait in the swim reduces. It knows there is bait there, it wants another little feed, but it struggles to find any food. In those circumstances encountering a stringer, or a hookbait, can induce that much sought-after momentary lapse in concentration. The element of preoccupation is built up through the bait being available that month, that week or earlier that day. A carp does not have to be picking up its fifteenth bait to know it is on a bed of baits. The carp is in what it knows to be a feeding area, therefore it has gone there to feed.

One other thought on induced takes brought about by a reducing food source. Have you ever watched a small group of carp feeding on bottom baits or floaters? When there is plenty of bait available, the feeding is a fairly leisurely activity. Pick off a bait here, have a mooch around, pick up another one. Then they wander off and the temptation is to top up the swim.

If you don't, the next time they come in to feed their reactions to the available bait can be different. Five carp and ten baits means two baits each, which is starting to stack the odds in your favour, but not making them odds-on. When five carp are in feeding mode and want the only two baits available, then the odds have swung your way. Competitive feeding when they are up for it leads to action. Red letter days come about when they are up for it over a period of time, or three rods roar off within minutes of each other. In the first instance, there is a chance you will get a succession of takes. In the second instance, a group of carp have moved in and cleaned you out. Either way, it makes for memorable fishing but it should also make for careful analysis afterwards. We can all get it wrong (and frequently do) but it isn't always apparent whether we got it wrong, or the fish were too spooky. The aim is to always get it right, so that when they are up for it, your feeding situation makes the best possible advantage of your good fortune in being there in the right place at the right time.

The 'starve 'em into submission' syndrome is particularly important at last knockings. The more bait you make available to them at dusk, the more chance they have of waiting you out until your disillusioned footsteps have faded homewards before they get stuck. (I've tried it. They know the difference between decoy footsteps and the real thing, although there was an occasion at Roman Lakes when my then ten-year-old son informed me, 'That thing moved up while you were gone, dad!' after I'd made the first trip to the car park.) Dusk seems to be a fairly natural induced feeding time on day-only waters and I have a couple of vivid memories of last minute captures at both Cuttle and Roman: in fact my first twenty-pounder was caught at Cuttle Mill as dusk was descending and Mrs Brewer was raising the whistle to her lips. Don't get within an hour of dusk and decide to top-up ready for the last-minute feeding spell. If you've done the job right earlier in the day, the carp will know there is a feeding area in front of you and when it comes to feeding time, they will go there to feed.

When you are in a swim for one day it is difficult to assess how effective a back-up feeding situation created with hemp, other seeds, particles or pellets may be. When the fish are at catapult range it is possibly a safer method than using a spod rod, which creates more disturbance. Again, it is a question of finding out what the fish in your water will tolerate, but when time is limited and I am fishing for nervous fish I am reluctant to feed them with anything other than the bait I want to catch them on. For me, there is a distinct but fine line between using a background source of attraction (as tends to happen with dissolving pellets, crumb or Micromass) and a background food source. Leaving aside the disturbance caused by the spod (which can be a source of attraction on some waters!) pellets are so instant that they should be the ideal background baiting situation on daytime-only waters. The only way you will be able to assess your carp's reaction to the use of a spod is to try it.

On waters where back-up food sources or attractor situations have not been used they can be devastatingly effective. The majority of anglers cannot be bothered with the effort involved in spodding baits into position, which means that coming to terms with the method may give you a temporary, but massive edge on waters which have not seen it. And it will pay to bear in mind that the Nash Ball Pellets enable you to create a background source of attraction without having to resort to the use of a spod. Ball Pellets represent a very subtle way of inviting the carp to re-investigate the swim during the day, the occasional introduction of a few Ball Pellets increasing the smell of food in the swim without increasing the number of baits available to the carp.

Tactically, you need an awareness of all the alternatives and a very open mind when you fish daytime-only waters. In terms of difficulty, they will rate from extremely easy, where you just pile the bait in and the fish come and feed on it, to extremely difficult, where a fish in a day is a result and you need to bring all your experience and thinking to bear to achieve that result.

The thoughts I've put together in this chapter will open the eyes of some of you to lines of attack you may have been missing, but please understand that anything you read in print is only a guideline. While I have been writing this section, my mind has been going back to carp captures which have entirely bucked the trend of the common-sense rules I try to apply to my fishing. I'll finish the chapter by recounting one such capture.

Greg Fletcher and I had a number of day sessions at Roman Lakes in the early 1980s. From memory, the first such session was in January 1982. We'd been let in on the hair via our southern Carp Society friends during the previous autumn and were keen to try out the method at what used to be a quite frustrating water in the pre-hair days. A spell of frozen lakes frustrated our efforts to get out, and when we did eventually make it to Roman, it was obvious that we were too soon after the freeze.

There was a cold north-west wind blowing across the lake, and the water was still gin clear after the freeze cessation of feeding activity. Greg fished the first swim in and I fished one of the middle pegs. Conditions were so grim that we were the only ones on the water for the entire day.

We put some early home-made boilies out, cast out a couple of hair-rigged bottom baits into position, and froze our way through a short, boring, bleak, actionless winter's day. Normally your expectancy level increases towards dusk at Roman but on this occasion it all seemed so hopeless (and there was possibly a hint of snow around to put the run back across the Snake Pass in peril) that by mid-afternoon Greg was round to my swim to see if I'd had enough. I went along with the idea of an early departure and we set about packing our gear.

I'd taken a pound or two of bait with me, and had only put about fifty out earlier in the day in view of the conditions. No point in taking it home with me, so before I reeled in the end tackles, I fired the rest of the baits out to the baited area. I'd almost finished when I was away on one of the rods and landed one of the lake's bigger residents, a known big double/low twenty. Needless to say, it was a tactic I repeated on subsequent sessions at the water, the lack of further response proving just what a fluke that particular capture had been!

19 OVERNIGHT SESSION FISHING

Overnight sessions throw up a different set of problems to daytime-only sessions. The problems are twofold, practical and tactical. Let us look at the tactical problems first, which nearly all centre around the likely timing of the feeding time or times. Night-feeding waters rarely fish all night and as in daytime-only fishing a badly timed introduction of bait can eliminate your chances for at least one of the possible feeding periods.

If you are arriving at tea-time, an evening feeding water can be a difficult proposition. You cannot turn up at the water and start piling the bait in. You have to fish on the back of previous efforts, with an established bait the fish are on the look-out for. Singles and stringers are again the right choice in this situation, although a trickle of bait over a wide area and across a period of time may well be a practical alternative.

The length of the evening feeding period will be important here.

If you are arriving at tea-time and the water fishes 'up to midnight' (which is not uncommon) the time span is such that you will almost certainly feel happier putting some bait in to alert the fish to the presence of food. But once the evening feeding spell is over, where does that leave you in terms of baiting-up and positioning hookbaits for the morning feeding spell? Quite simply, you have to step up a gear and become a far better technical carp angler, and a far more imaginative one. Baiting-up visually with the aid of a marker float is a simple enough process, but how many of you are capable of baiting-up accurately and positioning hookbaits precisely in the dark? The tactical considerations of overnight sessions centre around the timing of the introduction of bait.

Part of the tree line at Birch. An ideal spot for using the clipped-up casting method in the dark.

The practical considerations centre round learning to fish efficiently in the dark.

If you are fishing open water within catapult range, there are no great problems in introducing free offerings or casting into position. In the dark, beyond catapult range, presents greater problems, but they are by no means insurmountable. Once you have confidence in these alternative methods, it means that you can fish your overnight sessions through the dark evenings, provided getting to your swim in the dark is a practical proposition.

Very accurate baiting in the dark necessitates the use of a spod rod, or a few warm-up casts with stringers. If you are starting fishing in daylight, find the range of your spod, and clip the line at the reel (or fix it in some other way if your spool does not carry a line clip). You will have the precise direction of the cast from your horizon marker. When you need to introduce more bait you load the spod, aim at the horizon marker and cast. The clipped line will stop the spod in flight at the required distance. I mention the Bait Missiles elsewhere, and these are very easy to use (comfortably coping with distances in excess of a hundred yards) and very accurate. I find these modern bait rockets tremendous aids for introducing boilies, and when I am fishing with stringers, I actually prefer introducing free offerings in this way, to condition the carp to finding the bait in little clusters. The Bait Missiles carry 8 × 18mm baits or 12 × 14mm, so it only takes a few casts to create an adequate short-session feeding situation. If you are introducing bait by means of a throwing stick or a catapult, you will have to rely on muscle memory for accurate baiting.

Casting out with pin-point accuracy in the dark is again a question of finding your horizon marker in daylight, clipping or marking the line to the required casting distance, and casting to the full extent of the clipped line. If you are arriving at the water in the dark, you will need to have your spod rod and fishing rods clipped up in advance – as you leave the water from the previous session will be the obvious time if you know which swim you will be fishing at your next visit.

What do you do if you are not sure which swim you will be in? You will need different marks for the fishing spots in different swims and to clip the line when you arrive at the water. How? Either by overcasting in the swim in question and reeling back to the line marker – then clipping – or walking the line off the spool across a field, or along the bank, until you find the right mark. The latter course of action is the one you will have to adopt if one of your marks is a snag where overcasting is not possible.

Casting clipped line requires some practice. In open water, where 'thereabouts' is good enough, it is comparatively simple. Casting to snags where there is no margin for error isn't, and here you will learn that you have to err on the side of safety – which is no bad thing in the dark where the carp probably don't require the end tackle quite as tight to the snag as they do in daylight. The problem with casting clipped line lies in the effect of wind on the line while the lead is in the air. You need a heavy lead, and you don't need an exaggerated overcast. You'll learn that a cast which just takes enough line off the spool is ideal. The lead loses its momentum naturally, which means that the line maintains its forward momentum during the entire flight and during the descent of the lead.

In a cross-wind, an abrupt stopping of the flight in the air results in the wind having an unnaturally exaggerated effect on the line and the end tackle being pulled sideways and backwards at the end of the cast. On the other hand, be aware that any cross wind while you are fixing the stopping distance is having an effect on the amount of line in the air during the cast. I have found to my cost that when the wind drops, the cast that was right earlier in the day in windy conditions is a cast too far once the wind drops. Practise this method of casting in daylight and familiarize yourself with the variations in casting distances before you launch an end tackle towards a snag across the night air. Even when you are practised in the art there is still a nervous few seconds as you listen for the lead hitting water – or wood.

The 28lb Birch common which fell to a start-of-season midnight(ish) clipped-up cast to the tree line before I had even got the third rod out. Double Big Fish mix 20mm baits on the stiff link was the subtle presentation this fish fell for! I had a mirror of 27lb 12oz on the same rod an hour later.

There are two further points to bear in mind when you are casting clipped-up. One is that you are better using a heavy lead. This helps overcome any effect a cross-wind may have on the line. The second is that when you are casting to a feature or snag in deep water, the end result of clipping will be that the lead will swing back towards you as it hits the water. This is because the line is clipped to the distance of the cast hitting the water and the clipped line will then result in a loss of momentum and a pull back on the lead. Overcome this by being prepared to thrust the rod forward as the line hits the water.

All that sounds very complicated. I had read Zenon Bojko's writing about the method on a number of occasions before I actually got round to putting it into practice. Birch Grove at the

start of the season proved to be an occasion made for casting with clipped lines. I like to start on the Main Boards, but in the days when we had to cast out at midnight on the fifteenth, the cast to the far tree line was a problem because of the danger of casting into the trees, and because we have a celebratory drink at Birch at the start of the season and you need all the help you can get when it comes to casting out in the dark!

So I set the far tree line rod in the clip some time during the afternoon, went back to the caravan for the celebratory party, and returned to the swim in the dark for the ritual first cast of the season. The tree line rod went out first, the one to a hoped-for hot-spot second, and I was just preparing to cast out the third rod, when the first one roared off! There was a 28lb common on the end and I was instantly converted to the benefits of casting clipped-up. I had a mirror of 27lb 12oz on the same rod a couple of hours later.

There is one other method (at least one other method) of achieving the required distance on a darkness cast, and it is my preferred open-water method. I use stringers in almost all my carp fishing (other than extreme range) and I prefer to limit the distance of the cast by the number of baits in the stringer. When you use a marker float, it is easy to assess what distance you are achieving with different stringer loadings. Most of my fishing is done with small baits, so my stringer loading will vary from four small baits up to twenty. This arrangement suits me for ranges of ten to over a hundred yards. My optimum range for the multi-bait stringer set-ups is seventy yards in calm conditions, so I just limit the number of baits depending on how much further I want to cast.

I use this same loading scale to assess my casts against the distance I can achieve with a throwing stick with bigger baits. A dense bait like a fishmeal boilie of 18mm I can throw ninety yards with a throwing stick, which will equate to a three bait stringer of boilies of that size. With 22m baits, I can achieve the same distance with the throwing stick as I can cast a single bait. I know all this because over the years I have spent many hours baiting-up to a marker float, so I am not guessing at the distances and relative distances I am achieving during baiting-up and casting. When I change bait I have to reassess the formula in terms of the physical properties of the change bait when it comes to throwing stick work – but that's one of the other beauties of the underemployed bait rocket. This method of baiting removes muscle memory and the bait characteristics variables. The limitation factor is your own casting ability and the restrictions imposed by your rod, reel and line set-up.

In my experience, overnight feeding spells fall into three categories: early evening, early hours and around first light. Early evening we have taken care of by not embarking on an overbaiting situation. It is unlikely that a water will have

an early evening and an early hours feeding time, so this is a perm any two-from-three situation. I will skip the early hours for the minute and look at the combination we have on the Mangrove this autumn, where the fish have adopted a new pattern for the water. If you haven't had a take by eight o'clock in the evening nothing is likely to happen until four next morning at the earliest. If I've had no action whatever I leave the baiting situation *in situ*, although I may top-up with some extra baits if the conditions and overnight forecast warrant it. If I've had the odd unexplained bleep from the buzzer, I'll guess that the free offering in the stringer has been taken and the hookbait avoided. In these circumstances, I'll leave the end tackle till well past the evening feeding spell, then recast. If I'm at extreme range, I'll spod out some extra baits (no more than three or four casts). If I'm at moderate range, or down the margins, I'll recast with the multi-stringer set-up.

Once the evening spell has passed, you are in an overnight situation and there is no cause for touching the rods unless you have action. The overnight baiting situation is the morning feeding situation. I think a carp feeding in the right spot at this time is vulnerable because the baits have been in position for some time. No swim disturbance, the baits will have lost their human odours, and first light onwards is a very natural feeling feeding time when all nature is extremely active. On waters where such a feeding time occurs, I expect the carp to feed on the overnight free offerings, and I expect them to take the hookbait without too close an examination. The only circumstances in which I'll reel in a hookbait at this time is if I think it may have been taken, or partly eaten, by nuisance fish, or if it is palpably in the wrong place from an overnight cast. My bait is a food, not a source of attraction, and I think the carp will be more relaxed about a food which has been there for some time than about a newly introduced one.

Early hours feeding times are angler-friendly for overnight carpers. Midnight or one o'clock are popular times for the carp starting to feed (or starting to become catchable), which allows for

This striking 28lb Motorway Pond mirror fell to a precisely placed overnight PVA trap close to a weed bed, and gave me some anxious minutes before I put the net under it in the weedy, snaggy lake.

quite normal angling considerations to be employed. I like the baits to be in position at least three or four hours prior to feeding time, which means having them in position by early evening. The ability to fish in the dark makes all-year-round overnight sessions possible on early hours waters, the main drawback being that if you are going to work next day a succession of fish can make the following day a very long one. I used to fish day sessions on Roman Lakes while I was working night shifts, which was even worse. I can sleep by the water at night, but the Roman sessions meant going twenty-four hours without sleep, which was not fun. The things we do to catch a carp.

Angling considerations apart, I find setting-up and breaking-down in the dark irksome, but no great problem. You need a greater degree of organization so you know where everything is when you arrive (and when you leave) and your

swim choice may be tempered by the need to be within reasonable distance of your transport. But I have always been surprised about two aspects of overnight fishing. My first reaction was that I was amazed at the number of carpers who practised overnighters, particularly in the real hotbeds of carp fishing like Kent, Surrey and the Colne Valley. My second reaction was that I was surprised how many of these carpers stopped doing overnighters once the dark nights set in. I accept that they are mentally daunting, but overnighters are anyway. But, as we discuss in winter carping, carp can be a lot easier to catch in the autumn, through to Christmas, and this is a period when mid-week pressure on many waters is minimal. It's all a question of how much you want to catch. If you are determined enough to really want to catch carp, then I would give some thought to adding dark overnighters to your armoury.

20 LONG SESSION FISHING

Sussex big-fish angler Dave Lane, by reputation the most mobile carp angler on the scene. He is one of the most successful, too, with an amazing list of big fish to his name. He is pictured here with Mary from Wraysbury at a weight of 49lb 15oz. I guess that makes him one of the most honest of carp anglers, too!

I define a 'long session' as any session where bait application and tactics can be applied on a long-term, rather than a short-term, basis. On overnight and weekend sessions the immediacy of the plans to catch carp is limiting. What happens over the baited area on day three is merely of academic interest. The weather prevailing at the time you arrive at the water is of greater significance than any change which is likely to take place. When you go to fish for longer than two days, some of the planning may have to be long term.

I guess the first consideration of the long-term angler is an honest appraisal of his own mobility. Not to put too fine a point on it, I am not as mobile as I once was. Once I've put down roots at the water on a long session I'm reluctant to move unless I'm absolutely convinced that I've got it wrong and that the fish are going to remain somewhere other than where I am for the balance of the session. This isn't entirely due to inertia or laziness, but at the same time, I cannot kid myself that I have the energy or enthusiasm of the Dave Lanes of this world, carp anglers who travel light and only have to see a carp's nose emerge in a swim other than the one they are fishing for them to move and put a bait on it. And I have to add that I think I am in the majority, and Dave and his imitators in the minority, which is why he has aspired to the outstanding big fish record he has to his name on some of the most brutal waters in the country, while the rest of us settle for more modest returns from far easier waters!

There are mobile long-session anglers, and static ones. The mobile ones, I can only applaud and offer some obvious advice to anyone who wants to emulate them: travel as light as possible, treat every stay as a one- or two-day session, then reread what follows when you've burnt out, or old age approaches, and you decide to join the ranks of the bivvy dwellers rather than the bivvy movers. Phil Thompson's book *Waiting for Waddle* gives a comprehensive insight into the machinations of long session movers and I would unhesitatingly recommend it to anyone who is going to fish the big waters and has the focus and drive to pursue the carp they are after round the lakes.

There is a genuine angling-based conflict between moving and not moving, even on the big waters. Successfully anticipating the movements of the fish rather than moving onto them can be a very rewarding tactic. Some baiting situations do not come to fruition until day three or beyond. Some carp do not take kindly to having baits put in over their heads. Some swims will always produce, while others are less dependable. Certain swims produce known big fish, while others tend to produce smaller fish. Five possible reasons for selecting a swim, producing a baited situation, then sweating it out. Sometimes the tactic will fail, but then that is true of all carp tactics. You can only judge the

results of your efforts over a period of time and build your carp fishing tactics around what suits you best and gives you the best results.

The major drawback of static carping is that you have to get swim selection as right as possible at the first time of asking, which requires some advance knowledge of the water, the conditions and the feeding habitats of the fish. If you live some distance from the water, watch the weather forecasts for the week before your session. All carp anglers worth their salt know where the compass points lie on their waters, so if you don't, I'd advise you to acquaint yourself of this knowledge as soon as possible. Once you are in range of local radio, check the local forecasts on your way to the water, and listen closely. I've driven across to Shropshire with the national forecast telling me to go into one swim on the strength of anticipated southerly winds, and have had to change my plans on the basis of the local forecaster reassessing what was supposedly a southerly wind to south easterly. Southerly means a number of possible swims on the Mangrove while south easterly narrows the field down to one, possibly two.

Waters vary in terms of the time of day when carp show themselves. If there is a feeding significance in carp showing on your water, try to arrive before they start showing so you can take this invaluable location aid into your reckoning. If the carp show at feeding time, get on them but don't ruin your chances by filling the swim in when they are showing. Just put out stringers or hookbaits until the fish have finished feeding, then get on with the bait application when the feeding spell is over and the fish have gone quiet.

Assessing the long-term effect of baiting situations is an aspect of carp fishing that has to be learnt, then relearnt. I've learnt some salutary lessons during my years of fishing the Mangrove and Birch Grove, lessons which have stood me in good stead in terms of acquiring patience during long sessions. The most startling lesson goes back a few years. Bill Cottam and Brian Skoyles had been extolling the virtues of groundbaiting with crumbed baits for carp for some time, so I decided to have a shot at coming to terms with the method during a week's fishing on Birch Grove. I was on my own during the week and Mary was coming down at the weekend to join me. I put out the marker in a known producing spot, scattered a couple of pounds of crumbed baits over a suitable area, then set about emptying the lake, fishing Big Fish Mix over the crumb baited area.

The fish were singularly unco-operative, and when nothing had happened from over the baited area by the Wednesday I couldn't rationalize what was happening, changed tactics and started avoiding the spot. Mary duly came down on the Friday, and we fished through to Sunday. By the weekend, I'd quite literally forgotten all about the crumb area. From first light onwards on the Sunday morning, there was an unusual amount of fish activity in one particular spot, and it took me half an hour to realize that it was the spot I'd crumbed earlier in the week! I switched a couple of hookbaits to the area and had two carp in half an hour before the feeding activity ceased. Six days on the spot which had produced nothing was suddenly a centre of feeding operations. What was that about?

Well, the reality was probably that the fish had started feeding in that spot earlier in the week, but since that time I have noticed that it frequently happens that there is a delay between the baits going in and the fish starting to feed confidently over them. I think that what had happened in that particular case was that, by the weekend, the fish were feeding with frustration over what had become a disappearing food source. Either I'd put too much crumb in to start with, or I'd mistakenly topped it up after the initial baiting, or the fish were just feeding indifferently at the start of the week and with some abandon by the end of it. I've since come to recognize that this delayed start, or build up of action, over a baited area is a frequent enough occurrence to be a predictable one.

The simple explanation may be that the angler is sitting there waiting for a build up of confidence in the fish's feeding. To help my own confidence, I look at it this way. What starts out as a cautionary bed of bait gradually becomes accepted as a desirable natural feeding area.

More carp visiting the spot to feed may well lead to competitive feeding, and once you get the fish competing they become catchable. Applying the bait correctly can lead to the frustration factor starting to play a part in the carp's feeding, which will have happened on the Birch Grove occasion referred to. I stopped feeding the spot so the food source diminished until there was just the smell left.

When you are fishing long sessions, it is important to understand the significance of the delayed start in confident feeding. It may mean a very different tactical approach between the start of a week's session and the start of a three-day one. I am willing to keep the bait going in on a week's session, while I recognize a need to limit the food supply on shorter sessions.

I find the timing of applying bait important on a long session. When there is strong feeding activity and I want to keep adding bait to the swim, this has got to be achieved without spooking the fish. Carp on some waters will stand for baits going in over their heads while they are feeding. A number of us have learned the hard way that on the Mangrove it is a disastrous mistake to put bait in on top of the fish while they are showing – and the same consideration will apply to many other waters. If I am using a lot of bait, I put the main application in at what I know to be the quietest period in the fish's feeding – in the Mangrove's case, late morning. My routine is that I put out the baits, leave the water for an hour or two, then fish for the remaining twenty-two hours. I top up the baited area during other known quiet periods, but what you do learn fishing this way is that the common concept of very restricted feeding times just isn't realistic at all. The Mangrove has the reputation of being a night-only water, but I now consider late morning to be the only time the fish aren't going to feed strongly enough to get themselves caught. The important thing to me is that they come to look on the baited area as a feeding area which has always got food in it. As acceptance of the feeding area starts to grow, the carp will visit the area with increasing regularity and increasing confidence and hopefully become more catchable.

I have watched the effect of applying boilies on Birch Grove during the close season, admittedly when the fish are not under angling pressure. The fish will move back in on a new introduction of baits within twenty minutes to half an hour of their being introduced, but it takes them time to regain their confidence in their feeding on each new application of bait. Sometimes they are feeding nervously and are clearly not catchable. At other times they are competing with each other, and frantically stirring up the bottom looking to see if they have missed any baits. Carp have plenty of feeding times, but only a limited number of these are catching times.

Times without number I have watched anglers putting out bait at what I know to be a strong feeding time. If you do this on a long session, you are drastically cutting down your chances. For two reasons. Firstly, there is a chance you will be pushing the fish out of the swim. Secondly, even if they stay you may well have negated that particular feeding time by putting fresh baits in over their heads.

For me, there is an important point about long session fishing which many people seem to miss. Such a session gives the opportunity for continuity. Not continuity in the sense of a series of twelve- or eighteen-hour sessions. Continuity in the sense that there is always a feeding area in front of you and that the trap is always set. For instance, I am not sure that the oft-quoted principle of giving the swim a rest by having your lines out of the water is a particularly good idea. A carp will become familiar with a state of affairs which always exists, whereas the disturbance of reeling in, and recasting may give more cause for concern.

There will be a point at which your bait is at its most acceptable to the carp. Attractor levels are very arbitrary and cannot be at their most effective throughout a twenty-four hour period. In addition, it may well be that a bait which has been in the water for some time and has that lived-in look and smell may be more acceptable to a wary carp than a newly introduced bait. Albert Romp wrote of catching Sally from Savay on a hookbait which had been in position for three days. That's an extreme example, but I'm a great lover of hookbaits which have been in position and immersed for a long time. For me, a bait which has been out there overnight is more likely to be taken in the morning cleaning-up operation than a newly introduced bait, and I remember a quite startling instance of this on the Mangrove.

I was fishing four rods (without prejudice) and by the time I made my regular 7.45am phone call to Mary on the mobile I'd had a carp on three of them on overnight baits. I commented to Mary that conditions looked good and that I was still in with a chance because I'd still got one overnight hookbait in position. At 8am the buzzer sounded and I landed a fish on the one remaining overnight hookbait. Four takes over a three-hour period, all on overnight hookbaits. I had no action on any of the recast rods.

It amazes me the number of anglers who reel-in at first light and put on a fresh hookbait. If you are nervous that your overnight bait will not survive the attentions of eels and other nuisance fish, then come up with a hookbait which will. There are plenty of rock-hard hookbait mixes available now, Rod Hutchinson's Clawbuster mix being a good example. Alternatively, the addition of egg albumen and/or Nutragel to your mix will help you come up with nuisance fish-proof hookbaits based on your actual mix.

I see well-meaning companions reeling in the other lines when an angler is playing a fish. If the hookbaits have been in the water a long time, this action may negate a few hours of fishing while there are feeding fish in the swim. Even on long sessions, feeding activity sometimes comes in bursts after long periods of inactivity. If at all possible, leave the hookbaits in position until you have to reel them in to leave the water.

Understand that when you are occupying one swim and fishing with attractor baits, they may start to lose their effectiveness from day two or day three. Be aware that this may happen and have a change of bait available, or move to another part of the lake.

There are three other major points to cover in session fishing, learning from the water, passing the time and being organized.

Learning From the Water

Being static in one swim for a length of time gives you the opportunity to observe and learn. The water will tell you things, the carp will certainly hand you a great deal of useful information, and the actions and results of other anglers will also help you. I take notes in my head, but really I should keep written notes. For instance, one carp sighting in any particular spot may be of no importance, but a series of sightings will start to have a growing significance. It pays to watch others baiting-up. When? How much? Where? How soon after they bait up does the action come, if any? How long into the session does the action come? Are they fishing on the baited area or off it? If they put out a marker float try to cross-reference it to see if it's a spot you know. If you are going on for a week, find out where the weekend anglers have been fishing so you will understand the significance of unusual areas of carp activity during the week. All this information helps you build up an understanding of how the carp react to baits and pressure.

Passing the Time

How to pass the time? It is a question I get asked a great deal. There are those who have to get off the water as much as possible when they are session fishing. Others spend as much time as possible in the swims of others. I spend as much time as possible in my own swim and recognize that I have got to handle staying in one place for long periods of time with nothing happening to enjoy what I am doing. Session fishing is a state of mind, but then so is carp fishing. The ends justify the means, so the means have to be coped with, endured or enjoyed, and I suppose that to me session fishing is a mixture of those three. There are times when I have to force myself to stay at the water, others when I am actively bored, while knowing that boredom is just part of the price, and other times when just being there is an unmitigated pleasure and it is enough to sit, and watch, and think and let it all wash over me.

I have learned so much from observing carp movement that I can enjoy watching the water for every waking hour, a vigil which is punctuated by frequent cups of tea or coffee and the odd bankside meal. I learn more about a water from simply watching it than in any other way. I accept the boredom that goes with acquiring that knowledge.

Oddly enough, I find it difficult to read or write at the water. I listen to the radio a great deal, sleep a great deal but they are the limit of my non-carp fishing activities. I cannot get on with the concept of television by the water. I just wouldn't feel I was fishing if I diverted myself to that extent.

Organization

I am quite sure it wasn't always so, but I've become a very organized, routine session angler. The longer you intend to stay by the water, the more tackle and living aids you need to take with you. The more gear you have with you the more organized you have to become. My organized tidiness has been thrust on me through frustration at not being able to find things in a cluttered bivvy!

I will not give a list of session requirements because we all have our own ideas of what our creature comforts should be, but if you are new to session fishing, I'd remind you that the extras you might not think of are bait storage facilities, self-take photographic equipment if you are fishing on your own, and sufficient food and water for meals and drinks on the bank.

In winter, extra towels and changes of clothing are essential. On the waters I fish, the carp feed best in monsoon conditions, and the logistics of continuing to live in the bivvy when you are having to make trips out into torrential rain and heavy winds require a great deal of forethought and organization.

You can only really learn what you need through going without it a couple of times. I take more tackle, equipment and clothing than many people I know but that's because I live at the water for two or three days when I'm there. A mental itinerary and a place for everything in the

Bivvy life. The mobile long session anglers are in the minority, although Alan Smith (pictured here relaxing with a young protégé on the East Bank at Fishabil) is another very successful big-fish man who is more than willing to move when he feels it is necessary.

bivvy have become essential parts of my carping – particularly in winter – and if you are to be a successful session angler, this is just one of the aspects you will have to come to terms with.

Understand that I am not saying that what I have written above is the way it has to be – it is the way it may have to be if you want to catch carp consistently. For many, a long carp session is their carp-fishing holiday for the year. It may include taking your spouse, or even your spouse and kids, and in those circumstances some sort of compromise has to be achieved between a holiday atmosphere and a carp-fishing session. Within certain acceptable guidelines, carp fishing is what you wish to make of it. A major chance to come to terms with a water and its carp, a few days of the crack with friends, a combination of family holiday and carp-fishing session. More and more people are coming to recognize that session carp fishing is a very pleasant way of life. Whatever your perception of a carp session may be, I will make an impassioned plea regarding one important aspect. Wherever you are fishing, and for however long, leave the water and its surroundings as you found it. It is a sad fact of life that we are having to live with a minority of carp-fishing animals who deposit litter, excrement and soiled toilet paper on the bank with no regard for others or the environment. Living rough without leaving a trace of your having been there is one of the aspects of carp fishing long-term anglers must come to terms with. Please give this aspect as much priority as selecting your bait or arriving at the right end tackle.

21 BIG CARP FROM MIXED WATERS

This is a subject I get a lot of letters about. For many, carp fishing is about trying to catch big fish, although we have all got our own visions of what a big carp actually is to us. In my book *Big Carp* I defined such a fish as being one over 25lb in weight, which is a very arbitrary assessment – and an unnecessary one. The first carp we catch is big. Mine weighed 6½lb. I have recently interviewed the current holder of the carp record of 55lb 13oz. His first carp also weighed 6½lb , and it looked huge – as mine did. In other words, all carp are big. It is our perception of them that changes through familiarity. As with beauty, size is in the eye of the beholder.

So when someone asks how they catch 'big carp', I think they actually mean 'bigger carp'. This opens two lines of thought, trying to catch the bigger – or biggest – carp in the water they are fishing, and targeting new waters to try and catch fish bigger than any they are currently fishing for. Both categories raise the obvious question: how valid is it to selectively fish for big carp, rather than just fish and wait till it is your turn to catch the big one? The answer is that it is entirely valid. It is something the top big-fish hunters in this country have been doing for many years now. Many of the big fish are known, many of the waters they live in are accessible. I mentioned the current record holder, Terry Hearn, earlier. Terry is a remarkable angler. Since he was in his teens, he has been joining waters to catch the biggest carp in each water. He was successful to the point that he finished up catching a record carp. Luck? No! In the previous six years Terry had caught the biggest fish from up to ten different waters. That is heady stuff and a life to be pursued by a small minority of anglers.

Let us be more realistic and start by looking at the situation many of you will be in. You are fishing a water with one or two big carp in it, but they never seem to come your way. Are you doing something wrong, or are you just waiting for your number to come up? Probably a combination of both. Consider a number of scenarios we will all have lived through, and which some of you will be experiencing now:

- If you are not catching at all, your methods and bait just are not good enough.
- If you are catching occasionally, but never the bigger fish in your water, you may be fishing in the wrong place, or the bait (or your bait application) may not be good enough for the bigger fish.
- If you are catching your share of the fish, including some good fish, but never the biggies, the situation needs further analysis.
- You just cannot put in the hours needed to catch big fish. This is the toughest category of all, but one in which you can at least shorten the odds slightly in your favour by careful allocation of your available time.

If you fall under the first category, hopefully this book will help you resolve some of your problems. It will help enormously if you can find a water where you can watch fish feeding on the bait you intend using. Once you know the fish are treating your bait as a food source, you have eliminated one of the most difficult variables, and you can focus your attentions on angling tactics.

Next, your bait (or bait application) may not be good enough for the bigger fish. Many of you will have difficulty accepting the premise that a bait which catches carp does not necessarily catch the bigger carp. I have no doubts whatever about the validity of it. Particle fishing will often bring much more action than boilie fishing, but the majority of the fish will be the smaller ones in the water. This is particularly true of light-coloured particles such as maize, black-eyed beans, soya beans, etc. The majority of bigger fish fall to boilies, and this can be broken down further to boilies with a food content which is treated as a food source.

That is not to say that attractor and instant baits do not account for big carp. When boilies are first used on a water, the carp appear to have difficulty distinguishing between baits which promise them food and baits which actually feed them. There is a bait pressure cycle. Check the catch reports in *Carp-Talk* for the baits in use for the bigger fish in this country. The one thing they will have in common is that they will almost all have a good nutritional content, and very often a liquid food content in addition to the base mix. I have emphasized 'in this country' because most of our fish are subjected to the bait pressure cycle. The quality of the food increases in significance with the increased pressure through repeat captures. Once the awareness of the danger of a bait is established in the instincts of a fish in a given water, that bait will gradually become less and less effective. The bait is no less worthy; it has simply become less effective through its own success. Till the pressure starts to mount the carp can be much less discriminating in their choice of bait than they later become. If you use a food bait you take all the guesswork out of what they will and will not respond to, but what is important to grasp is that carp live on food, not flavours, and the bigger the carp is, the more food it needs to eat just to live.

Fishmeals are food baits with built-in attractors. If they are new to a water, get on them. If they have been in use on a water for some time and have accounted for the big fish a number of times over, a variation on a theme may be the simple answer. Nutrabaits' Big Fish Mix accounted for most of the Mangrove's big fish on a number of occasions between 1989 and 1995 and I suspected that fishmeals may have started to lose their effectiveness. I was wrong. Paul Selman went on with Premier's Aminos with Betaine and had a stunning summer. John Lilley switched to Kevin Nash's S Mix and the bigger fish were straight on it. Richard Skidmore continued to fish Big Fish Mix and continued to catch big fish on it. When I came off Big Fish Mix, I went for a change from fishmeals and switched to Mainline's Grange Mix with CSL. No flavour, no other additives; that was the bait. Within two months, I had pushed my personal best up twice, and Conan, one of the big fish in the water, has fallen to the same bait half a dozen times in the last two years.

I should add that results on Big Fish Mix since I came off it have been exceptional and that the big fish have continued to fall for it. Big Fish Mix with caviar flavour and black pepper oil seems to be a combination the big fish just have to eat, the only problem with fishmeals being that they may not be as effective from autumn onwards: if you are fishing a winter campaign at some stage you may have to change baits.

I've named four of the best big-carp baits I have come across: Big Fish Mix, Aminos, S Mix and the Grange with CSL. I am sure they have not all accounted for all the big fish in your water, but given the chance they will. There are other consistently successful big-fish baits, Rod Hutchinson's Super Fish and Liver Mix, most protein and HNV mixes (preferred by many for the late autumn and winter) and those birdfood mixes which pay as much attention to the food content as they do to the attractors. Check out the adverts and the catalogues, choose a bait, speak to the bait company concerned and get their advice on additives. Tell the company what you want the bait to do and how much time you have available, then fish the end product with blind faith, not for a session or two, but until you have caught the fish you are after. Most of the quality food baits available now are so good that provided you fish well they will do the job for you. Just don't undermine what you are trying to do by overloading with attractors, fishing with baits that are not fresh, or by fishing a rig so complicated that it will actually discourage the fish from picking up the hookbait.

The important thing about your big-fish bait is that it has to have an element of selectivity and I have seen the baits I have named consistently catch bigger fish from waters with big heads of smaller fish in them – the Mangrove and Fishabil. In addition, these baits have featured in numerous catch reports of big fish which appear in the press.

Selectivity can be important on some waters, particularly where the bigger fish are the older fish and in the minority. I have caught ten English thirty-pounders, and they all had this in common: each capture was isolated in that it was either the only one on that day, or the first. I have had numerous multiple twenty-pounder captures when I hoped that the next sounding of the buzzer would herald a thirty-pounder. It never has done. Of the thirty-pounders I have caught, only Mangrove's Scaley seems to be at all communal. The others appear to be loners. I thought there was some great mystery in this till Rod Hutchinson patiently and logically explained that the older fish are often survivors of a generation, and tend not to mix with later generations other than at spawning time, which means they are loners when it comes to feeding.

This is an aspect that needs analysing in terms of the habits of the fish in your water. If you are fishing for a loner, you need to understand that is the case. A bed of a thousand baits is not a situation that is likely to account for a lone feeder, or the first fish in. Catching big fish is not necessarily an extension of just fishing for anything that comes along. It is not just a question of coming up with the right bait; you have to get the baiting situation right too. Reflecting on my *From the Bivvy* summer and autumn on the Mangrove at a later date, I was disappointed that of the known bigger fish in the water, I only landed Scaley. Analysing that now I think that I had too much bait in front of me most of the time, although the selection of the swims I concentrated on may have been a contributing factor too.

This brings us to the point that location requires analysis also. Some big fish are markedly territorial, and some seem to prefer some areas of the lake to other areas for no readily definable reason. In the early 1980s I caught Waveney D Lake's magnificent mirror Big Scale twice at thirty pounds plus, both times from under the Big Oak. I would guess that he was hooked in that tight area the majority of times he was caught in the late 1970s and early 1980s. I caught another D Lake thirty-pounder, the Leather, on one of the sessions when I caught Scaley, and in terms of bait placement that was undoubtedly one of my better captures.

After a couple of days in the swim, I got to thinking about Scaley, the Big Oak and the Leather. I knew that the Leather fell to margin baits, but as far as I knew the fish never came from under the oak. Was this because Big Scale was territorial to the point that he actually commandeered any bait that was under the oak? Would the Leather actually have to skirt the oak on his patrol route round the margins? I guessed he might well be doing so, kept a bait positioned just off the branches of the oak throughout the second half of the week, and that was the bait the Leather fell to. In that instance, catching one of the water's big fish was a question of eliminating an area from the equation rather than identifying one.

The Mangrove fish are not territorial in the sense that Big Scale may be, but they certainly seem to be lone feeders. For the last few years the water has held up to ten or twelve thirty-pounders, but there has been just one genuine brace of thirty-pounders from the mere, Joe Bertram's capture of Trio and Scaley within three-quarters of an hour of each other on the same rod in 1989. The best known of the Mangrove thirty-pounders get caught four or five times each season and it is interesting to note that they rarely come from the same swim twice in any one season. That may seem a small detail, but it is an indication that even though they continue to eat bait, they react adversely to the pressure of being caught by associating an area with that capture and avoiding feeding there for some time after. The big fish in your water may just

John Lilley with the mirror known as Conan from the Mangrove at an early season weight in excess of 37lb. The run came at 11.00am, notoriously one of the quietest times for action on the Mangrove.

react in the same way, which will help you eliminate areas to fish as the season wears on and the capture record builds up.

Big fish are big feeders and their feeding times do not always coincide with the accepted feeding times for a water. I can quote many instances of this variation on a feeding time principle. For much of the season, feeding time on the Mangrove is the early hours – one o'clock through till seven, or sometimes as late as eight. I have caught both Scaley and Conan during the afternoon and John Lilley who, like me, tends not to leave the water and prefers to fish throughout a session, has had a number of thirty-pound captures at times well removed from what is accepted as the feeding time. I look on late morning as the dead time on the Mangrove and do my main baiting then. Others bait up late afternoon or

evening, times when I consider the chances of catching a big fish to be good. Study the capture records of the big fish in your water in terms of both location and timing and plan your sessions accordingly. Never mind the herd going up to the pub, the café and the Indian restaurant. If you want a big fish, stay put and fish through all the possible feeding times; don't fish part-time and fish through the probable feeding times.

This point about the big fish apparently feeding on their own is absolutely vital and can be the key factor in catching them. They may not be lone feeders. There may be another simple explanation for them usually coming as individual captures, in that they may steer clear of an area where a fish, or a number of fish, have just been caught. This may be why they are often caught at off peak feeding times. Smaller fish are not feeding so nothing is getting caught and there is no disturbance in the area of the end tackle.

On the other hand, most big fish are big feeders so there is a realistic chance that they will feed more often than other fish, which is why many of them tend to get caught more often. Statistically, big fish are hard to catch: the odds against catching one target fish from a water may be high, but that is because you are after one or two fish out of a population of ten, fifty or a hundred. I can think of many fish in the Mangrove which are far harder to catch than the known big ones, but their irregularity of capture is largely unremarked on because they are not considered huge. I have included a picture of one very coveted Mangrove mirror. I caught this fish twice in my first season on the water in 1983, and caught it again at 27lb 12oz in the *From the Bivvy* season. I can trace one other recorded capture of this mirror, and that was to John Lilley in the mid-1980s.

The fact is, that if you want a biggie you may have to avoid other fish. This will involve some self-discipline. Food bait, moderate attractor level, moderate quantities of bait, a careful study of the timing and location of your target fish's capture record, then make a plan and stick with it. Don't get side-tracked into trying to bag up because that can be the kiss of death to big-fish hunts.

One of my favourite fish. This Mangrove mirror of 27lb 12oz is on record as having been caught just twice since 1983.

Calendar timing can be of great significance. Keep a record of the dates and times of the captures of the big fish you hope to catch and see if there is a pattern in terms of the time of the season when the fish gets caught. One particular season I was having a good run of fish from Birch Grove during the opening session. Someone commented that they were all males, and that the females wouldn't have a good feed until they had spawned out. I don't even known if that's true or not but if it is, it's something worth knowing if your time is limited and you set your stall out to catch a big female at the start of the season!

If there is a repeating pattern of captures, it is worth planning your campaign around those peak periods. The fact that all captures do not conform to the pattern does not mean to say that the fish was not vulnerable at the peak time; it simply means it did not get caught then. If you

concentrate your efforts on the predictable peak times you are increasing your chances even before you start fishing.

If you keep a record of the nationwide big fish captures in *Carp-Talk*, you will find that they have peaks and troughs. This is partly seasonal. On occasions it may just be that the conditions were right for the big fish to feed in a number of areas of the country at one particular time, but there are also what appear to be natural highs and lows in the big-fish capture pattern. I could quote many examples, but I will limit myself to one or two.

I caught a personal best mirror of 36lb 8oz during the first week in December 1994. I wouldn't have said that the conditions were at all carpy, but within a couple of days of that capture, Martin Locke caught his fifty-pounder from a Herts club water, and Zenon Bojko landed his third English forty-pounder, from the Manor. Go back further and Dave Cumpstone's magnificent Wraysbury brace came out the very same week. It is probable that other big fish were feeding that week both years, but if they weren't being fished for, they wouldn't have been caught. The first week in December is hardly the first week to be filled in on the holiday rota when carpers are planning their holidays, and even full timers can find their motivation starting to wane at that time of the year!

The change in the close-season laws has revealed that late April and May is an excellent time of year for big fish captures. This is not simply a question of the big fish's calendar telling that it should be safe from capture at that time of year. The period has been revealed as a natural heavy feeding period during which the fish are recovering their condition from the low level feeding period through the colder months, and building up towards what their system tells them is the approaching spawning period. I have still got a built-in aversion to fishing through this period, but I accept that it is an illogical one based on custom and tradition rather than practicality. Fact is that if you want to catch a big fish and your water is open during April and May, this period may be one of your best chances of putting your target carp on the bank.

It is important to understand that a big fish may be vulnerable once, twice or three times a season. If you are not there, in the right place at the right time and fishing well enough to take advantage of any momentary lapse in concentration on your target carp's part, then your chance might have gone for another season. Catching a big carp really is as simple as that, being in the right place at the right time and getting it right. I know I was a bit stunned by my first thirty-pounder. I think I had caught a handful of twenty-pounders at the time and my personal best was of the order of 21lb 8oz. I went to Waveney D Lake to try and improve this figure to over twenty-five pounds. I caught Big Scale at 32lb and felt a bit embarrassed by the jump of over ten pounds, but I'd been in the right place at the right time, and the big fish completed the rest of the equation for me. My first thirty-pounder was my second fish from a water holding in excess of a hundred carp. Oh yes, I do think you need a bit of luck on your side at times.

People scoff at the idea that certain baits increase the likelihood of catching a big fish. Food baits have a good big fish track record, and unless your time is very limited and you have to pursue the instant bait option, I would make sure your base mix has a good food value when you have big fish in mind. Apart from boilies there are other baits which have accounted for more than their fair share of big fish. Tiger nuts immediately come to mind, as does sweetcorn on waters where it has not been used, or where the carp may have forgotten the dangers it can carry with it. These two baits apart, particles can have too great an appeal for the smaller fish to make them consistently successful for the bigger fish, but there are no rules to be made here, merely historical guidelines which help us eliminate certain baits from our reckoning.

But where an element of selection has to be part of your planning boilies are the usual choice. Beyond the use of food-value bases (quality fishmeal based baits have a particularly impressive big-fish track record) some smells have accounted for more than their share of the biggies. People scoff at this concept, but, quite

simply, it is true. Ask your bait dealer about this aspect. Do they have a smell, or combination of smells that have accounted for a disproportionate number of bigger fish? Every bait dealer will have a special big-fish puller which may help to do the trick for you.

I think that when it comes to scoring one or two big fish from a well-stocked water, you may need an element of luck, but there is another aspect I believe in which others are probably less convinced about. I have noticed numerous examples of newcomers to a water catching the bigger fish almost immediately while syndicate members of some years standing, or locals who fish the water regularly, tend not to catch them. I am not talking about startling differences in angling ability here. I am talking about experienced talented anglers not catching known target fish over a long period of time, while others come up with the goods first chuck. This happens on so many waters that it is not coincidence; it is part of an established pattern which I explain – rightly or wrongly – as follows.

The adverse reaction to the smell of humans is well documented. It is possible that we all have our own personal odours, and I suspect that over a period of time our personal scent becomes a danger signal to the carp. Paradoxically, the scent of some humans is – and remains – an attraction. Think of your smell as an additional flavour which affects the overall smell of the bait. To start with, it may attract and aid an instant capture of a curious big eater. Gradually it may start to blow, to start to act as a danger signal. If the big-bait eating fish manage to avoid your hook bait the first few times they come over your baits, then they may have your smell and become extra difficult for you to catch. Your own success with the other fish in the water reduces your chances of catching the target fish and starts to act as a handicap: the fish learn from experience, associate your smell with danger and become much harder for you to catch.

I have had a recent startling example of this. There is a fish in the Mangrove known as the Linear (as there is in most waters!). I caught the fish during my first year on the water in 1983. I

A Mangrove margin-caught common of 30lb 6oz. I arrived to fish on the Saturday afternoon and only went in the swim I caught it from because I could not get in any of the swims I wanted! The take came at 1.00am on a freezing, foggy night in what I considered to be impossible conditions.

haven't caught it since. My mate John Lilley has fished the Mangrove since 1984, has spent thousands of hours of his life there in the intervening years, and has caught literally hundreds of fish from the water. He's never caught the Linear. I recently took Paddy Webb on as a guest and the Linear was the second fish he caught, from the swim John usually fishes! I am sure you can all bring to mind examples of this syndrome relating to the waters you fish, and I could give dozens of examples. Long term, the fish like the smell of some humans and switch off to the scent

of others. The only suggestion I can make for those of us who do not act as instant and ongoing additional attractors is to find an alternative method of putting the bait on. Surgical gloves, a female companion to put your hookbaits on for you, forceps, soak the baits in something which will override the human scent. Don't just sit there knowing your chances are reducing by the hour. Try to find a way of reversing the trend because if your bait is good enough, the big fish are eating it, but if they've got your scent, they may be studiously avoiding your hookbait.

22 BIG CARP FROM BIG CARP WATERS

By no means all of you will have big carp in your water. If you have not and you want to catch one, you will have to get on your bike and go and find one, or preferably some. Locating waters with big fish in them is no problem these days. Such waters are well documented and many of them are very accessible. Where would I start now if I had to do it all again and I had no private doors opening to me? I would probably do much as I did first time around, except that there are now far more alternatives than there were in the early 1980s, and I would probably add one or two of those to my list.

Darenth and Waveney remain two of the best possibilities. Waveney is a ticket venue with big fish in a number of the waters. Do not make the mistake of rushing off there early in the season until you really know the place. Go in the autumn when the pressure has died down a bit. I found D Lake to be a terrific October and November water for big fish. The fishing is slow at that time of the year but if the buzzer does sound there is a chance it is one of the biggies, and this can be true of most big-fish waters which continue to fish at the back end.

There are now a number of big-fish waters at holiday venues. Zyg Gregorek's Anglers' Paradise venue in Devon is a very popular holiday/angling centre which anglers visit on the strength of the prolific carp fishing, with two waters holding carp to well in excess of thirty pounds. The Warmwell complex in Dorset is proving to be an incredible big-fish venue, having produced a forty-pound mirror and the country's first fifty-pound common. The fishing at these venues is open to anyone going there on holiday so you do not have to have access to an expensive syndicate to fish for the big fish. You can make it a once or twice per year pleasure crusade combined with a holiday in pleasant surroundings. These three holiday venues are just examples of the many such waters growing in popularity with the growing army of pleasure big fish anglers who make up a significant percentage of the current crop of carpers.

Although it contains a limited number of carp in the thirty-pound range, Cuttle Mill is a big fish water on which many would-be big-carp hunters have cut their teeth, and I can recommend it unreservedly. It is situated in the middle of the country, opposite the National Golf Centre of the Belfry, near Tamworth in Staffordshire. At five acres, it is not a big water, it contains numerous twenty and twenty-five pound plus carp, is extremely well run, and the carp are bait orientated. It is so popular that actually booking a session may not be easy, not in the more popular carp-fishing months, anyway, but the angler pressure does ease off towards the back end and in winter. I caught my first twenty-pounder from Cuttle Mill in the late 1970s and have a very soft spot for this lovely, aggro-free carp pool. Cuttle is an ideal stepping off point if you are about to launch yourself on the big fish circuit waters. When you move off your local waters you can sometimes have an elevated idea of your carp catching abilities. Catch consistently from waters like Cuttle Mill and Waveney and you have the grounding to go onto any water in the country and succeed – eventually.

Apart from the fact that its geographical location is a bit remote for most of the country, Darenth is an ideal big-fish starter water. It's a season-ticket venue where you will be fishing alongside some of the best carp anglers in the country. Even if you start by feeling out of your

Contributor Mike Willmott with the big common from Warmwell. Mike caught it at 38lb 12oz when it was on its way to its high weight in excess of 50lb. This was one of the most sought-after fish in the country, but sadly this great fish died while this book was being compiled.

depth (which you may well be) you will learn as you go along and see how successful big-fish anglers go about their craft. Rob Hughes and Simon Crow have been travelling round the country to report on day-ticket waters for *Carpworld* for a number of years now, which is why I have asked them to contribute a chapter detailing a number of day-ticket venues readers can target for a big fish (*see* Chapter 25). Their ongoing series in *Carpworld* is worth checking for other big-fish waters appearing on the scene, but before you set off for any distant water, ring in advance to make sure that the published details are still relevant, and that the venue can be still be fished by visitors.

The waters I have listed above are what I would term 'pleasure/big-fish waters'. There are smaller carp present and when you are easing your way into big-carp hunting, the odd consolation double or low twenty-pounder doesn't come amiss. There are other such waters in the country in the form of day-ticket, syndicate and season-ticket waters. If you see the name of a water producing big fish, it's up to you to discover its status and how you set about gaining entry.

After the pleasure/big fish waters come the 'headbangers' – the coveted, largely restricted entry lakes containing a handful of huge carp that the best big-fish anglers in the land are focusing their attentions on. Typical of these are Withy Pool, Horton, Wraysbury, and the group of waters at Yateley. The status of these is that Withy is day ticket, Horton very limited entry syndicate, Wraysbury season ticket with the odd place coming up occasionally, and the same goes for the Yateley waters (night syndicate).

If you follow the catches in *Carp-Talk*, you will get the impression that there are a great many big carp caught from these waters, which is a misleading impression. Almost all the carp caught from these lakes tend to be reported and publicized because they are big fish. The lakes in question are under constant heavy pressure from the best carp anglers in the land. The waters are not impossible but you have to recognize that for most anglers time on the bank is a large part of the equation in catching from these waters. Your chances of catching from them are much higher if you live in the area and can keep a bait going in, keep observing what is happening and keep putting the time in. The regulars know the degree of difficulty of these lakes. On some the equation will be twenty nights per fish, on others longer – and that is for the most successful anglers on the lake! But then again, that was the equation for catching any carp on many waters back in the 1970s.

The successful pursuit of the very big fish from the headbanger waters cannot be explained, or analysed, because at that level success is a very individual thing which requires a massive personal input in terms of thinking and application. You need to be very determined and very focused just to get on some of the big fish waters, and even more determined and focused to catch from them.

The waters you are able to join and the areas you choose to fish will depend on where you live, how far you are willing to travel, how much time you have at your disposal and just how serious you are about wanting to catch big fish. Once it really gets a hold of you, very little will stand in your way and you'll probably finish up spending far too much time on the road like hundreds of carp anglers before you. Hairy Friday afternoon drives to the lake ruined by over anxiety about the swim you want to be in and hairy Sunday-afternoon drives back through overtiredness are all part of the big-fish scene, I'm afraid.

Making the jump from just carp fishing to fishing for big carp is largely an act of faith. Big-carp fishing is based around belief, determination and single mindedness. I am tempted to add experience to that list, but I think it is possibly the wrong word. In his book *The Carp Strikes Back*, Rod Hutchinson commented that Ritchie McDonald had the knack of catching big fish – which he had. Ritchie at his peak certainly had belief, determination, single mindedness and experience, but you have to go a step beyond that.

I have fished with a great many very capable carp anglers over the years on waters containing big fish. Some catch more than their share of the bigger fish, some less, some none at all. In the final analysis, I can narrow the difference in approach down to three aspects: bait, baiting situation and swim. Many of you will have differing concepts of bait but I know of very few consistent catchers of big fish who swap and change bait. Once they have decided on a bait for the water for the season, that is what they use. Most of them will use attractors they are either familiar with, or which they have had strongly recommended to them at the known correct levels. Many of the most successful will have gone out of their way to watch carp feeding on their proposed bait over a period of time to make absolutely sure it is acceptable. I can name three who I know go out of their way to do this: Alan Smith, Martin Clarke and Terry Hearn. It is not always possible to watch the target fish in the water you intend fishing feeding on the bait you intend to use there, but try and make sure you have a water available to you where you can watch the carp's reaction to the bait. If their acceptance is enthusiastic enough, you can be pretty certain that the carp in your target water will react similarly. Big-carp fishing is a very slow business and it is a total waste of time sitting behind silent buzzers for very long periods if the bait is wrong in the first place. Bait is the confidence factor in carp fishing, but especially so when you are fishing for one, two or a handful of takes each season – at best.

None of which explains 'the knack' that Rod Hutchinson referred to. Well, if we could explain it, or define it, or buy it, the knack would be available to everyone and there would be nothing unusual or extraordinary about it. It is the extra dimension in carp fishing that no one can explain, the old 'many are called but few are chosen' syndrome. All you can do is stack the odds as much in your favour as possible and

Carp record-holder, Terry Hearn from Surrey, returning the record-breaking fish to Wraysbury. The lovely mirror is Mary at a weight of 55lb 13oz.

hope that you have been born with – or somehow acquire from accumulating experience and understanding – the knack of catching big carp.

I have kept this chapter brief because when it comes to fishing for big fish all anyone can do is give rough guidelines. But I will make one final point about the baiting situation. On the waters I fish regularly, I catch more than my share of twenty-pound fish, and less than my share of thirty-pounders, which I think is down to swim selection and baiting situation. The swims and situations that produce bags of good fish tend not to produce the biggest fish in the water. Do I go in a slower swim and sweat it out for a biggie, or go where the action is with the possible reward of four or five twenty-pounders in a night? Before I get to the water, I can rationalize the first approach. In reality, when I arrive I head for the action, and bait accordingly.

But – and it's a big but – while I've never caught a big carp after the swim has already been disturbed by a carp capture, the same consideration doesn't seem to apply to the capture of bream and tench. A big carp can follow a succession of bream or tench, an observation based not only on my own experiences, but on the experiences of others too. So while a big bed of boilies may work against you, a bed of hemp, Micromass, Response Pellets, Rod Hutchinson's new pellets, or any mass baiting situation which gets the coarse fish feeding in your swim may well work for you. Don't shy off a baiting situation because it's producing bream and tench; it may well mean you are on the right lines and that the next sound of the buzzer will be from that elusive biggie.

Big carp are fish other people catch until you accept the simple premise that their very size makes them big feeders, which therefore makes them vulnerable. They will eat most days, possibly every day. Half a dozen times in a season they may be catchable. Just keep doing it right and hope that one of those occasions occurs in your swim while you are fishing. If it hasn't happened after five seasons, go back to the drawing board and start again.

23 CARPING FROM GRAVEL PITS – MARTIN CLARKE

Martin Clarke is from Luton, and has acquired a reputation as being one of the most successful big-fish anglers in the country. As a regular contributor to *Carpworld* and *Carp-Talk*, he has proved that he can convey to the reader what it takes to come to terms with a concept or a set of circumstances. He could have written about any one of a number of subjects, but as he has had considerable success on a number of very difficult gravel pits, I asked him to pass on some of his experiences regarding coming to terms with this popular type of carp fishery here. My own gravel-pit experience is too limited for my time spent on these waters to be meaningful in the context of this book.

Tim Paisley

I would guess that the majority of lakes south of Luton are gravel pits, all varying in sizes, age and characteristics. Most of these lakes were formed before I was born in 1960, with a few more pits becoming available each year up and down the country, which means we are now approaching the millennium with an abundance of ever-maturing gravel-pit carp fisheries.

My earliest recollection of fishing gravel pits was in the very early 1970s, fishing under the wing of my father on a couple of lakes run by the London Angling Association, one of which was in the heart of the Colne Valley. My father always caught the quality fish and as time went by, much of his knowledge was passed on to me. I progressed from catching roach and bream weighing ounces to tench and carp up to double figures in a relatively short space of time. Since then I have fished rivers, canals, huge clay pits, reservoirs and gravel pits, and during the last ten years have been fishing further down the Colne Valley and having success on two very different gravel pits. I suppose I

must have been doing something right, and I have learned along the way. One thing is certain, there is more than one method of catching carp. To make the point, I have caught both the carp in my pictures twice and they come from two very different gravel pits.

Like any other type of carp fishery, gravel pits cannot be mastered overnight. The starting point is a thoughtful walk round to start to get a basic feel for the venue. Once you begin to fish the water, it is then that you discover that in most swims a knowledge of the terrain in front of you is essential in order to pick areas to actually fish as the carp travel around or along the features in the swim. I have always been a great believer that on every lake I have ever fished, almost every swim has a productive spot within casting range. Some swims have more such spots than others and gravel pits are certainly no different in this respect. At any given time, though, only half a dozen of the productive spots have the potential to produce action in any one given period of time; it all comes down to fishing in the right spots at the right time. Each productive area or spot will only be productive for limited periods of time, though this can be dependent on a number of factors: time of year, angling ability, angling pressure, and so on. Selecting the right spots in the prevailing conditions, keeping one step ahead of the carp, and getting the results are my aims – and that's what successful gravel-pit carping is all about.

The two very famous gravel pits I have had some memorable moments on are two very different waters, each with their own problems to come to terms with. 'The Madhouse' is a 45-acre Colne Valley venue with a reputation as a battlefield filled with water, and 'The Doghouse',

The water Martin refers to as 'The Madhouse', Harefield Lake in the Colne Valley. The water is a notoriously difficult big carp gravel pit controlled by Boyers Angling.

a 22-acre mind-blower close to old Father Thames. Neither of these lakes is what you could term typical gravel pits, but then what is a typical gravel pit? In comparison, they are like chalk and cheese, although both have similar productive areas and respond to similar tactics when it comes to catching a few of the residents.

'The Madhouse'

'The Madhouse' got its name because you have to be mad to fish there, with its razor sharp gravel bars and deep gullies to contend with when you get a take. In the 1990s tackle to withstand the problems of the bars has improved, and the bars themselves are not as fierce as they used to be: the continual washing of gravel has caused the gullies in some areas to shallow-up. For all

that, it is still a hostile environment for terminal tackle in some parts of the lake, but year by year the under water terrain is mellowing at a much faster rate than it tends to on other gravel pits. Over the six years or so I have fished there, I have known bars to disappear completely, and some of us can remember that the Car Park Bay used to be over 6ft (2m) deep, and now it's almost dry land!

I dropped my ticket for this water at the end of the 1992/93 season, having had more winter action than any other angler had managed in previous winters. I dropped out because I did not have enough money to renew my ticket and fish the other venues I wanted to fish that summer. In the seasons I fished there, I think it would be fair to say that a lot of other very good carp anglers from all over the country fished there with the same objectives as myself – to

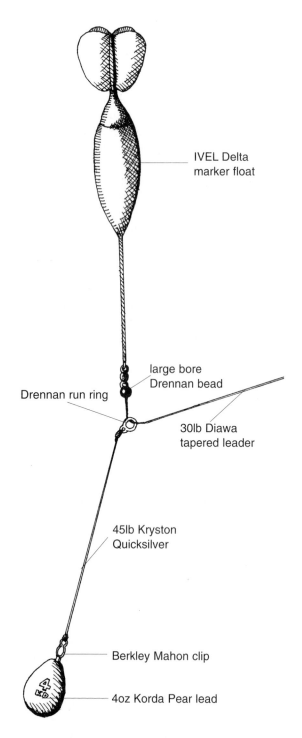

IVEL Delta marker float

large bore Drennan bead

Drennan run ring

30lb Diawa tapered leader

45lb Kryston Quicksilver

Berkley Mahon clip

4oz Korda Pear lead

Martin's marker rod set-up.

catch a few whackers. With a syndicate of one hundred members plus bailiffs there was hardly a day in the season when the water wasn't being fished, so angling pressure was just as much an influence on the carp's feeding as the weather. During that period, a lot of famous names fished there, and the injection of big carp from two other gravel pits – Willow Pool and Rodney Meadow – turned the lake into what you could term a high-pressure circuit water. It held about two hundred carp, and I have mostly fond memories of my times on there. I made plenty of friends, and certainly came away a better angler. Who knows, one day I may even go back.

I have mentioned the water's rapidly changing features and depths and the angling pressure; apart from these factors, the 'Madhouse' is just another gravel pit with perhaps more features than most. Being in the region of 45 acres with just over forty swims means each swim has plenty of water to cover, with the only inaccessible areas being those out in the centre of the lake. Degree of inaccessibility would depend on the strength of the wind and what bank you were fishing from. The majority of gravel bars are not hard to find using a plumbing rod. They are extensive, with some continuing into the next swim. When the water level is down in summer the tops of these bars are often out of the water. Accurate casting, marking (or sometimes clipping) lines proved to be very useful tips passed on by my dad in those early days of my fishing in the 1970s.

Plumbing is without a doubt a brilliant method for learning any lake's topography, although if overdone at the start of your session, it can prove to be detrimental. The best time to explore a swim you intend to fish is when you are not actually fishing. On gravel pits, casting-out blindly into unknown depths is not advisable as you can later discover that you have spent the weekend fishing in under a foot of water. Believe me, I've seen people do it!

The purpose of plumbing, if done correctly, is to obtain more information than just the depth of the water. By slowly pulling back, every vibration or movement on your rod tip will tell a story from which you can decide on your hookbait's form of presentation and the dimensions of your rig. In most gravel pits, there are bars and features of every size, from little humps to some the size of houses; nearly every one of these can be found through plumbing around with a marker rod, or better still, with two marker rods. Personally, I find pear-shaped leads the best for plumbing purposes, giving good feedback to the rod tip, not only on the harder, featured patches of bottom, but also in the softer silty areas. Use a marker float in conjunction with a strong leader and an abrasion-resistant bottom link to avoid cut-offs on zebra mussels, sharp rocks or edges of bars. It goes without saying that when it comes to spotting features – and fish – climbing trees can give you a visual picture of the features to back up the work with the marker rod.

I mentioned that selecting the right spots in the going conditions at the right time was what I aimed to achieve on each of my 'Madhouse' sessions. Locating carp each visit was, as usual, a must if I was to be in with a chance of catching. Actual swim choice was down to either visually seeing the carp, either on the surface or a few feet below, or poking their heads out somewhere where I could present a hookbait to them. Generally, the carp stayed in two or three shoals in the 'Madhouse'. Sometimes they would spread themselves out over three-quarters of the lake, but as a rule they were to be found in just a quarter of the lake's total area at any one time. The art was to be in the right place at the right time as they moved around the lake, particularly when they were feeding at distinct feeding times. Observation was essential and actual positioning of hookbaits or baited areas was then a question of fishing the best swims available from previous knowledge, the aim being to fish the features or areas that the carp frequented with feeding in mind.

In the summer, each swim has its moments and the timing of such activities as fish spotting, moving swims, moving hookbaits, changing tactics, baiting-up, etc. has to revolve around not only the carp's position on the lake, but when they are at the right depth too. Every swim has its range of depths and productive areas, and almost every inch of the swim will be inspected by the carp in the course of a season. Some depths and specific areas will be frequented, and feeding will take place in some spots more often than in others, depending on the prevailing weather conditions. Success lies in fishing each potentially productive swim and fishing your hookbaits in the best spots at the best times. Fishing in unfamiliar swims may have to be based on calculated guesswork to begin with, but becoming familiar with the swim – and the movements of the fish when they are in it – are vital steps in the learning curve in getting to know and come to terms with the water.

The 'Madhouse' has numerous productive areas around the lake which is why quite a few carp are caught from the water each season, and my understanding of the water and its fish meant I certainly caught my fair share. For the record I will list what I perceive to be the twelve most productive gravel-pit areas:

1. Natural feeding areas.
2. Shallow marginal areas between 2ft and 5ft deep.
3. Island margins.
4. Unpressured extreme range areas.
5. Tops, sides and bases of bars.
6. Gravel-bar endings and intersections.
7. Gravel humps and mounds.
8. Gullies and silt pockets.
9. Lily pads and weedbeds.
10. Other unpressured (unfished) areas.
11. All the corners, bays and out-of-bound areas.

I have caught both fish pictured twice (*see* overleaf and colour pages). The big fully scaled mirror came from 'The Madhouse'. First time around I caught it at 36lb 2oz fishing the shallow silty margins of the workings from the Mad Swim, a cast of just over a hundred yards into four feet of water with a very silty

Successful big-fish angler Martin Clarke with the fully scaled mirror from Harefield, in excess of 36lb. He caught this highly prized fish twice while he was fishing the water.

bottom. The actual area is now a well known big carp swim. The fish wasn't my first thirty-pounder from the swim, or my last: small wonder when the swim offers six examples of the productive areas on the above list (1, 2, 4, 6, 10 and 11). The second time this lovely fish fell to my rods was when I caught her the following season at the other end of the lake fishing a swim known as Goose Spit. I was fishing a spot on the side of the bar which is, in fact, the spit itself and which offers five of the productive spots listed in one (1, 2, 5, 6 and 10). I recall I had two takes at the same time that day, so I must have stepped in something!

As the summer turns into autumn, and then finally winter, fewer and fewer carp are caught; they tend to shoal up into tighter groups and occupy just a fraction of the lake's total acreage. I always found that as the season wore on, the bulk of the carp were less inclined to feed in shallow water, seldom coming out at depths of less than five feet, with fewer and fewer captures coming from the summer productive areas. Come the winter, the only places I received any action in was in areas deeper than seven feet, though normally not deeper than twelve feet. Most of my action came from the base of a bar, in open water or in a gully, with virtually all my takes coming from silty areas.

'The Madhouse' in winter is a tough nut to crack. Very little or no weed on the bars means that in most of the swims you've got to play any hooked carp with your fingers crossed and someone upstairs looking after you. The productive areas will be determined by the carp, not the anglers, as next to nothing is introduced by way of bait due to the winter influx of tufted ducks. The vast majority of takes I had in

The Madhouse.

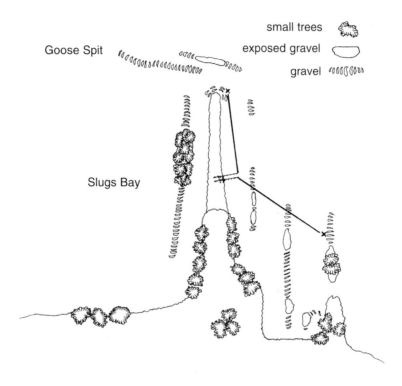

small trees

exposed gravel

gravel

Goose Spit

Slugs Bay

winter came from the Road Bank casting out into the middle zone beyond the third bar towards what I presumed to be a gap in the fourth bar (not on the map), on/in thick silt which took the full test curve of the rod to ease the 4oz lead out.

Other takes came from similar types of bottom, a few in Slugs Bay, a few from the Causeway, and also a couple from the Stick Bar swim, fishing tight to the bottom bank which hardly anyone ever walked along. All winter takes came in short feeding spells from small areas the size of a snooker table over which carp had shown, presumably feeding on natural food, as no bait was introduced. The vast majority of my winter fish fell to pop-ups rigs. My personal best 'Madhouse' carp came during my last winter on the water at a weight of 39lb 8oz, so I left on a high note. The fish came at extreme range, but thanks to Diawa's 30lb tapered leads I could reach it and land it.

'The Doghouse'

'The Doghouse' was – and is – a totally different kettle of fish, if you'll excuse the pun. At just over 20 acres, it is half the size of 'The Madhouse', but with about thirty swims. Features-wise you could say that the bottom is pretty barren with only a few small mussel-clad bars in the main body of the lake, and a couple of bars in the Clubhouse Bay. Plumbing around with the marker float reveals that it is of pretty uniform depth all over – between 7 and 11ft (2–3.5m) – with areas of weed, silt, sand, gravel and mussel beds, much as you tend to find in most gravel pits.

I gave the water its nickname to avoid upsetting the locals by referring to it by its real name. The nickname has a certain relevance, as behind one of the swims there is a big house with boarding kennels which normally house over a dozen dogs barking from morning till night. Just like

'The Madhouse' you must be part mad to fish there, although for different reasons.

1. Size: 22 acres.
2. 30–40 buoys dotted around the lake.
3. Speedboats and skiers.
4. Yachts and windsurfers.
5. A 48-hour limit on fishing is in operation.

The stock of carp in the water at present is slightly different to when I first fished there. A few of the original big mirrors have died and these have been replaced by some nice-looking stockies from a Berkshire source which are growing well. Six months prior to my catching the fish in the photograph (*see* colour pages), the stock was twenty-three original mirrors (thirteen over 30lb with four over 40lb), around a hundred commons (mostly doubles with a few twenty-pounders), and loads of tench and bream, with a few going into double figures. All the carp were over thirty years old and had been fished for since they were doubles: they had seen all the baits and methods every other gravel pit in the south of England had seen, but without the publicity. To some of you, a 22-acre lake with thirteen different thirty-pound plus carp in it must sound like heaven, which it was, but the fishing was by no means easy, as location of the fish could be very difficult. I should make it clear that virtually all the carp anglers who fished the water – myself included – were looking to catch the bigger original mirrors and not the commons.

With little in the way of features in open water apart from weedbeds, it was important to use the lake's most prominent feature in as efficient a manner as possible to extract the big fish, meaning its margins and marginal slopes. Open-water features tended to be subtle variations in depth and bottom make-up. Finding these subtle variations wasn't easy and plumbing with a high-tech braid such as Berkley Gorilla Braid (which has no stretch compared to mono) proved to give a much more sensitive feel on the rod top and, therefore, better feedback.

The water sports on this lake proved to be one of the major influences on the carp's day-to-day activities and I had to learn to adapt my methods to get some action. When I started fishing the venue, it soon became apparent through observation that they could feed at any time during my normal 36-hour sessions: the boating activities didn't put them off feeding during daylight one little bit. When the boats entered the water by the clubhouse and started their activities, it either made the carp keep their heads down where they already were, or they would drift into the sheltered marginal areas, such as weedbeds, overhanging trees and corners.

When fishing at any sort of range on gravel pits, the only method I would recommend to overcome water sports if you cannot lower your rod tips into the water far enough to avoid problems, is a method I came up with when I fished a local day-ticket venue back in the early 1980s. That is to use captive back leads, which allow you to position your back lead a few feet under the surface, but not on the bottom of the lake. A back lead fished on the bottom can cause your line to rub against unseen obstructions between you and the fish when you get a run. This can cause damage to the line, or even a cut-off. I did notice some strange looks when I first used this method, but the other anglers couldn't deny their effectiveness when they converted to them after losing fish on conventional back leads, as I had done before coming up with the alternative method.

The first time I caught the Fat One was at a new lake record of 44lb 4oz, stalking with one rod in just under three feet of water in the margins of Dead Body Bay. This happens to be a bay in the north-east corner of the water which screams 'Fish me!' every time there's a good south-westerly wind blowing in there. The actual spot I placed my hookbait in just required lowering my rig under the rod tip and slackening off the line. I could see my rig on the bottom and, funnily enough, I had to spook a twenty-pound plus common from taking the hookbait by throwing a couple of boilies on its head! Only minutes later, the Fat One came in with another forty-pound carp, and made a mistake by picking up my hookbait – much to my delight.

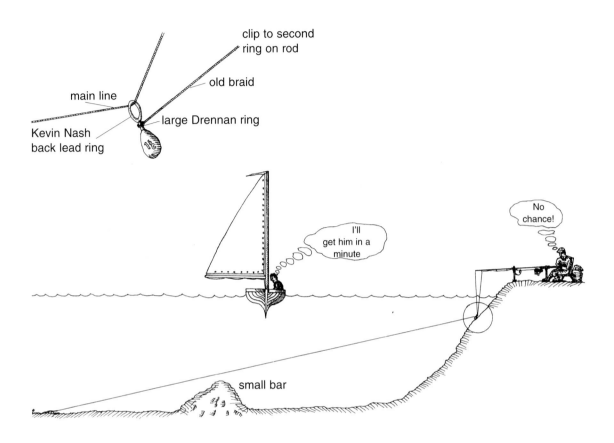

Martin's captive back lead method.

I caught her again 18 days later, fishing a more static style about a hundred yards away, again in the margins but in a totally different swim, using the same bait and rig as before. This was a swim in which I had seen my main target carp feeding in the margins a week earlier. In my fourth short stint in the swim, the first of the original mirrors to grace my net wasn't the one I had hoped for, but the Fat One again, this time at 44lb 3oz. I went on to catch a couple more mirrors from this spot, along with more tench and bream. The producing spot had no real distinguishing features close by, which is probably why I never saw anyone else fish it. Neglected swims have at least one good thing about them, and that is that other anglers pass them by.

On the occasion of this capture, hookbaits were placed with one at the bottom of the marginal slope in seven feet of water and the other on the slope at five feet. The two hookbaits were no more than one-and-a-half rod lengths out on a weed-free bottom. I must have caught at least thirty tench and bream from this spot before it produced its first carp, one of the double-figure commons. Over a period of two weeks, I kept this spot topped up with boilies and particles as well as fishing other swims. Funnily enough, I came close to catching the Fat One up at the other end of the lake in that time on a very visual looking spot similar to the one in Dead Body Bay. On that occasion one of the thirty-pounders beat her to my hookbait, which was exciting for me and a couple of my friends who stood and watched the events taking place before our very eyes.

Sadly 'The Doghouse' has lost some of its big

Martin checking out the margins at 'The Doghouse'. His attention to this oft neglected area paid great dividends.

mirrors, although thankfully not all of them. Having gone on to catch all the original mirrors, I am now looking at other gravel pits in the area with the potential to satisfy my dreams, although I know it will mean taking on a new challenge and starting from scratch. Gravel pits; love them or hate them, do your homework and treat them with respect and you'll be rewarded.

24 CARP FROM SMALL WATERS – MIKE WILLMOTT

Mike Willmott is from Bridgwater in Somerset and is the proprietor of his own tackle and bait firm, Essential Products. I have watched Mike give entertaining, perceptive slide shows and have read details of some of his successes with carp from small waters. He struck me as being the ideal carp-fishing/writer to provide this chapter and I was delighted when he agreed to do so. Like all the other contributors, Mike has had outstanding success at home and abroad, and from waters large and small, and his observations in the pages that follow are based on a wealth of carp-fishing experience.

Tim Paisley

My involvement with fishing for carp in small environments stems right back to the mid-1970s when I abandoned my quest for all other species to fully concentrate my efforts into fishing solely for carp. In those halcyon days any water over 10 acres seemed a daunting prospect, a far cry from my more recent exploits when fishing some of the 10,000-acre inland seas found on the continent. Even the size of these waters fades into insignificance when compared to other waters found on a wider global scale to which the growing army of carp anglers seems to be aspiring. Oh, how far we have come!

Ashlea Pool, a magnificent small water for learning about the carp's behaviour.

Personally, I gain a great deal of satisfaction from fishing a variety of waters these days. Apart from eliminating the monotony factor, it decreases the chances of becoming stereotyped in approach. Having said that, there is no getting away from the fact that small waters always hold a personal fascination for me. Perhaps it is that intimate feeling which exists between the angler and his quarry when fishing at close quarters, or it is the 'early days' carp-fishing literature which was available to the up-and-coming carp anglers of my era. After all, aren't the early exploits of the Carp Catchers Club at Redmire Pool instilled deep within the roots of many of us in our early days?

The most inspiring piece of carp literature I have ever had the pleasure of reading came from that great book *Quest for Carp* by the late Jack Hilton. A prominent part of this book focused on Jack's experiences on that famous little water Ashlea Pool, which I later had the good fortune to fish for almost a decade.

Before elaborating any further on the subject of small-water carping, I think it would be best if I categorize what I would consider as being a 'small water'. Certainly any water up to about 8 acres I would class as being small. From this point upwards to, say, 40 acres I would evaluate as being medium-sized. In my book, expanses over 40 acres within the UK would have to be classed as being large, the emphasis there being on the 'UK' because my opinion would be quite different if I were classifying waters on the continent.

Undoubtedly, two of the most famous small waters I have had the pleasure of fishing are Ashlea Pool and Warmwell. Both waters share the statistic of being approximately 1½ acres in size, but this is where the similarity ends. Ashlea Pool is gin-clear with an abundance of weed, whilst Warmwell is quite the opposite – thick, muddy brown in colour and, as one would expect without the benefit of light penetration, little in the way of weed growth. Both waters, however, share a record of producing big carp, which in turn puts to rest any theory that such fish can only successfully thrive in big waters rich in natural food.

Small-water carp are usually subjected to more angling pressure than their bigger water relations, not necessarily due to more anglers fishing for them, but on the basis of what I term 'nowhere to hide'. The smaller the water, the more relevant this term becomes. Basically, it is where the carp consistently come into contact with anglers' presentation in virtually every part of the lake, and for much of the time.

After a few years of this intense pressure, the carp can eventually become paranoid in many situations, and Warmwell above all waters stands out as a classic example of this. My association with this remarkable little water has predominantly been centred upon winter fishing, due to the fact that the pressure is just too intense during the summer months for it to warrant my attention. Over the past five years, angling pressure has resulted in the fish drastically changing their behaviour patterns. I have witnessed the 'wind of change' at first hand during this time, and it has changed from being a water which just five seasons ago I would have classed as being relatively easy to one which is, at the present day, nothing short of being very difficult indeed.

During the past six months of June to December, I have collated some interesting statistics from this unique little venue. For instance, a total of 300 different carp anglers have fished this tiny water during this period of time, and actual rod hours (angler hours multiplied by the number of rods fished) have amounted to a staggering 82,656!

Now, I don't wish to enter into the complexities of dividing these rod hours into the tiny acreage in an attempt to discover the average pressure measurement of each square metre of water, but from the statistics shown it goes without saying that the water is subjected to immense pressure twenty-four hours a day, and for nine months of the year. (A close season still exists on the water.) The fish have no sanctuary areas whatsoever, yet probably one of the most sought-after fish in the country, 'Herman', Britain's largest known common carp (50lb 8oz at its biggest recorded capture weight) has only been landed once from the water during the six months referred to! I find this quite remarkable considering the statistical circumstances.

For those not quite as convinced by the significance of these figures as I am, take Mary (the current British record) from Wraysbury as a contrasting example. This fish has been caught four times during the same period of time, yet it resides in a huge expanse of 120 acres, with plenty of sanctuary areas. I also fish Wraysbury and know how difficult the venue can be, but to be fair, this is mainly due to its size coupled with its very low stocking density. The main difference between the two waters as regards carp behaviour is mainly due to the fact that the Warmwell carp are subjected to far more pressure than the Wraysbury carp. When the latter encounter a carp angler's baits or rigs it could be the first such contact over a period of several weeks. During this period they would have consumed a totally natural diet from within their environment with no real pressure upon them. When confronted by anglers' baits, they are unlikely to act with as much caution as a carp which comes under constant pressure, twenty-four hours a day.

Small-water carp will generally not have the escape route of sanctuary 'freedom', and the pressure exerted on them will undoubtedly have an effect on their behaviour and the way in which they evaluate their food sources, particularly anglers' baits. Such behaviour patterns have inevitably been born through intense pressure, which in turn has fuelled the carp's ability to cope with situations which they associate with danger because of previous bad experiences. Their ability to change has been developed through their animal instincts, and it is remarkable how quickly they can learn. This is called 'progression', and it is a typical phenomenon associated with small-water carping.

When approaching a small water, I adopt a completely different strategy to that of fishing a large expanse of water, where location is the most important consideration. On small waters, most of my emphasis is laid on rig presentation

and bait application, because I believe these are the two areas in which carp anglers can become very stereotyped. Offering something different is often the key to circumstances in which carp have wised-up to standard presentations and situations through association.

Location of fish on small waters does not present a problem in real terms; however, on all waters – even the smallest – carp will have their own hot spots, and such areas may be frequently visited. Locating these spots will inevitably lead to a more consistent string of success.

One vital area of importance when trying to locate feeding spots is to build up a picture of what lies beneath the surface, i.e. the topography of the lake bed. Often the smallest of features can turn out to be productive hot spots. This may be a slight depression on the lake bed, or silt pocket, possibly a patch of clean gravel surrounded by silt, or even a small gravel hump. All are areas which the carp will recognize within their environment. Indeed, some of these features could have been created by feeding carp and may therefore be revisited on a regular basis.

Searching for these spots can, at times, be a tedious and prolonged exercise, but having said that I have lost count of the number of times my efforts have been rewarded by the location of these spots.

The method I use for finding such features is very simple indeed. It incorporates the use of a 2oz lead fixed directly to the end of my line. This is then cast out into different areas of the lake before slowly drawing back the rod tip at a 45° angle. The rod-tip behaviour and the feel of the lead as it drags along the lake bottom will then provide enough clues to enable me to evaluate the necessary features on the lake bed. This is nothing new or fancy; just plain simple, but extremely effective. This method can be modified to greater efficiency if your monofilament reel line is substituted with a braided line, particularly one of the extremely fine polyethylene-type braids. These materials possess 20 per cent less stretch factor than mono, which in turn allows every single bump and depression on the bottom to be felt right the way through the rod. The difference is amazing.

There are a number of ways to ascertain any variations in depths of a given water, most commonly by using a sliding marker float in its various forms. However, unless I feel it is critical to plumb a particular depth within inches, I am quite happy to use the above leading-around method, and count how many seconds it takes for the lead to hit the bottom, which in turn will provide the necessary information needed to give me the approximate depth.

One very important aspect of carp location usually worth taking into consideration, even on small waters, is weather conditions, particularly wind directions. I say 'usually' because this would certainly be an important consideration on medium-sized waters and above. However, I have not found it has any real correlation to where carp are likely to be found on small waters. This is particularly true of those very small venues which rarely possess the necessary expanse of water surface for the wind to play any major role in terms of underwater currents and food location.

The gin-clear water of Ashlea Pool makes the lake the perfect venue for learning about carp behaviour, and it is here that I have spent thousands of hours observing the carp's reaction to certain rig presentations, methods, baits, bait additives and formulations, with some very interesting findings. I have always maintained that one season's observations on a water such as this is worth ten years experience in comparison to other waters, where carp cannot be observed, when it comes to the learning curve.

Anyone who has had the experience of observing pressurized carp at close quarters will be able to appreciate just how cautious they can be, and how much can be learned from just watching them. Ashlea Pool really opened my eyes to such findings and was the first water on which I actually witnessed carp communicating with each other. My first experience of this was a real eye-opener and made me look at my carp fishing from a completely different angle from that point on. It was a very hot June day as I sat

balancing myself amongst the branches of an ash tree thirty feet above the water. This provided the perfect vantage point to view a group of small carp (16 to 20lb) which I was trying to get interested in my Chum Mixers. The group of carp showed a definite interest in the free offerings, but their body language showed signs of extreme caution as they repeatedly circled the area, occasionally bolting several yards and sending the Mixers whirling around within their vortices before returning to them for a closer inspection. My aim was to get the carp feeding with confidence before I even lowered a baited rig, but they were having none of it.

Eventually, after gingerly pinching one or two Mixers, the carp swam away from the baited area across the width of the pool and confronted what appeared to be a very large carp; certainly one of the thirty-pounders judging by its comparative size. After circling round the big fish, the group proceeded to make their way back in the direction of the free offerings, only this time with a big black mirror on their tails! On arrival at the Mixers the big carp (which I could now recognize as the big mirror known as Humpy, a fish of approximately 35lb) took over the role of being chief investigation officer. The big carp only had to circle the endangered area once before sensing that all was not well and promptly vacated the area with the smaller fish in tow. In fact, they hurriedly made their way to the opposite end of the pool, not to be seen again that afternoon!

I had witnessed a classic example of fish communication and I had yet to lower a rig into their watery home. This turned out to be only the first of many similar occurrences at the magical pool. In fact, after witnessing such events, it makes you wonder how on earth we catch carp at all.

Rig presentation and bait application were two crucial areas of coming to terms with these carp, crucial because pressured carp are more prone to individual inspection of baits. If the statistics were known, the majority of anglers would be shocked at the number of times their hookbaits are picked up and ejected, or the free offerings consumed and the hookbaits left in hopeless isolation. Anyone who doubts this has surely not experienced witnessing pressurized carp feeding on anglers' baits.

I can vividly recall from my Ashlea days that a favourite trick would be for a carp to come in over a baited area and cautiously wave its pectoral fins back and forth, which in turn would create a disturbance around the baits. If using a balanced hookbait or pop-up, the behaviour of such a bait as it wafted around on its tethered leash would appear totally unnatural, particularly in comparison to the free offerings in close proximity, which would stay in place. Basically it was very easy for a carp to differentiate between a carefully balanced hookbait and a free offering. Once the carp had finished their evaluation, they would proceed to consume the free offerings, avoiding the hookbait in the process.

This scenario was particularly apparent when fishing the rigs on gravel, and a switch to unbalanced bottom baits with no extra buoyancy in an attempt to imitate the free offerings was a big improvement. On the soft, more silty areas, my success on balanced hookbaits or pop-ups was, interestingly, far greater. My own theory as to why this was the case was that such areas were usually abundant in the underwater weed known as 'cabbages', as well as various other forms of plant life. The introduction of free offerings into such areas would often lead to them getting caught up in the weed; as a result, the carp were accustomed to picking up food particles at various levels in such areas, as opposed to clean gravel where the food items would invariably be located hard on the bottom.

One of the most successful hooking methods I have used when carp become wary of pop-ups is to 'overbalance' them so they can't behave unnaturally when they are inspected. By doing this, you still have the bait off the bottom and the hook in an upright position which I think is advantageous when carp are mouthing baits. The overbalancing effect does not allow the hookbait to waft all over the place to the extent that one which is critically balanced does. This effect can be further enhanced if the shot or putty used to create the overweighted effect is situated as closely as possible to the base of the hook. By doing this, the actual hookbait will be sitting in close proximity to the lake bed and, in my opinion, not viewed in the same light as a more easily identified pop-up presentation. In fact, such is the successful effect of this presentation that I really do believe the overweighting effect, in conjunction with the bait being positioned as closely as possible to the lake bed, makes it look and behave in similar fashion to the free offerings.

Supple braids as opposed to mono are a far better option to use in conjunction with this type of presentation, mainly because their suppleness factor allows the hook to sit in an upright position, whereas mono tends to have a 'keeling over' effect on the hook, which in turn minimizes the rig's effectiveness.

The crazy thing about fishing in the situations described above is that there are times, albeit few and far between, when the carp completely throw caution to the wind and, within reason, no matter what rig you are using, it is difficult to fail. During these times, the textbook can be thrown out of the window! Unfortunately, these occurrences are not frequent enough these days. When such an occasion does occur I look on it as a nice bonus, but obviously by setting up my rigs to what I believe is the best choice for each situation, I know I am covering all eventualities.

When trying to make a generalization on small waters as a whole, it is virtually impossible to stipulate which type of bait is going to prove the most effective. Some waters respond better to particles or seeds, whilst others to boilies. I do not believe there is any major tactical difference between fishing small and large waters when it comes to bait choice, so while I am tempted to discuss choice of baits, such a wide-ranging topic would have me wandering too far from the original concept of the chapter to do it justice.

Having said this, it has to be emphasized that bait application does have a major role to play on small waters, particularly those which are subjected to a great degree of pressure. The greater the degree of pressure by way of the number of anglers fishing a water invariably leads to a greater introduction of anglers' baits. Such increased food-availability levels will not only lead to less competition for food, but the likelihood of a greater variety of foods for the carp to choose between. Both these factors will have the effect of minimizing the chances of your hookbait being encountered; therefore, careful consideration and thought must be given to the amount of bait you are going to use.

The correct levels can only be arrived at through logic and building up an understanding of how much bait is being introduced by other anglers. Size of water, stocking density, pressure and time of year will have a big influence on the quantities of bait to be used, and all these factors must be carefully considered.

If there is one area in which I observe anglers becoming very stereotyped, it is in bait application. Arrive at the water, cast out the rigs, introduce fifty freebies around each hookbait, sit back and wait; you know the score. Unfortunately it doesn't always work, and the fish soon realize that, despite them being an easily obtainable source of nutrition such beds of bait can spell danger.

I have witnessed situations at Ashlea when carp have literally spooked away from beds of bait. The last few years at Warmwell has undoubtedly seen fewer fish being caught, which I am convinced is partly due to the increased food availability by way of anglers' baits.

Bait application is not simply a question of the amount of bait used in any one session. Baiting patterns, techniques and variations on the theme can often be used to your advantage. Groundbait is an obvious example which springs to mind; chopped baits is another; in fact, anything which could be different to the baiting situation which is commonly being used on the water concerned.

PVA bags are a brilliant example of an idea which allows an original bait application concept to be put into operation. When I started to use these bags consistently in 1990–91, I had some outstanding results. Okay, I will accept the bags proved to be an exceptional method for the weedy waters I was fishing, but I am also convinced that

The use of PVA bags can provide a totally different form of bait presentation.

much of their success was due to the fact that they presented a completely different baiting pattern to any the carp had encountered before. I am also convinced this was why I was fortunate enough to catch the bigger fish from most venues I fished at the time. The bigger – often older and wiser – fish did not look at this baited area with the same caution they would normally associate with larger, more orthodox baited areas.

Several years ago, I wrote an article for the *Fifth British Carp Study Group Book* in which I gave details of a baiting pattern technique I first adopted during the winter at Ashlea Pool. I have used the same method on numerous occasions since (particularly on pressurized small waters) with some very pleasing results. The technique involves fishing the hookbait several yards away from your baited patch, the theory being that the carp are attracted to the baited patch but act with caution in that area, possibly picking up a few baits during each visit. However, a single hookbait presented in isolation not too far away would be considered as being 'safe' and hence picked up with confidence.

This is a bit of trickery, really, but it works well, particularly against such features as marginal snags, where the free offerings can be introduced on one side of the feature and the hookbait on the other side. Small islands are another ideal feature for this method, placing the free offerings at one end whilst the hookbait is positioned at the other end. There are numerous other examples of spots which lend themselves to this very successful alternative bait-application tactic.

If I find myself in a position to string two or three consecutive days together on a small water, I often use a similar tactic which again has worked well for me. On my arrival I will introduce my free offerings to several areas (obviously providing this does not interfere with someone else's fishing). If possible, the areas selected will be safe areas (e.g. snaggy areas), where the carp will consume the bait with less caution and hopefully build up confidence in availability of the food source. I then fish with very few, if any, free offerings around my baited rig, with the theory being that when the carp encounter the hookbait, they will have already built up a certain level of confidence.

I will now move away from bait application and on to another subject which I consider to be important on small waters, that being line-shy fish. Carp can become very paranoid over lines cutting through the water on hard fished venues, and back-leads can be an absolute necessity under such circumstances. Anyone who has had the opportunity of witnessing the reaction of a carp swimming into a line will know what I mean. I have seen carp stop in their tracks at the sight of a line going through the water on venues where the clarity allows maximum visibility.

Unless the water has an abundance of weed, I prefer to use the back-leads I make myself. These leads have a nice, smooth friction-free nylon ring which runs nicely down the line, when required, without getting caught up. They also have the benefit of a flat underside, which in turn minimizes movement in windy conditions.

For all my close- to medium-range work, I prefer to use a 1oz back-lead. This is placed on the line and allowed to settle on the lake bed just a couple of feet past the rod tip. This ensures that the majority of my main line between the rods and the rig is held on, or close to, the lake bed. If the conditions turn very windy, or I decide to use terminal tackle leads of over 3oz, then I would change the 1oz back-lead for a 1.5oz version for extra stability. I have not found back-leads to have any detrimental effect on bite indication; in fact, I believe they can even enhance the situation, particularly when using the quiver type of tensioned indicators which really keep the line under constant pressure and show every movement if your terminal lead is moved.

I am convinced that carp will often circle and evaluate a baited area in an attempt to see or feel if any line is present. In fact, I first experienced this happening back in 1983 whilst fishing a small clay pit of roughly 2 acres. The chosen bait was hazel nuts and they were having them big style – that was until I presented a baited hook in among the free offerings! After doing this, all I would experience would be short-line lifts – obviously line bites – then nothing. It was very frustrating. I decided to adopt the use of back-leads and it completely solved the problem. No more line bites and a lot more carp on the bank.

It may not have escaped your notice that during this chapter I have constantly made reference to the connection between small-water carp and pressurized carp, and to be fair there is a close relationship between the two which cannot be ignored. Having said this, it has to be admitted that the level of pressure from water to water will vary. Happily, there will always be tranquil, willow-fringed carp pools tucked away from the madding crowd, completely alien to any form of pressure, although sadly such exceptions to the rule are now few and far between.

One of the great problems with small, well-known venues is that the pressure exerted by the mere presence of anglers day-in day-out is immense. I never cease to be amazed by the

Mike Willmott with Humpy at 35lb 2oz. This wise old warrior evaded capture for three years at Ashlea, but perseverance paid off in the end for Mike.

antics of some carp anglers on these tiny venues, apparently thinking that carp are blind, deaf and stupid to boot! Most of my Ashlea experiences centred around me having the water to myself much of the time, periods during which I would be as unobtrusive and as quiet as possible, and still the carp were extremely nervous in the presence of baits. Bankside disturbance aggravates the situation. To some extent, you are in the hands of other anglers when it comes to this vital aspect of carp fishing, but whatever the behaviour of others, you can ensure that you do all you can to make the area of the lake you are fishing as quiet and undisturbed as possible. Small water carp in tiny, pressured venues are never far from the anglers, and are hard enough to catch without anglers themselves carelessly and thoughtlessly making them impossible!

Small waters will always hold a special fascination for me. Perhaps they do not possess the mystique that some of the larger, less well-known venues hold, but in their own special way they create a challenge from a different angle. It goes further than just the angling though. There is no substitute for small waters when it comes to learning about the carp's behaviour and habits. The wise angler will be the one who remembers that it is not just us, the anglers, who change tactics according to the carp's behaviour, but the carp themselves who change their habits on the basis of how the anglers approach their quarry.

25 CARP FROM DAY-TICKET WATERS – ROB HUGHES AND SIMON CROW

I have asked Rob and Simon to write a chapter on day-ticket big-fish waters because they have a unique insight into, and knowledge of, this type of fishery. For the last few years they have been writing a popular day-ticket series for *Carpworld*: their research programme has been arduous, and has been slotted into a 'normal' working/student lifestyle. Their lives revolve around carp fishing, and in addition to catching numerous carp from a variety of waters both here and in France during the last decade, in 1996 they flew the flag for Britain in Europe by winning the prestigious 'World Carp Cup' at Fishabil in France. They are both in their mid-twenties, Simon hailing from Wolverhampton and Rob from Oswestry.

Tim Paisley

The last few years has seen us travelling around the country undertaking research into some of the country's best – and indeed worst! – day-ticket venues. During this time, we are pleased to say that we have, in the main, been pleasantly surprised by what we have found.

For many anglers the thought of a day-ticket venue conjures up images of crowded banks, litter and damaged fish, but these days day-ticket fisheries represent a commercial venture, with businessmen investing thousands of pounds in to such fisheries. As a result, the quality and standard of most of the venues, and with them the fish, has increased dramatically.

Our brief through the pages of *Carpworld* and *Carp-Talk* magazines is to visit and evaluate the day-ticket waters. Our usual approach is to arrive at our chosen venue on a Friday night and fish a weekend session before returning to our respective homes in the Midlands on the Sunday afternoon. This approach is followed for two reasons. Firstly, we like to see the venues at

the time most anglers reading the features on them might visit them: a midweek visit when the fishery is quiet would not always give a realistic impression of popularity and bankside pressure. Secondly our work and study commitments mean that our mid-week fishing time is restricted to fishing venues close to home in order that we can pack up, get home and get cleaned up in time for work in the morning, leaving the weekends our only free time for reviews.

The trouble with fishing venues a reasonable distance from your home, as anyone living within a twenty-mile radius of Birmingham or any other major city can corroborate, is that the road networks are not always too kind, and indeed the M6 in the Birmingham areas is an absolute nightmare. Nevertheless, a man must fish, and sacrifices have to be made, even if it does mean sitting in the car for a protracted period of time, thereby not usually arriving at the venue till around nine o'clock at night. That's not so bad in summer, but when you consider that there are only a few months in the year when it is still light at 9.00pm, most of our day-ticket fishing takes place following an arrival at the water in the dark, never having seen the venue before, and with usually about thirty-six hours left to try and extract a fish or two.

As a result of our short trips, we have had to come to terms with methods that will give us the best possible chance of a fish in the minimum time available to us, and we think that readers of this book who find themselves in a similar situation to ours may benefit from the lessons we have had to learn.

When we arrive at a venue, one of the first things we do – and it doesn't matter if we arrive at midnight and it's chucking it down with rain –

Simon Crow with a lovely, long linear mirror of 25lb from Orchid Lake.

is to walk round the water to consider which swims we should choose. Even at midnight, we can see where the wind is blowing, whether there are any visible features in front of any of the swims, where the other anglers are fishing, and how much water each swim covers/reveals. It is vitally important when visiting a new water to put yourself in a position where you can see as much of the lake as possible. This way, when daylight comes, you are in a good fish-spotting position and can consider a move to another swim, vital if your gut feeling about swim selection the previous evening turns out to have been misguided.

This leads us to another point that has been made many times before, but one which is worth repeating here, namely that you should be prepared to move if you are not catching and prospects look better in another swim. An hour in the right swim is worth a day in the wrong one.

As far as tactics are concerned, we generally have a set routine for approaching day-ticket venues. We aim to be successful in a very short

period of time, so always look to cover as much water as possible. Unless conditions tell us otherwise, we would spread the rods out in as many different areas as possible, subject to the permissible rod limit. Almost all swims have some kind of feature within them, be it only sand, silt or gravel, and rather than putting all our eggs in one basket, we would try to multiply our chances of finding the feeding spots. Obviously, if you have reasons for doing so and conditions dictate such a course of action, then there is nothing wrong with fishing all your rods in the same area, but remember if you are arriving at the water for the first time and you have absolutely no background knowledge of it, then this tactic could prove detrimental.

Bait and rig selection follow a similar course for us as we base all our decisions on that one particular strategy. Bait choice needs to fulfil certain criteria, with instant attraction and confidence in the bait being the fundamental factors behind its selection. For the past two years we

Rob Hughes with a 24lb mirror from day-ticket water Borwick Lake.

have continually used Kevin Nash's 'S' Mix on the day-ticket venues we have fished. Although Kevin himself does not consider the mix to be very instant, our findings have been quite the opposite. When we are fishing for the weekend, we are not great believers in piling the bait in, and usually opt for baiting on a little-and-often principle, similar to the in-vogue winter strategies of some anglers. Our baiting would normally consist of half a dozen freebies with the first cast, which would only be topped up if and when action has occurred.

As with bait, rig selection would also be based on the confidence factor ahead of anything else, even the advice of other anglers. We both prefer simple rigs, and unless a situation tells us otherwise, we will always stick to reliable tried-and-tested methods. There is little time for experimenting when you are at a water for a very limited period of time. You need to be sure that when you hook into a fish your chances of landing it are high. For this reason, our rigs always consist of strong materials, products and knots which we know will not let us down. In addition to durability, hooklink selection should also take into account visual appearance, and, if the situation allows, a hooklink which lies flat would be our preferred choice. Hook preference will also take into account both sharpness and strength, to be capable of dealing with the hard mouths of many of the fish we encounter in day-ticket waters.

The 1990s have, without question, seen an improvement in the size of the fish being caught. This is possibly a product of an increase in the quality and quantity of anglers' baits, the process of eutrophication (fertilization) of some venues via the seepage of fertilizers and other nutrient sources into watercourses, and finally favourable weather conditions over the last few years. Not long ago it was normal for a day-ticket venue to have as its average stock mostly double figure fish with a few twenty-pounders thrown in for good measure. Until recently, the target fish for most anglers on these venues would be a twenty-pounder, but now it is possible to fish for upper twenties, thirties, and even carp as big as forty-pounds plus in some venues.

Although day-ticket venues tend to be overstocked, there is now a trend towards anglers preferring to catch bigger fish, and the stocking levels of some venues have been revised to allow a better growth rate of the fish already present. There is certainly a higher rate of fishery owners taking more of an interest in their fisheries, and managing them appropriately; this can only be good news for the day-ticket anglers looking for exciting new venues.

As to what constitutes a 'big fish' from a day-ticket venue, whilst many such waters hold carp in excess of 30lb a fish of over 25lb is still a very creditable fish, and a carp of 20lb is still big enough to make a weekend's session worthwhile for most anglers. On some venues (e.g. the magnificent Orchid Lake in Oxfordshire), there is a large head of carp present in excess of 25lb, and at the time of writing there are nine known carp in this water in excess of 30lb. However, on the general scale of things, a 25lb day-ticket fish can be classed as a big day-ticket carp.

On the other hand, going right to the top end of the scale Warmwell, which cannot really be classed as a day-ticket venue as such, has produced a fish in excess of 50lb, and is home to another one of over 40lb! Fish of such a size are rare in pay lakes, but there are now a few venues which house forty-pounders.

Unfortunately, as with all things commercial, there are always people out there looking to make a few quick bob, and one or two of the venues have chosen to introduce 'unannounced' foreign fish into their venues in the hope that they can pass them off as home-grown fish. This practice not only has the effect of putting the introduced and resident fish at risk of disease, but it could also make a mockery of the record list should such a fish be caught at a weight above that of the current record carp. There is no disguising the

Day-ticket delight. A striking sunset on Rob and Simon's favourite day-ticket venue, Orchid Lake in Oxfordshire.

fact that many of the fish imported into this country in recent times have ended up in day-ticket 'pay as you play' fisheries, and indeed as long as the stockings are legal and above board, why not? Our concerns are that the fish are finding their way into waters disguised as English fish. There should be a duty – if only a moral one – on the fishery owners to explain that not all of the fish in their water are of English origin.

So what, exactly, are the qualities of a good day-ticket venue? These days, anglers demand much more from their fisheries than just a chance of a reasonable level of sport. There have to be facilities for obtaining drinking water and using the toilets, as well as tackle purchasing options and the availability of meals or snacks. With these increased levels of facilities comes an increase in cost, and it is not uncommon to see the price of a day's fishing costing out at in excess of £20.

The current going rate for a fishery with average size fish (mainly doubles but with odd fish to upper twenties) is around £10.00 per day, but there are venues which charge in excess of £30 for the privilege of twenty-four hours' fishing. These tend to be the big-fish waters where target fish can be in excess of 40lb, and most carp anglers accept that it costs more to fish for beasts of this size.

The days of noisy behaviour on day-ticket venues has long gone – on most of them anyway. The quality of angler visiting these fisheries has increased with the increase in quality of the sport being offered. Security is another consideration to be taken into account by anglers fishing these venues, and those running these waters have to make the effort to ensure safe fishing for their visitors. Our advice is that if you want to start down the big-fish trail and have no knowledge of waters holding the size of fish you hope to catch, day-ticket venues may well be the ideal starting point for you.

Here is a run-down on our top ten big-fish day-ticket waters in this country. No doubt there are other venues around the country which offer bigger fish, but the list offers what we consider to be venues with a variety of ranges of difficulty, top-class fishing and, for some, the facilities to match. They are not listed in any order

of preference and we have tried to offer as good a geographical spread as possible.

The details of the waters described in this chapter are as accurate as possible, but the status of waters does change, as do phone numbers. Please check the information about the waters listed here before setting off on a long journey hoping to fish one of them.

Cuttle Mill (Warwickshire)

This well-known water lies near Sutton Coldfield, very close to the famous Belfry Golf Course. At only five acres, it is heavily stocked with carp in the 20–25lb bracket, with the biggest being around the 35lb mark. The lake is so well stocked that we would not like to hazard a guess as to how many carp the water holds. Just take it from us, it is absolutely stuffed. Out of all the day-ticket venues we have fished this venue almost certainly offers you your best chance of a fish over 20lb. The fishing can be fairly easy and it is not uncommon for multiple catches to occur in a single day. Day tickets are limited and have to be booked in advance, and on the day of fishing anglers have to draw for swims. Further details can be obtained from the owner Tony Higgins, telephone 01827 872253. There is no night fishing allowed at this venue (although you can stay on the premises overnight), and there is a close season in operation.

Dorchester Lagoon (Oxfordshire)

This venue lies on the same site as Orchid Lake and is owned by the Dorchester Sailing Club. It covers an area of 40 acres and is very underfished as far as day-tickets are concerned. The lake contains some awesome-looking snags and weed beds, but there are some cracking carp well worth fishing for. There have been two recorded stockings of the lake with the initial one comprising thirty Galician race carp and the second two hundred fish of the Dinkelsbuehl race. The original fish, which were stocked some

East Yorkshire's Motorway Pond is controlled by Hull and District Angling Association. The water holds carp of almost 40lb and is a big fish venue for the future.

time in the mid 1970s, have reached weights in excess of 38lb, and the dinks have reached mid-twenties since their introduction in the early 1990s. There are five known thirties in the water as well as a couple of unknown biggies around the same weight. The unknown fish are not myths, and evidence which substantiates this came in 1991 when an uncaught common of 39lb was washed up dead. It is certainly a water with a challenge and both day and night tickets are available throughout the year. Telephone 01865 341810 for further details. The fishing is fairly easy for some of the dinks but much harder for the originals. However, some of the dinks are growing fast and look set to make 30lb in the near future.

Manor Farm (Oxfordshire)

This Linear Fisheries owned water has become well established as a day-ticket water in recent years and hit the headlines in a big way in late 1996 when it produced its first forty-pounder. It contains some gorgeous dark-looking mirror carp as well as being rumoured to contain a very big uncaught common (authenticated sightings). This 12 acre gravel pit has an abundance of features and natural food stocks, and can be a bit hard going for the inexperienced carp angler. There are six known fish over 30lb in the water as well as a good head of twenties and doubles. Day and night fishing is available January to December and tickets are available on the bank. Details can be obtained from Linear Fisheries head office: telephone 01908 645115.

Motorway Pond (East Yorkshire)

This 18-acre lake holds, as far as we are aware, the largest carp available on day ticket in the North of the country. Although there is a fairly good head of carp in the 20–25lb bracket, Kevin Clifford informs us that there are also at least three different thirties present, with the biggest

Storm clouds over Savay Lake. Big carp conditions on a premier big carp water.

a mirror weighing around 38lb. It is a water with plenty of features to fish to, but it is said to be a fairly difficult venue. There are no night tickets available but don't let this put you off, as fish are caught during the day and the early part of the evening. The venue lies alongside the westbound carriageway of the M62 motorway, hence its name. Fishing is only available through purchasing tickets in advance. Contact Hull and District Anglers for further details.

Orchid Lake (Oxfordshire)

Despite being situated alongside a couple of Oxfordshire's major roads, this 17-acre water lies in extremely picturesque surroundings. In the height of summer, the greenery includes some absolutely gorgeous overhanging willow trees. The venue is one of our favourite day-ticket waters and we make frequent visits. There are loads of features to fish to, including reeds, weed, gravel bars, etc. The water contains at

least nine genuine known thirty-pounders. To date the biggest fish is a 38lb common which, judging by previous growth rate data, looks certain to make the magical 40lb mark at some stage. Besides these big fish there are plenty of quality back-up fish, with up to an estimated seventy fish going over 20lb. The venue is owned by well-known specimen hunter Marsh Pratley and further details about the fishing can be obtained by telephoning him on 01865 341810. Day and night fishing is available for twelve months of the year, but be prepared to work for your fish.

Savay Lake (Middlesex)

No list of big-fish venues would be complete without mention of this famous water. Savay is possibly one of the most talked-about venues in England, if not Europe, and also one of the toughest. It is a water which is not for the faint-hearted, especially as far as day-ticket fishing is concerned, so don't expect to take the place apart if you do decide to pay it a visit. The head of big fish is impressive, with an excellent chance of a thirty-pounder should you be lucky enough to receive a take, with the biggest fish in the mid-forty-pound range. There are rumours of uncaught monsters and it would come as no surprise if one of these fish suddenly turns up out of the blue. There is no night fishing on ticket, but don't let this put you off – it is worth fishing, if only to say that you've been there. Day tickets are available from local shops. Contact Peter Broxup on 0860 594856 for further details.

Warmwell Country Park (Dorset)

This venue is one of the many holiday-type angling venues which are now cropping up all over Europe. It is an extremely popular water and is fished constantly throughout the year by a swarm of anglers from all over the world. It has become famous for its two big residents, known as Herman (a common which exceeded 50lb at its heaviest, but which sadly died during the compilation of this book), and Bertha (a mirror in excess of 40lb). This small water also contains a good head of other decent-sized carp which are well worth pursuing. Because the fish are so pressured, the lake is just not as easy as people seem to believe, and very often it becomes a long-term waiting game if you are after one of the big fish. The water is open twelve months of the year, but fishing is restricted to holiday-makers staying on the site. There are no individual day or night tickets available and anglers have to book a week in a chalet to qualify for fishing rights. Further details can be obtained by telephoning the booking office on 01305 852911.

Waveney Valley D & E Lake (Norfolk)

Another famous water now, but this time in the far east of the country. Primarily a holiday venue

which can only be booked in conjunction with a caravan booking in the summer months, this venue does offer day and night ticket fishing from 1 October until the end of February. Its most famous resident is a mirror known as Big Scale which weighs in the upper thirty-pound bracket, but there is also a good head of back-up fish present into the thirties. Day tickets are restricted and it is recommended that anglers telephone before visiting. Although the fish have seen almost everything and can be very cute, the fishing is not the hardest available on day ticket as the carp's main diet does appear to be baits. Telephone Tony on 01986 788676 for further information.

Withy Pool (Bedfordshire)

This lake needs no introduction to most carp anglers as it has been at the forefront of the sport for a number of years now. For many years a private syndicate water the venue surprised everyone by turning day ticket at the start of 1997. It is owned by big-fish angler Kevin Maddocks and holds an impressive number of big fish. It is far from easy compared to most day-ticket waters, but contains huge fish to mid forty-pound range, which add to its attraction for many serious carp anglers. At the start of 1997 it contained four forty-pounders, as well as grass carp to over 20lb. The lake also contains a huge catfish which has been caught at over 60lb. It is not a cheap venue to fish but the rewards are there for the catching if big fish are your aim. Day and night tickets are available the year round. Telephone Kevin Maddocks on 01462 816960 for further information. Kevin Maddocks is also the proprietor of Beekay International, the publishers of the book *Beekay Guide to 2000 Carp Waters*. This is available from many book shops and is an invaluable source of information about numerous waters, in addition to the few mentioned here. If you can't get hold of a copy ring Beekay at the above number for details of availability.

26 COLD WATER CARPING

Prior to the 1990s I would have considered this chapter as minority reading. In percentage terms, winter carpers may still be a minority, but there are now so many people carp fishing that this particular minority now represents a significant number of anglers. Having spent hundreds of hours carp fishing through the winter, two things have become apparent. The first is that I love winter carp fishing. The second is that while the fishing can be slower, it can be more hectic too. Add to those two points the fact that the majority of my modest collection of ten fish in excess of 30lb have been caught after the first of November and you will start to understand my considerable attachment to this form of fishing.

If you are going to carp fish through the winter, you must have two immediate objectives. The first is to kit yourself out properly and condition yourself to what lies ahead. The second is to convince yourself that at some time during the colder months, the carp you are after will occasionally have a little feed. Then you go and

Birch Grove, Shropshire, in a heavy frost. I am convinced that at least some carp feed almost every day throughout the winter, although some days actually catching one of them is a different matter!

take root as often as possible for as long as possible and wait for the fish to have their little feed.

Here is some encouragement. I am inclined to believe that some carp on most waters feed at some time during the winter. Do not be put off by a marked tailing off in feeding activity through the first cold spells of the winter when the water temperature is dropping. Yes, the feeding slows down, or even stops, but this seems to be a temporary situation. This lull apart, some carp feed fairly normally up until the end of the year, and then less frequently thereafter. These are generalizations, obviously, but there have been some remarkable carp catches during December in particular. In fact results in that most unlikely of carp-catching months have been quite spectacular some years when you consider the number of carp anglers still fishing at that time of the year. The first week in December in particular turns up some very big fish, but there have also been spectacular results in the run up to Christmas and over the Christmas period.

The fact that overall results decline sharply in the winter is a deceptive statistic. Even given that an increasing minority of carpers carry on carp fishing, how many save a week of their holidays for December, January or February carping? Not a lot. So while there are still a significant number of anglers carp fishing in the winter months, the collective rod hours aspired to by this minority will be significantly lower than the summer and autumn months. And yet catch reports to *Carp-Talk* have made it absolutely clear that a significant number of carp are caught throughout the winter – some of them very big ones.

Some of you will have been put off winter carping by either brief experiences of the long, cold, boring nights, or by writers emphasizing this aspect. I think I have done so in a negative fashion in the past. For me, they are the difference between winter and summer carping. Summer is a pleasure and a challenge. Winter is a challenge which can become a pleasure if you can condition your state of mind to an acceptance of the long hours of nothingness. At any

time, the effectiveness of your carp fishing depends on your state of mind, your ability and willingness to get it all right then let it happen. Successful winter carping exaggerates this situation. If you are mentally and practically equipped the worst part can be setting up and tackling down. During the actual session, you do not have to leave the bivvy unless something happens, and if it does happen, you will be quite prepared to leave it whatever the conditions (nervous drop-backs from bream being a notable exception ...)!

I will just expand on that comment a little. Comfortable and reasonably spacious living quarters are a must for winter-session carping. You may be able to travel light in summer and autumn and put up with a level of discomfort, but in winter you cannot. You need to look on the bivvy experience as an extension of home life. Make yourself comfortable, find some way of occupying your mind through the periods of what in advance you perceive to be unmitigated boredom and you will start to find winter carping to be the ultimate escape, and a very mind-easing experience.

I take the kitchen sink with me all year anyway, so my winter quarters are only a slight extension of my summer set-up. I cope with the possible boredom by splitting the twenty-four hour periods up, and settling into a routine based around them. I have periods of greater expectation than others – suspected feeding times – but for the most part, my mind is focused on the self-discipline of the routine. Self-discipline and determination are the base on which a winter campaign is built. You must want to catch and be determined to stick to your winter-session routine, come what may. It is easier to be discouraged by a blank in winter than in summer, and when it is winter, it is easy to forget that you actually suffered blanks in summer. If you realistically compare your winter results with those of summer, you may surprise yourself.

So given that your carp may be catchable, and that you are determined to fish the winter through for them, how do you set about catching them? That part you will have to plan for yourself, but your winter carping should begin long before winter sets in. Carp can be very difficult to locate during the colder months, and if you can keep track of their movements and whereabouts through the autumn, you will make swim selection and choice of potential feeding areas a more viable proposition than if you arrive at the water 'cold' and clueless in December.

The other vital aspect of establishing a winter campaign is the prebaiting. Leaving aside all other considerations, accept that carp are harder to catch in winter than in summer, in the sense that, even if you do get them over the baits, their reduced need for food reduces their catchability. Your prime requirement is an acceptable, established bait. My biggest mental barrier to winter carping is not the cold, or the long dark nights, or even the location aspect; it is the knowledge that I have a bait the carp will feed on. There has been a great deal written about the difference between summer and winter baits. I have been down the route of changing baits from summer to winter, and find it difficult to work in practice. While ever the summer bait is working I do not want to change, and I do not even want to distract the carp from the ongoing food source by introducing a new one. But if you are using fishmeals, I think it is universally accepted by most winter anglers and bait boffins that you will have to change. The most painless way of doing this is by introducing a couple of pounds of the new bait at the end of each session from the end of September onwards. If you can get down to the water to supplement this baiting between sessions, this may help, but once the season starts almost all my prebaiting is done as I leave the water. This is certainly true of my autumn and winter carping.

Once you have a going winter-bait, keep it going in. I introduce up to 5lb of bait into a couple of swims as I am leaving the water, whether I have caught or not. If the bait is not being accepted, I will know because sooner or later it will float to the surface. That has not happened to me yet in winter. The principle that you need the carp feeding on your bait to catch them is just as important in winter as it is in summer, because

you need reluctant feeders feeding with confidence to induce that momentary lapse in concentration you are seeking. To fish single hookbaits and stringers through the winter 'because the carp aren't feeding' is an admission of defeat. Think of their winter feeding as having a little feed and your thinking will focus more sharply on the tactics I have found successful.

I find the advice that location is the key to winter success is very discouraging. I cannot argue with it, but the point I am trying to make is that there is a great deal more to getting the carp to give an indication of their presence in winter than merely finding them. I learnt that aspect of winter reality back in my Snowberry days in the 1970s. There were not enough minutes in the year for me to do all the carping I wanted to do in those days, but I found Snowberry a real struggle through the worst of the winter. On one occasion, I found half a dozen carp lying up close to the bank in the lily pad area. It was my first sight of carp for some weeks. Bait-up or not? I did. I had been having success with sweetcorn and maggots, so I fired a few pouchfuls onto the carp, and was relieved when they didn't swim away. I set up two light link legers and swung them into position. The buzzers and banksticks were quietly eased into position, the rods set up, and I sat back behind the hedge to wait for action. Nothing happened. After an hour or two, I carefully peered round the hedge, thinking I had spooked the carp out of the swim. They were still there. They were still there next morning... They were still there the morning after that when I had to leave! The fish were inches from the baits and lines but the buzzers and indicators didn't give a single warning of their presence.

There is more to winter carping than finding the carp, but find your carp you must. On most waters, carp give no indication as to their movements or presence during the colder months other than when they move the indicator. Tracking down the carp is more an exercise in deduction and detection that one of watercraft, although it is probably fair to argue that detection is all part of watercraft. Sometimes location is made easy. I once read an article which suggested that location was a question of finding out where other anglers were catching from! I winced when I read the advice, but I cannot argue with the logic of the observation. It is one form of location, but one which may not make you too popular, and one which will have no basis if you are the only angler winter fishing your water!

Having said this, it is a fact of winter life that carp can be far more tightly shoaled and located in one area in winter than in summer. All waters have their going swims at any time of the year, but this can be exaggerated in the colder months, to the extent that all those fishing one water want to be in one particular swim and fishing one particular spot. I do not think it is a fact that all the fish in the water are in that precise area, I think it is more a case of them being hard to pinpoint, which means that when someone does find a hot spot, it becomes *the* hot spot for the water throughout the winter.

The basis of winter location includes the successes of others, previous winter-capture history, observation of the carp through the autumn and early winter, and watching and listening for carp movement during daylight and the waking hours of darkness. Failing these, location is down to inspired (or even uninspired, but do not even think that!) guesswork, which is how many winter campaigns start. Inspired guesswork and the assistance of the weather man.

It may not be true of all winter waters, but it is my experience that low pressure and oxygenation are strong influences on winter feeding. Oxygenation is brought about by big winds and rain. I am not of the opinion that any wind is a good wind, because when there is a chill factor (which to me means that the wind feels colder than the actual air temperature) feeding seems to stop in its tracks, once the effect of the wind starts to be felt. But any wind which feels warmer than the prevailing air temperature, and particularly westerlies of any sort, can lead to feeding activity. Continuing mild, still conditions have not proved to be consistently good feeding conditions during my winter carping, but such conditions can be special after big winds or heavy rain.

Rain is different things to different waters. In his revealing and entertaining book *Waiting for Waddle*, author Phil Thompson dismisses rain as being an absolute non-starter where feeding carp are concerned. On the Mangrove and Birch Grove in winter, it can be like a dinner gong, and if that is true of those two very different waters, it will be true of many others. The arrival of rain often follows a sudden lowering of air pressure (which is probably the actual reason for the sudden feeding activity) but to have everything in place when it starts raining can mean a fish on the bank which you would not otherwise have caught. I do not like fishing in the rain any more than anyone else, but I now accept that I have to be geared to coping with winter carping efficiently in torrential rain, and a great many of my winter carp have been caught in gale force and/or very wet conditions.

I will enforce the observation that good feeding conditions can occur unexpectedly and very briefly. In *From the Bivvy*, I recounted the tale of two good winter carp in the landing net at the same time late in November. They weighed 51½lb in total, and the fish came from two spots forty yards apart; the runs came within minutes of each other. In that instance, the reason for the sudden burst of feeding activity was not obvious, or definable, and that is the way of many winter feeding spells. You cannot plan them, or foresee them, but to know that action may be only minutes away results in an underlying optimism far removed from the more predictable known feeding spell anticipation of warm-weather carping.

My best winter campaign of all (my Mangrove winter of 1994/95) was based on finding a tight holding area, fishing it hard, and catching when the carp had a little feed. My summer carping is based on two main thrusts, a bed of bait which I feel sure they will feed on, but which will not always result in them making a mistake in that area, and a concentration on what I perceive to be feeding spots which the carp visit naturally. In winter my tactics are different, and during the bulk of that winter, I concentrated on one tight area where I had seen consistent carp movement

November 1995. Sometimes it just does not stop raining. Dave Chilton took this shot of a gutty Mangrove common using the flash from inside my bivvy. The picture was actually taken mid-morning and conditions were as awful as they look.

over a couple of seasons, but which was not a producing area. This suggested that it might be a holding area. During an excellent slide show in Sheffield some years ago John Harry, the author of the book *Savay*, made an interesting point about winter-holding areas. He suggested that finding a holding area can be a key to success in the winter months. When conditions fall right for them to have a feed, the food source is there on their doorstep and they do not have to waste energy going looking for it. He made the further point that carp coming out of a lay-up may not have their full wits about them, which means they may be easier to catch, and that you may catch the odd fish which would not normally fall to baits.

The success I had from the one tight area convinced me that I had found a winter-holding area, but if it was such an area, it emphasizes the difficulty with winter location. There was nothing whatever to distinguish that spot from the rest of the featureless open-water 18 acres of silt. Not to the angler, anyway. The carp (or at least a pocket of them) were apparently comfortable there, and that is where they were to be found during most of my sessions throughout the winter.

I did explore the area, and found one or two spots which I took to be features. This included a deeper hole about fifteen yards from the hot spot which excited me enormously, but which did not produce a single bleep to the rod I fished in it for a few sessions. Was the producing area

December 1993. More Mangrove rain. Torrential overnight rain raised the water level by over 12in (30cm) and I had to reluctantly abandon the session, having caught during the worst of the rain during the night. That fish determined me to have a crack at the difficult winter water the following winter. During the close season we raised the level of a few of the platforms to avoid a recurrence of this minor disaster.

the site of an underwater spring? Did the blood-worm hole-up there in winter? Was it just that it was on the end of the westerlies? Or did the carp just happen to be there during most of my winter sessions? I don't know. All the takes came from an area approximately three yards by three. Other rods fished away from that spot didn't produce a single fish during the period that one small area produced nearly forty. Their presence and the resulting action does open your mind to areas beyond the oft-recited winter hot spots of snag areas, gullies between bars, dead lily pad beds, reed beds and so on. For the record, there are no bars whatever on the Mangrove, but there are snag areas, hundreds of yards of lily pad beds, and similar expanses of Norfolk reeds.

Having decided where to fish, my winter campaigns are based on a steady introduction of bait when I am not fishing, and the possibility that the fish might have a little feed when I am. This

'little-feed' concept was born of winter frustrations on Birch Grove during a previous winter campaign. For a number of years now, I have fished small baits in winter and I have been happy enough with the bait and the feeding situation. But through two winter campaigns, I was getting a repeating pattern of landing a fish early in the session then having no follow up action in the next two or three days. Was half a pound of bait followed by a topping-up after the early action too much for the fish? Or was it that those fish that were willing to feed were satisfied by the initial baiting and there was no further feeding during my stay at the water? The 'one fish then nothing' phenomenon did not occur every time, but certainly often enough to be part of a pattern and to make me rethink the baiting situation at the start of the Mangrove winter.

In the end, I settled for fishing the Grange CSL mix with 5–6mm baits as the main feeding situation, with Micromass (which was then at the development stage) as a back-up disappearing food source. I started each session by putting in ½lb to ¾lb of bait in total (half and half), spread over an area roughly five yards by five yards. It is exceptional, although there are other products which will do the job I used Micromass to do that winter. Ball Pellets, Crumball, breaking-down pellets, crumb; all these will create the required background disappearing food source/scent feeding situation.

I use tiny baits for two reasons. One is to make the carp work harder for its meal. The more times it has to pick up a bait to complete its meal, the more likely it is to take its mind off what it is doing and make a mistake with the hookbait. You are trying to take its little mind off the possible source of danger while it is having its little feed. Obtaining a supply of tiny baits is not easy, and I appreciated the help I got from Mainline in this regard. But the supply that first winter was a limited one, and by the time it had run out, I'd discovered that a pound or so of tiny baits was sufficient for a three day session. So before each session, I laboriously made 1½lb of tiny baits to make sure I'd got sufficient for the next session. It's a boring process but only takes about three hours to make the required quantity of maple-sized baits. Baiting-up at the end of sessions was carried out with my existing supply of 14mm or 18mm baits.

The back-up breaking-down baits or pellets are there to create a smell of food in the feeding area while keeping the actual available food to a minimum. To start with I would top up the Micromass and the Grange baits if I had had action the previous night, but I discovered that was apparently a mistake. For my two or three night sessions I was better sticking to the original baiting, and fishing over the original bed with twelve or fifteen baits stringer set-ups, which came to represent the little-feed food source always available in the swim.

I became very confident in this baiting arrangement and for the first time in my winter fishing, I was as likely to catch on the third night as on the first. There was often a strong temptation to top-up after catching, but results were definitely best when I restricted the fresh supply of food to the hookbaits and stringers. In other words, I was playing on the carp's frustration based on their awareness of the disappearing feeding area, the smell of food in the swim and the difficulty in locating an actual food source. The stringer set-up was a feeding spot within a feeding area. A few misplaced casts do not come amiss in this situation. It means the carp are not just encountering clusters of bait which spell danger. In the most difficult of the conditions, it would sometimes take three or four casts to achieve the correct end tackle/stringer placement, which meant a number of free meals in addition to the loaded one.

I found that it paid to vary the situation as the winter wore on, fishing a pop-up or a balanced bottom bait on one rod. Some sessions the stringer trap worked. On other sessions, I had fish which fell to the variation bait. My thinking was that if the fish did not have much of a feed, they might still be willing to get hold of a single bait, and that a pop-up might be easier to find in very cold conditions when the smell of the bait might represent minimal attraction.

Bream can be enthusiastic about the Grange, and of course the tiny-bait situation was very much to their liking. Early in the winter, I landed rather more bream than I wanted, which resulted in me making the mistake of going onto bigger baits for a couple of sessions, which minimized the bream action, but slowed the carp action down too. It did not take me long to realize that the feeding activity of the bream was probably a big help in drawing the attention of the carp to the feeding area. From the middle of December onwards, it became apparent that the bream were not allowed onto the baits until the carp had finished their feeding spell, a bream take meaning the carp's feeding had finished for the night.

I think the important thing about this baiting situation is that however strongly the carp feed, or want to feed, there is a chance of a take. I always keep disturbance to a minimum and have the baiting situation and end tackle in position long before a possible feeding spell is due. I had blank sessions, but I have long had the philosophy that a blank simply means that the fish did not feed strongly enough to get caught. I kept introducing the bigger baits at the end of the session, and my confidence was kept high through not having more than four blank nights on the trot.

I think that keeping making the bait available to the carp is critical, even for those of you who prefer to fish singles and stringers. I realize that those of you with an ongoing coot or tufty problem will be reading this with some scepticism, but I actually developed this method on Birch, where there is a coot problem in winter. When the birds are overactive, I concentrate more on the disappearing food source with a single bait fished over the top. In this situation, my own preference is still for an established, prebaited bait, but I am sure it can be made to work just as well with one-off attractor baits fished over pellets, Micromass, Ball Pellets or whatever your preferred background feeding noise is. Frustrating them in their attempt to feed on an apparent food source is the key to success here.

I will make it clear that the Mangrove does not exactly surrender its fish in the winter. In fact, prior to my run of winter success, the winter carp from the water could be counted on the fingers of one hand. The fact that the trap accounted for almost forty carp from the start of November to the close of the old season on 15 March suggests that the method should work well on most potentially productive waters during the colder months. In fact, a surprising number of people have come up to me at meetings and conferences to tell me how their success rate has increased dramatically since they started fishing this disappearing food source/tiny-bait combination.

I think running lead set-ups are essential in winter. My winter takes are a mixture of screaming runs, stop/start takes and a succession of bleeps from a tightening of the line. I've experimented with fixed leads during the colder months, but I think they give the carp too much room for manoeuvre without you knowing about it. Running leads are dealt with at length in Chapter 8 so I will not elaborate on the theme here.

There is one other technical point to emphasize and that is concerning PVA. Other than with stringers and single bottom baits, I use PVA for every cast I make in the winter, whatever the conditions. As much of my action comes during torrential rain, I need a PVA which does not die on me when I am putting the stringer trap together, casts well, but dissolves fairly rapidly (within minutes) once it is in the swim. Kryston's Meltdown does this for me. It also comes

Winter is not all doom and gloom, although peaceful winter sunsets like this one on the Mangrove usually mean a quiet night for the buzzers, unless the pressure drops and the clouds come rolling in.

in protective tubs, which is a crucial storage factor. I need the PVA out on the bivvy table for immediate use, so I need it protected. Continuing damp conditions without the PVA coming into contact with water can start to have an effect on PVA in the form of a toughening-up process.

Your priority is that your PVA must dissolve. Check the effectiveness of your PVA in the water temperatures prevailing at the time you are fishing. When I was starting a Birch winter campaign, a number of us tested the PVAs we were using in the November lake water. One of them dissolved inside an hour. The others hung around indefinitely. In the even colder water of February dissolving times were even longer. I am sure there are PVAs other than Meltdown which do the job you demand of them, but check them out. Do not just take their winter effectiveness on trust.

One final word of warning about winter carping; you must keep warm and dry to fish efficiently. I have mentioned catching carp in gale-force winds and torrential rain. In these conditions the results are rewarding, but the practicalities are problematical. You have to be prepared for the buzzer dragging you out of the bivvy in the worst conditions imaginable, and

you have then got to plan for resuming life in the bivvy with water running off you in all directions. The sleeping bag you are going to sit on has later to be slept in. Your hands have got to be dry while you recreate your little feeding situation. You need weatherproof clothing, but you also need a supply of towels. I spread a big towel on the bedchair to sit on, and have a number of smaller towels available so I can keep drying myself off should the best possible scenario occur and I have to launch myself out in the storm more than once in the course of a feeding spell.

In the early 1980s, the 'winter' chapter in Kevin Maddocks' book *Carp Fever* encouraged me to go winter carping because it made winter carp sound catchable and gave me the confidence to go out and fish for them. I found winter carping very difficult prior to reading Kevin's chapter, and I found it becoming increasingly difficult again until I stumbled on a bait, baiting situation and bait trap which would encourage them to feed, but still catch them in the little – and sometimes reluctant – feeding situation which prevails in winter. Rod Hutchinson coined the phrase 'scratching time' to describe carp which are reluctant to be caught. I look on winter carping as permanent 'scratching time' and adapt my tactics accordingly.

Most of my winter trophy shots are taken on the remote set-up using the tripod. This pretty common was part of an evening's two twenty-pounder brace after four successive blank nights had me wondering if the fish had moved from the productive area.

27 CARP ON THE BANK AND MISCELLANEOUS MATTERS

This book is concerned with the tactics of catching carp from the bottom, but it feels incomplete without brief reference to some other areas of carp fishing. I should really make an attempt to justify the decision not to include a chapter on floater fishing or stalking. I really should say a few words about carp care, because now you have learned how to catch them, you must learn to look after them! And when you have that long sought-after whacker on the bank, you need to be able to take a good picture of it. The more successful you get, the more waters you will want to join, and the more likely you are to want to go and fish in France.

Playing Fish

Playing fish starts at the tackling-up stage. Your tackle set-up has to be designed to cope with the pressures you are going to have to put on the fish. Don't hit-and-hold unless you absolutely have to, but if you are in a situation where you know you will have to, your hook and line must be capable of meeting the demands you and the fish make of it. Always have something in hand in terms of strength of tackle. Use a hook that will go in, and stay in, and line the fish cannot break and which will withstand any snags in front of you.

When I hook a fish in open water, I always presume it weighs in excess of 40lb. A fish is at its strongest just after you have hooked it. Show it some respect, and if it wants to run around a bit, let it do so. Only try to stop it in its tracks if you have absolutely got to. Don't baby it,

Playing a fish on Birch Grove. The fish is still some way from the bank here. The usual danger times are just after hooking, and when the fish is under the rod tip, particularly with stiffish rods.

though. Keep the pressure on at all times and watch the bend in the rod. If you let the bend go out of the rod at any time, you are increasing the chances of the carp getting rid of the hook.

Keep the pressure on and wear the fish down. If it starts to kite towards bankside snags, try one of two tactics. First try flattening the rod to parallel with the water and heaving. A carp is far more likely to respond to a horizontal rod than a vertical one. But when you lay the rod flat, ensure that you still keep the bend in it. If the carp does not respond to the flattened-rod treatment, you will have to try pulling it towards the snag it is headed for. With some carp this works well; with others it doesn't. If it clearly isn't responding to this trick, go back to the flattened rod and heaving.

If you have overhanging branches between you and the margin spot the carp is headed for, bury the rod tip under the water and carry on heaving.

When the fish is under the rod tip, there are three things to think about. The first two are critical. The nearer the fish comes to the surface, the more it will be affected by bankside noise, and the greater the pressure is on the hook. I am paranoid about people speaking, or shouting, or moving quickly in bright clothes when I've got a fish within ten yards of the bank. However nice other anglers may be, at least some of them will be jealous that you are playing a fish; they couldn't care less whether you land it or not, and one or two would be happier of you lost it! Insist on quiet while you are playing your fish.

The third point is that you should exert as little vertical pressure as possible. Carp do not respond to it, and it is a situation in which the pressure on the hook is at its greatest. Lay the rod over to left or right to bring the fish up through the water. When the fish goes down again, repeat the treatment. Don't just crouch there (crouching, rather than standing, reduces the angle of pull and makes you less conspicuous) allowing the fish to swim around under the tip. You must exert as much pressure as possible as safely as possible. I have watched inexperienced anglers play fish for up to three hours at Fishabil, simply because they had a loose clutch and couldn't exert any pressure –and apparently didn't understand that they should be doing so. When you want to bring the carp to the net, encourage it to make a little run out from you, then try to get its head and ease it in across the surface. Pulling upwards stresses the hookhold;

easing the fish across the surface for the final few yards minimizes that stress. But remember, you must keep the bend in the rod while all this is going on.

I play carp on the backwind. Modern tackle is so good that there is no need for a clutch to tell you whether the line is at breaking point or not. It never should be. You play a fish – rather than just haul it in – because the hooks we use are the lightest and smallest we can get away with in any given situation. A clutch cannot feel the pressure on the hook, that is down to a second-by-second assessment by the angler. In addition the rods we use much of the time make the efficient use of a clutch something of a compromise. When you are using a 12 or 13ft rod your clutch setting has to be set far too soft for the reel to respond to a fish under the rod tip because of the inadequate bend in the rod when the fish is that close in.

I use the clutch when I am margin fishing, then get on the backwind as early as possible in the fight. When I am fishing at range, I have anti-reverse on and the clutch screwed down tight to maximize the power of the strike, then switch to anti-reverse as soon as I've set the hook. I then play the fish on anti-reverse until I have led it into the net. If you follow this course of action, make sure you are familiar with your reel controls. Over the years I have lost a couple of carp through fumbling for the anti-reverse on a new reel and discovering – too late – that the lever is not where it used to be on the previous model!

Be very patient when the fish is under the rod tip. If someone is netting the fish for you, make them crouch and keep still, and keep the net still until you quietly tell them to lift. Ease the fish in across the surface. If you fish on your own, use a modern carbon landing net; they are lighter and much easier to manoeuvre than their glass counterparts. Make yourself stay calm throughout the fight. Putting the net under the fish is what you are fishing for. Make sure it happens every time the buzzer sounds. If you never try to net a fish until it is on its side, you will have few landing net losses.

Sacking

Make sure sacking is permitted on the water you are fishing. Use a sack which allows a good flow of water. The quicker the sack drains the better the passage of water (and therefore oxygen) for the sacked fish. I use a Gold Label sling/sack so I have just the one carp transference to make, from landing net to sling/sack, which is used for weighing and sacking.

Find a suitable sacking spot before you start fishing, or while you are fishing and before you catch. You want a spot with a good depth, which you may not find in your swim or without paddling out. Sort all this out in daylight.

Use a long, securely tied cord on your sack. Check and recheck the knot joining the cord to the sack: there have been instances of carp swimming away in the sack. The long cord allows the carp to find its own level in the water. Once they have settled down they usually lie up on the bottom. Too short a cord prevents them from doing this. Securely fasten the sack (mine are zipped) or you might suffer an instance of a carp swimming away without the sack and without being photographed, a surprisingly common phenomenon which happens to most sufferers just once!

When you have first sacked a fish, keep checking the sack to make sure the carp is upright and breathing freely. Don't try to push it down into the water. Sacked carp seem to like to lie near the surface until they have recovered from the exertions of being played, then go down to the bottom or such other depth at which they feel comfortable. Some fish take much longer than others to drop into the lower layers of the water when sacked.

Once you have sacked a fish and checked that it is comfortable, leave it till you are ready to photograph it. Never subject the fish to the extra stress of dragging it out of the water to show it to your mates. I've seen it happen! Never put more than one fish in one sack. Photograph the fish as soon as conditions permit. When you have returned the fish, check the contents of the sack. They can be very revealing!

Unhooking Mat

Always have an unhooking mat with you. There are numerous versions available and while some are better than others any mat is better than no mat. I use Kevin Nash's Continental Monster Total Protection mat, which is well padded and has a far more realistic surface area than most mats. It is bulky to carry though, and I have used a number of perfectly satisfactory alternatives. Fox, Hutchinson, Cobra, Leslies of Luton, Tails Up and many others make excellent unhooking mats. Shop round for the best buy then carry it with you at all times.

Weigh Sling

In addition to the Gold Label sling/sacks, I carry a Nash weigh sling for those waters where sacking is not allowed or for weighing fish I am not going to sack. Wet the sack or sling before you put the fish in it and do not include the weight of the sack or sling in the weight of the fish.

Weighing

Always carry an efficient, accurate, reliable set of scales which will weigh the biggest fish you are likely to encounter in the water you are fishing. Zero the scales to the weight of the wet sack or sling before weighing, or deduct the weight after weighing. If you are using scales which involve more than one revolution of the needle to arrive at the weight (e.g. Avons) make sure you have selected the right revolution. There are more misweighings than accurate weighings. Many weights include the weight of the sack, sling (or even landing net!), while we all see some very embarrassing fish weights based on the incorrect reading of multiple-revolution dial scales.

I use Kevin Nash single-revolution 56lb scales. He also markets a 112lb version. (I am an optimist, but not that big an optimist!)

Suspend scales from the top. If you hold them from the bottom you get an incorrect weighing.

Reliable weighing set-up. Tackle Box Weigh Hook screwed into a storm rod and the reliable and easily read Kevin Nash 56lb dial scales. Support the storm rod during weighing.

Hold them by means of a bar, or suspend them from a branch, or the Tackle Box weigh hook (which screws into the top of a storm rod).

Don't get a reputation for being a 'fancy weigher'. The carp world has already got a fair collection of such anglers: most of them are known and simply not believed when it comes to weights of fish. A fish weighs what it weighs, not what you want it to weigh.

Photography

The extent of your carp-fishing involvement will probably dictate the degree of trouble you will take over your carp-fishing photography. As a magazine publisher and regular writer, I take literally hundreds of pictures each year, and the quality of the pictures is important to me.

Because I spend a great deal of time fishing on my own, a percentage of my trophy shots are self-taken, therefore my camera equipment has to be geared to that eventuality. For the self-take and most of my general shots I carry a Nikon 601 35-mm SLR camera with an air release screw-in fitting and built-in flash. With the camera I need a stable tripod and an air-release extension. The camera is fully automatic, which means that I just have to set up the equipment, pose with the fish, then keep squeezing the air-release bulb and shifting the pose slightly until I have taken the number of shots I require.

'Framing' self-take shots is a matter of commonsense. I judge the height from the background foliage and the width from the unhooking mat dimension. If in doubt, err on the side of making the image too small rather than too big. As long as everything is in the shot you can always have prints done of the essential area of the end result. If there are bits missing, you can't add them afterwards!

A fully automatic camera is important for self-take shots: the light conditions can change rapidly and you need the camera to monitor these changes and self-adjust the exposure.

Common faults in trophy shots are poor depth of field, which means that either the angler or the fish are out of focus, and/or poor exposure. These faults can happen with foolproof fully automatics and manual cameras. Poor depth of field is more likely to occur in poor light conditions. The poorer the light, the wider the aperture has to be (meaning a low f reading). The wider the aperture, the harder it is for the camera to focus on two different lengths at the same time. So someone holding a fish well forward in poor light is likely to cause focus problems. Hold the fish close to your body at all times (but particularly in poor light conditions) and you will eliminate depth-of-field problems. Flash also eliminates the problem because it permits the use of a narrower aperture.

A shutter speed of $\frac{1}{60}$ second is the slowest you can safely use for hand held shots. For readings below this figure, you should use a tripod or switch to flash.

The trusty Nikon 601. Screw in remote fitting, adequate built-in flash, and reliable fully automatic controls make this mid-range SLR camera ideal for self-portrait trophy shots.

Poor exposure can arise from the angler wearing clothing lighter than the colour of the fish, or where there is too much light in the background. The camera will adjust – or read – to the brightest light source in its range of vision, which can result in the fish and the angler being too dark. With a manual or automatic camera take the exposure reading from the fish. Some lenses now have a spot-monitoring facility, which means that the reading is taken from the centre of the image, which narrows it down to the fish in trophy shots (or should!).

Always use good-quality film which has been stored in a refrigerator. In theory, the poorer the light conditions, the faster the speed of the film has to be, but where you want to work to publication standards, you want the lowest speed film possible to avoid grain. Such is the quality of the best of the modern films that 100–200 ASA is an acceptable compromise, and you can go even higher where circumstances dictate (e.g. action or trophy shots in low-light conditions).

When you want to up-grade your camera equipment and you are on a limited budget, go to the best camera shop in town and ask them what they have got in terms of second-hand cameras. These are not rejects. Photographers are always seeking to buy better equipment and they trade their previous model against the new equipment. It is like buying a second-hand car. You can make substantial savings by buying second hand, and aspire to much better equipment than you could have afforded at new prices.

Getting friendly with the camera shop staff will enable you to seek advice when you need to come to terms with some aspect of camera work that you cannot figure out for yourself or from the camera manual.

This lovely self-portrait trophy shot was taken shortly after a November sunrise, the morning sun accentuating the superb autumn condition of this mid-20lb mirror.

Most of us have had some very disappointing pictures of our treasured carp. Be prepared for that fish of a lifetime and, if necessary up-grade your camera equipment now, not after the next major disappointment.

I have seen some awful prints from perfectly good negatives. If you are not happy with your prints, check the negatives. The fault may lie not in your work but at the development and printing stage. Developers can be very careless about printing the correct area of the shot, and missing heads or tails may be on the film. If the quality of a print is not up to the standard of the negative, ask the developer to do them again.

All my photographic work is done with transparency films, usually Fujichrome Provia in 100 ASA, but I also carry 400 ASA film for use with the telescopic lens I carry. I have the transparencies developed in sheet form, and only have prints done of those shots which I think warrant one.

If you are using a manual camera, check the ASA reading before you have the film developed. If you have shot the roll at the wrong ASA, the developers can make an adjustment at the developing stage with no loss of quality.

Always carry a spare battery for your camera with you. These are items you cannot buy from the local corner shop at seven o'clock at night or five o'clock in the morning.

Buzzers

You use buzzers so they will warn you when you have got a take. If I am fishing the same lake as you, I don't need to know that. I can understand pleasure anglers being irritated by the sound of buzzers. If you must play with them, or have them switched on while you adjust your indicators, or have them set so sensitively that they announce every minor zephyr of breeze blowing through your swim, then please turn them down or use an extension box.

Stalking

What a subject to cover in a couple of paragraphs! The thing is, I am not sure that you can explain stalking in print. Stalkers are born, not made. Most carp anglers don't do as much stalking as they should do. I stalk on floater waters, but not on others. That's largely because I like to sit and look at the water, but seeing carp on top invariably gets me off my butt.

I can tell you this about stalking. There will be a number of spots in the margins of most lakes that the carp visit. Ambush the fish in one of those spots by baiting them regularly, then checking them out every hour or so. Stalking lends itself to night-feeding waters where nothing ever happens during the day. If you are fishing such a water, find the fish, watch them, learn how to catch them.

There has been some excellent stalking material published by such writers as Chris Yates, Albert Romp, Brian Skoyles, Chris Ball, Brian Mills and others. If you can't figure it out for yourself, hitch your wagon to the star of one of these gifted and successful stalkers.

Floater Fishing

I agonized over including a chapter on floater fishing, then decided against. There is some excellent material available covering successful floater fishing, in particular the book of the same

name by Chris Ball and Brian Skoyles in the *Carp-in-Depth* series. Regular up-dates of floater developments, methods and tactics for floater freaks appear in the carp periodicals.

I do not think it is my imagination that floater fishing is becoming an increasingly minority pursuit, in terms of the number of waters that now respond to floater fishing. It is an ability you should have in your repertoire, and you should always have the necessary baits and tackle with you in case. Carp which respond to floaters seem to be a disappearing breed, a situation presumably brought about by pressure over a period of time. I can now go a whole season without catching a carp on floaters, whereas up to a couple of years ago I expected to catch at least a few off the top each season.

Hammering

There are times and places when some hammering on the bank is unavoidable if you don't want your bivvy to blow away in the first big storm to hit the water. However, one of those times and places is not within a few yards of another angler's baited area when feeding time is approaching, or just as the angler in the next swim has got the fish taking floaters. Show some regard for your fellow anglers and time your hammering to cause as little disruption as possible to the anglers already fishing when you arrive.

Joining Waters

When you are new to carp fishing, the next step forward seems very urgent. You've got to catch a twenty-pounder, you've got to catch a thirty, you've got to get onto that big-fish water you keep reading about. Just bear in mind that no one else shares your urgency about you achieving these objectives. Accept that in terms of fish catching, your achievements will be judged by your fellow anglers over a period of years, not in terms of what you have caught in your first month or two, or even year or two. Acceptance comes from being around and becoming recognized as an habitual carp angler. The carp world is all too well aware that there have been a number of carp-fishing shooting stars with something to prove, who apparently proved it to themselves and shot off over the horizon never to be seen or heard of again. In your formative years, you may be looked on as one of these. You achieve acceptance by not disappearing, not by getting up everyone's nose!

In terms of getting into waters, look on your objectives as a long-term thing. Write to the owner/lessee. Tell him who you are, how long you have been carp fishing, why you want to join the water and can you please go on the waiting list? If you are still around five years later and you haven't heard anything, write again. Carp fishing goes on a long time and five years isn't very long when it comes to waiting lists for prime syndicate waters.

Fishing Abroad

Those who do not fish abroad may look on this subject as a minority one. Those who do fish on foreign soil and struggle to get in the productive swims on the best waters know it isn't!

Fishing abroad has a culture of its own now. Part of that culture are the organized trips to waters like Dream Lake, Les Quis, Domaine des Iles, the Hermitage and other French lakes which are advertised regularly in the carp press. If you are going to France for the first time, arrange to go on one of these organized trips where all the arrangements are made for you. Such a trip will give you an insight into what's involved in fishing in France, and you will hear about the popular waters, and possibly some not-so-popular ones.

Don't start your foreign fishing by going to one of the big-fish venues like Chantecoq or Orient and finding that you can't get in a swim, and that you are out of your depth when you do.

Leon Hoogendijk is writing a perceptive, in-depth series about carp fishing in France for *Carpworld*, Tony Davies-Patrick is writing up his globe-trotting carp fishing experiences in his ongoing series in the same magazine and Fred J. Taylor, among others, writes of the prolific carp fishing to be found in Canada. In addition there will be regular articles by other writers in other carp and angling periodicals which will give you an insight into overseas carp-fishing developments.

Carp fishing abroad is growing in popularity and future monthly carp publications will reflect this trend. The fact that it is growing at such a pace was one of the reasons for not including a full write up of it in this book. Such material dates very rapidly.

The Carp Society

The Carp Society is a national organization open to all carp anglers. It is the biggest single-species angling organization in Europe and is run by a full-time administration and a voluntary committee. The Society runs national conferences and regional meetings and publishes a bi-monthly magazine, *Carp Fisher*, which is free to members.

The Society runs a number of carp waters and is committed to acquiring more, either on lease or by purchase. The organization owns the magnificent Horseshoe Lake near Lechlade in Gloucestershire and, the famous Redmire Pool on the Welsh border, big-fish water Farmwood Pool in the north-west, Chimneys Pool in Bedfordshire, Tutton Pool in Surrey, and a new water in Gloucestershire which is currently known as Project 2000.

However long you have been carp fishing you should be a member of the Society, which is working hard to protect the future of carp fishing. The address to write to for details of the Society's membership and waters is The Carp Society, Horseshoe Lake, Lechlade, Gloucestershire.

28 WHEN IT NEARLY COMES RIGHT: SUMMER

It is not difficult to pinpoint the start of the session, even without referring back to *From the Bivvy.* As I was setting-up Bob Tapken, who was fishing the swim round to my right, suddenly proclaimed to anyone who happened to be listening that Linford Christie had just won a gold medal in the Olympic 100-metre final. It was early August 1992 and I had arrived on the Mangrove on a Saturday afternoon for a session through to the following Tuesday (later extended to Wednesday).

I had arrived at the water with no doubt in my mind as to the swim I wanted to be in: Lightning Tree. During the previous session, when I had fished the Swamp, there had been fish showing in front of Lightning Tree about 50yd out in front of the swim. Now there was a big westerly blowing straight into the swim and I just knew that was where I had to be. On the drive down, I didn't want it too much. Not being able to get in a swim you want too much can undermine your confidence for alternative swims, so I have always got a few alternatives in my mind before I arrive, but on this occasion I knew that really anywhere else would have been second best.

When I got there, I hesitated about going into the swim. Dave Treasure was fishing Fallen Tree and Bob Tapken was fishing the Swamp, the swims either side of the one I was fancying. I walked round and checked them out. There were fish all over the place at that end of the lake, and both anglers were pulling off the next day. They had no problems over me going into Lightning Tree.

The swim had a strange reputation in those days. It was awkward to fish because it was set back in the pads, and it wasn't really a prolific

swim. Up to that season, Fallen Tree and the Swamp had been far more reliable, but the numbers of fish out from Lightning the previous session has convinced me that either there was a bed of natural food out front that hadn't been there in previous seasons, or the fish had suddenly decided that the swim was a pleasant place to be. Their strong presence during the previous session could have been a one-off, but the big westerly made Lightning Tree a fair prospect in any case.

They were there when I got in the swim. Dave had caught the previous night and during the morning prior to my lunch-time arrival. I was happy enough with that. The fish were in the area, some of them were feeding, Dave's captures might have pressured the fish that had been in front of him down to me. That was the good news: I created the bad news! At that time, I hadn't figured that the Mangrove carp didn't like baits over their heads when they were showing, so I put a few pounds out to keep them interested, chucked a couple of stringers out for a quick early capture, then set up shop.

I'd got 10lb of the going bait in the swim with me in freezer boxes, and another 15 to 20lb in the freezer up at the farm. This was the summer I was determined to put five pounds of bait out per night irrespective of conditions or feeding activity. Looking back there are times when I think that was dumb, but it made sense at the time, and carp fishing tactics are based on what makes sense at the time. Fact is, that the fish were responding to generous helpings of the Big Fish Mix. That particular day they were unusually active: I figured there were so many fish in the area that it needed a few pounds of bait just to hold them there, and that it was going to take

Early August 1992. Big wind into Lightning Tree during the session described here. I was sitting wondering if the wind was not too strong for the carp when Scaley roared off with one of the baits at 3.30pm.

all I had got with me to keep them interested. In retrospect, the thinking and the tactics weren't far out – it was the timing that left a great deal to be desired.

The wind continued to pummel the eastern end of the lake. Dave had one and lost one during the night while I think Bob had one of his rare weekend's blanks. Sunday morning came without so much as a bleep in my swim. The lads packed up and departed for civilization and I settled in to wait, expecting action at any second in the brilliant conditions. Late morning, I topped-up the swim, then again during the early evening, both predictably quiet periods from experience. The fish were in the area, I knew they were eating the bait with confidence: no sweat.

By Monday morning, I was beginning to sweat. Still no action. Overnight feeding usually finished by eight o'clock at the latest, by which time I was having a real crisis of confidence. The swim's reputation was proving to be more accurate than my revised assessment of it. The action during the last session achieved by casting across from the Swamp had been a one-off: I had been wrong to assess it as a new feeding area on the basis of one session's observations. My confidence was plummeting

By half-eight I was planning a move. I'd decided that although the fish would feed in front of the swim, they didn't like anyone occupying it: last time out I had caught from there because I had been casting across from the Swamp. I have no doubt it also briefly crossed my mind that the bait had blown, but I had built up so much confidence in it through the pre-baiting and the previous sessions' action that I dismissed that doubt as soon as it surfaced. Rig? If they were eating the bait, the rig was good enough. I was sure I hadn't run over any black cats, or broken any mirrors, and from the look of the night sky Uranus appeared to be in alignment with Jupiter.

Half-eight, I'm sitting in the bivvy doorway, racked by doubt when the rod fishing what I had hoped was a newly identified hot spot screamed off. Ten minutes of major league anxiety and I had a common of 24lb 15oz in the landing net. A run at eight-thirty after no previous action was an unusual occurrence, but not one that I was about to complain about. As I wrote at the time, 'What a difference a fish makes...' I took some unsatisfactory pictures on the air release set-up and the old Canon AE1 and settled in for some more waiting. Thoughts about moving had been pushed to the back of my mind – like they would be.

Seven hours later, I was sitting in the bivvy doorway shaving, wondering if the big wind was too strong for feeding activity, when the same rod was away again. Scaley was on the end at a new personal best of 35lb 10oz. I was pleased, but not overexcited. I was due the fish, and if I couldn't catch him in those conditions, I'd never catch him. I didn't risk the air release though. I went and got Stoney to do the honours on the Canon EOS with the great mirror, although we almost didn't get any pictures. I spread some sacks on the unhooking mat on the platform, and as I went to lift the lovely mirror, he made a determined effort to return to the lake a few minutes early. It was a close-run thing, my restraining tactics being singularly undignified, but happily successful.

I fished on with anticipation at a high level. Two big fish in a day was the sort of build up of action I could live with. The wind kept roaring in, I kept putting the bait in, and over the next thirty-six hours, I hooked five fish – and lost three of them! As the fish I landed were both seventeen pounders I suspected that two of those I lost were doubles too. In fact I saw one of them at fairly close quarters as it did a determined back flip just as I was bringing it over the drawstring and threw the hook – and it looked

Scaley at 35lb 10oz from Lightning Tree. I went to get Stoney to take the pictures with the Canon EOS, which meant I finished up with one decent set of trophy shots from the session!

to be a mid-double mirror. One of the other lost fish was a big-looking golden common that I had on top coming through the pads for a while, but then it got bedded down and finally managed to get rid of the hook.

I am normally a calm-enough player of fish (although I feel anything but calm until they are in the net) but playing them in through the edge of the heavy pads was a new experience. When I ran back over the two lost fish I decided that I had been a shade too anxious to keep the pressure on and keep them moving. When fish snag up in pads you have to take the pressure off, then let them move sufficiently for you to realign them and get them moving again. I felt I had got to take some responsibility for at least two of the losses.

The last two losses came within ten minutes of each other at about ten in the morning, one from open water and one from the edge of the pads. I was using Super Specialist size 4s fished with the line aligner, and such had been my faith in the strength and reliability of this set-up that the losses stunned me and had me rethinking the hooking arrangement. The hook had partially opened out on the last lost fish.

I checked out the range of hooks I had in the rig wallet, then went to consult with Ray and Dave, a couple of local carper friends to see if they had any patterns more suitable than those I had with me. I retied the end tackles with a change of hook when I got back, but only on a confidence-boosting, temporary-solution basis. I would have to think it out again when I had finished the session and could address the problem dispassionately.

I had had action during the two previous afternoons so I was a bit put out when the Wednesday afternoon hot time produced no run. Four o'clock, I topped-up the swim, rebaited the end tackles and put them back in position. I wrote at the time that I felt as though I was sitting on a powder keg. The fish were still there, and conditions were getting better and better with warm rain being added to the strong westerlies. I was so convinced that conditions were right for a result that I'd extended my stay at the water by twenty-four hours, which meant I was stacking up an even more frantic end to the week than usual when I got back.

The carp fed to a strange pattern that session. The main early hours feeding time produced very little action. They fed later than usual in the morning spell; afternoon had been better than usual, with the other likely time of mid-evening producing only one fish. The ongoing bait application was geared to slot into these feeding times.

Wednesday afternoon passed without action. I topped-up the swim between four and five, the next anticipated feeding time being eight o'clock onwards for a couple of hours. The wind was finally calming off, which I told myself might be a good thing, but deep down I felt it wasn't.

Stoney called in to see me soon after six o'clock on the way round to Erewhon to see someone. He'd call back on his way home. I made a coffee, took my chair to the front of the platform and settled down to sit and watch for fish movement. The noisy big westerly battering in for three days had been really unsettling and it was lovely just to sit in the gentler conditions. The calm after the storm. The urgency went out of the session and I was ready for away next morning. I am usually like that when I have stayed an extra day: it rarely works out and I start to think of the things I should have been doing during the stolen twenty-four hours.

Half-six, the right hand rod slammed off. It was fishing a possible new hot spot long to my right. Fish had shown there all three evenings of my stay and I hoped it was a natural feeding spot. I can't remember the fight other than the anxiety after the run of losses, but the aftermath is indelibly engraved on my memory. The fish was a heavily scaled mirror I didn't recognize, weighing comfortably in excess of 20lb.

The front of the platform is ten yards out from the bank, and in those days I always used to walk the fish back to the bank to weigh them. Getting past the bivvy with the made-up net was awkward, and the Solar Bowlocs net was ideal for breaking down, rolling the mesh round the fish and carrying it to the back of the swim. On that occasion I had just detached the arms and rolled up the mesh when the other hot spot rod was away – the spot that had produced two big fish on the Monday. I froze and my mind raced. Let it run and it would be a long way out when I hit it, with increased chances of it kiting into the pads on a long line. Hit it and then put the rod down? Which I did even as I thought it. Wallop, rod back in the rests, reassemble the net with the fish in it, mesh in the water, foot on the handle, carry on playing the fish.

This one was mental. It came into the edge much too quickly, which meant it was far livelier than I could live with in the heavy pads. But live with it you must! There was no way the hook could stand the pressure I had to put on it at such close quarters, but it did and with my heart in my mouth, I eased a big-looking mirror into the net. I had acquired a nice sort of problem. I had got two twenty-plus mirrors in the net! I considered the logistics of moving them from the front of the swim to the bank.

The first fish had already been unhooked. I needed both hands to carry the near fifty pounds of lively carp, which meant I would struggle to carry the netful of carp and the rod: the second carp had to be unhooked, too. I lowered the net onto the unhooking mat at the front of the swim. As long as I kept the front of the mesh up there was no danger of either fish making a bolt for the water (I thought) which was true provided I could keep the front of the mesh up, which I couldn't ...

One of the poor-quality shots from the 'nearly' session. I set the exposure control incorrectly for a number of good fish and then up-graded my remote trophy shots camera equipment as soon as I could afford to.

I'll not labour it. The first fish (which I see from the book was actually my twentieth twenty-pounder of the season) made a muscular, gymnastic back flip from a standing – or lying – start, and returned whence it came, unweighed. Its premature return probably made its capture more memorable than if it had been photographed. The second fish weighed in at 25lb 2oz; a big-framed mirror which I hadn't seen before, and haven't seen since.

I sacked the mirror, sorted out and got the end tackles back out there. It was still early evening. I was expecting Stoney to call in on his way back from Erewhon, hoping he could take the pictures on the Canon EOS rather than me have to set up the Canon AE-1 on the tripod for some self-take shots. (I should make it clear that I did not have a facility for using the Canon EOS for self-take shots.) In addition, I'd just got to tell someone about the extraordinary burst of action I had just experienced.

While I was sitting drinking coffee, experiencing the mixed emotions of delight at the double capture and disappointment about the premature departure of the twentieth twenty-pounder, the fifty-yard hot-spot rod was away again. This was the animal to end all animals: a bit of a psychopath. Again the pressure I had to apply in the edge scared me, but again the hookhold held and eventually I thankfully pulled a big-looking common over the mesh. She weighed in at 26lb 15oz and I was so excited by the sequence of events that I just can't attempt to describe my feelings – so I won't embarrass you by trying. You know those over-the-top goal celebrations that have you squirming in your seat? No, I said I wouldn't try...

Stoney didn't materialize and I didn't want to keep the fish till morning so I took the pictures on the partly automatic, partly manual AE-1 and returned the fish. The common I had slightly mixed feelings about. I had caught a personal best common of 26lb 14oz in July and thought this very similar looking fish weighing an ounce bigger was the same fish, which disappointed me slightly. As it turns out, they were different fish, have both since made thirties, and the common

I caught that evening has gone on to make 37lb plus. Later that night, I had a fourth twenty-pounder, this one weighing in at 21lb. Two of the fish came from the fifty-yard hot spot and two from the new spot.

I finished the session with three doubles, five twenties to almost 27lb, including two twenty-five pluses, one of which was a personal best common, and a personal best mirror of 35lb 10oz. I would guess that on the drive home and in the immediate aftermath I was fairly pleased about it all.

But, at best, I was only ever fairly pleased. I had made too many mistakes for it to be a really good session, whatever the end result. I had got the initial baiting wrong which had set me back the best part of two days: I had had a run of three lost fish which had me rethinking my hooking arrangement and thinning the heavy pads in the immediate area of the platform: I had let a lovely twenty plus mirror make its escape in the unhooking process; and to compound all that, the self-take pictures of the 24lb 15oz common, the 25lb 2oz mirror and the 26lb 15oz common were very substandard, because I had made a mistake in setting up the camera.

I know that for some of you that would have been the session of a lifetime, so I am not trying to be blasé, or churlish, or dismiss it as a non-starter. In a lifetime's carp fishing you have bad sessions, indifferent ones, run-of-the mill ones, good ones, really good ones, and truly memorable ones. After the initial passion – when all sessions are memorable, whatever the outcome – has abated exceptional sessions come your way but rarely. I have had many special sessions, and (in terms of captures) a mere handful of really memorable ones. Two big fish from Darenth Tip Lake within a couple of days of each other; the Waveney week described in *Big Carp*: the five twenty-pounders in a Mangrove night a fortnight after the events described above; the two fish in the net at once on Birch

the following November, and the 18 December Mangrove session described elsewhere in this book. Those, and the session described here, are the one-offs, the sessions that creep into your mind at unguarded moments when your memory is freewheeling and wanders off to one of your favourite swims.

I have a suspicion that this early August session should have been the best of the lot. The fish were there, I know they were feeding because Dave Treasure had caught a couple and lost a couple before I arrived, I had a bait they were feeding on with confidence and conditions held up for five days. Truth is, I did what so many of us do so often at carp fishing and messed up within minutes of getting in the swim. At least I had five days in front of me which gave the session a chance to come partly right, despite my continuing efforts not to let it! I can't help but reflect that on a two nighter I would have been packing away when I had that first confidence restoring common.

Looking on the bright side, it is a fact of life that we all learn by our mistakes and I made so many in that particular session that it must have been worth a season's carp fishing in terms of lessons learnt. As a footnote, I just can't get that session right at any stage of the proceedings. Three years after *From the Bivvy* was published, I've only just noticed that this session was incorrectly annotated at the page-layout stage, in that a date was left out. The error has had me trying to figure out what happened when. Then, finally, the above account details the three fish of the final evening in the wrong order. I am trying to find someone else to blame for these ongoing errors but I am afraid they are all down to me! Presumably this is what they refer to as a 'chapter of errors'.

Finally, the good news. Having spent some time coming to terms with the hooking problem and refining my methods I had just one hook pull on the next seventy-odd fish I hooked from the water!

29 WHEN IT ALL COMES RIGHT: WINTER

On 5 December 1994 I caught a mirror carp of 36lb 8oz from the swim known as Lightning Tree on the Mangrove. The fish came on the second afternoon of a three-night session and was the prelude to an amazing December and an extraordinary winter's fishing. The mirror, Conan, was a landmark fish for a number of reasons. It was a personal best, it fell to a set-up and baiting situation which were still at the experimental stage, and it came in awful weather and water conditions, which had me on the verge of rethinking my winter campaign and pulling off the water. Winter fishing is a battle of mind over matter and the big mirror took at a moment when the unwilling flesh and the unconvinced mind were screaming 'Enough!' The fish convinced me that I hadn't had enough, that the methods I was using were definitely headed in the right direction, and that even in what seemed hopeless flood levels, and apparently appalling weather conditions, the carp were willing to have a little feed. What follows is a minor rewrite of the article 'December Song' I wrote following the next two-day session. The facts and tactics are as I described them then.

I caught Conan at 36lb 8oz on Monday 5 December, left the water on Wednesday 7 December and couldn't get back until Sunday 18 December because of the *Carpworld* publication schedule. Even then I was not keen to go. I'd only got time for a two nighter, Christmas festivities were looming, the weather was cold and damp, and the nights were at their longest. But the only way you will catch is by being there, so I went.

The forecast swung it. Westerlies and north-westerlies. I'd fished Lightning Tree through the autumn and early winter and I'd caught Conan from that swim. But the swim known as Fallen Tree was pulling me, and a north-westerly wind would make it a must. I didn't particularly want to be in that swim: I'd just got to be there.

My enthusiasm rose on the two-hour drive down. I didn't get away from home until nine o'clock so I didn't think I'd see any of the weekend lads (if any had been), which would leave my mind completely uncluttered. When you're getting a strong gut feeling for a swim, influencing factors based on logic and the practical experiences of others can undermine you. On this occasion I didn't want undermining; I wanted to go in Fallen Tree.

There was no one there, and nothing to tell me if anyone had been there or not. The wind was pushing straight down the lake into Lightning Tree. Cool, steady, with perhaps too much clear sky around to suggest good fishing conditions, but the forecast promised rain coming in so a little feeding spell was on the cards.

I went into the familiar routine. Everyone's amazed at the amount of gear I take into the swim with me, but I think it's all essential for a two or three nighter in the winter. Once I'm committed I'm driven and there's nothing half-hearted about my attitude, or the session. I want to fish for however long I'm at the water and I'm equipped accordingly.

Paddling across in the laden boat I hesitated. The wind was bang right for Lightning Tree and it didn't make sense to turn my back on a producing swim which had seen a steady introduction of the bait I was using over a two-month period. On the other hand, I had baited Fallen Tree twice when I was leaving the water, and Tony had fished it a couple of times during the

19 December 1994. The Fallen Tree island platform with the water level up.
The morning after the night before.

colder months. The debate went on in my head, but the gut feeling was for Fallen Tree, so that's where I went.

The water level was higher than I expected and the platform was an island. I hesitated. Lightning Tree was a nicer swim to fish in the winter. I pondered a further ten minutes before I started unloading the boat. In the end, the influencing factor was the gut feeling, which was fuelled by a couple of practical considerations.

The first was that I'd had a run of fish from Lightning Tree and every one had moved left (towards Fallen Tree) on the run or after I'd set the hook. I'd been getting the feeling that the fish were coming to me for their little feed, and as the conditions got worse, they would be far less likely to do so. Once they decided to put down roots through inactivity, I would have to get on top of them to catch them; up to the end of November they had possibly still been moving with the prevailing conditions.

The second factor was that I'd caught a fish from the swim the previous December. That fish had come on a gut feeling based on a number of fish sightings in one spot through the autumn. That same spot would be my starting point now. I finally convinced myself to fish the swim and started unloading the boat.

When you are in a routine you become very organized. Up with the Titan; down with the two ground sheets. When it's not raining I arrange the bivvy contents before I put the front on the Titan and fix the Canopy over the top. An hour to set up home, then an hour and a half to get the baits out and the end tackles in position. The formula was starting to work and I wasn't about to change anything.

Because of the baiting situation I was using, I wasn't really expecting action the first night. I put out half to three quarters of a pound of a mixture of tiny Grange baits and Micromass. The fact that the bream were eating the baits made it difficult to assess ongoing levels and meant that I tended to start out by possibly overbaiting. The Micromass breaks down and leaves the silt smelling of food, while undetected feeding activity makes the quantity of Grange bait in the swim at any one time a very inexact science. The fact that the bream were getting hooked meant that I had some means of monitoring what was going on, and the three hookbait and twelve bait stringers trap meant that each end tackle represented a feeding situation in its own right. Buzzer activity meant the baits were being taken – obviously – but on the other hand no buzzer activity didn't mean the free offerings weren't being taken.

After the initial baiting I'll only introduce further free offerings in circumstances that indicate the fish have clearly had a strong feed. Whether there's bait left out there or not the smell of bait will be in the swim and the tiny patches of food represented by the hookbait and the stringers will gradually become the only obvious food source available. That's the theory. (I'll update that. Following that session, I stopped topping up after feeding activity and relied on the ongoing disappearing food source smell and loaded stringer traps. It was a very successful winter tactic.)

Sunday 18 December. There was a lot of football on the radio: three consecutive matches as I recall. That's a nice start to a session: it eases the early session restlessness that almost always comes with the sudden realization that after the activity of preparing, travelling, arriving and setting up you are suddenly faced with the unwelcome reality of staying in one place doing absolutely nothing for two or three days. From memory we had Reading and Wolves, Chelsea and Manchester United, then Scotland and Greece.

In situations like that, I'm fishing for next day, really, although the knowledge that the main feeding spell was likely to be in the evening was

Looking out from Fallen Tree. The strong wind and the build up of cloud in the north-west means that the pressure is dropping and the carp will feed. The winter hot spot is 60yd out, just out of shot to the right. Or was it 80yd out, in shot, to the left …?

never far from the front of my mind. Logic might have suggested that the following day was most likely but the eternal optimism undoubtedly insisted that that particular evening was going to be different. You just sort of be there and wait. Sometimes something happens; sometimes it doesn't. If you don't hope too much, you never get too disappointed.

Soon after I'd finished setting-up, the rain came sweeping into the front of the bivvy, which meant having the door down. It also meant the wind was quartering into the north-west, as promised. Some time during the Greece/Scotland match, the rain relented and I was able to put the door up. It was cool but not unpleasant, with winds and heavy rain forecast locally. I'd enjoy having the door up while I could.

I rang Mary to tell her I was in residence, made a brew or two, had an early evening dinner, then lay on the bedchair listening to the football and looking out at the rods, the darkened water and the approaching weather front. The sky had cleared late afternoon but there was a distant bank of heavy cloud coming in from over the Irish Sea. After the capture of Conan on the back of a wet front during the previous session I recalled that the previous December's mirror had also come as torrential rain hit the water. As a result, my previous dread of torrential rain in winter changed to a sort of welcome dread. A severe weather front possibly meant action.

At about seven o'clock I had a double bleep to the middle rod – the green LED. Line bite? Stringer gone? Fish sitting out there trying to shake the hook out? I always agonize about such occurrences, and almost always finish up leaving them. A double bleep was less unsettling than a single one because there was more likelihood of it being a line bite – up and down.

An hour drifted by. Scotland lost 1:0 and the summarizer started to explain why it had happened. The bank of cloud was halfway up the sky but the consequences of its approach didn't seem particularly imminent. I'd got my weatherproof top on, but not my waterproof trousers. I was relaxed, warm, comfortable and had no reason to move for a while, until the buzzer sounded.

Five to eight and the green LED was in action again. A short run which stopped, but the indicator stayed up tight. I took a few turns on the handle then whacked it. I remember thinking that I'd felt it go solid just a shade far back in the strike, a bit beyond the vertical, and hoped the hook would stay in. Conditions had been calmish and dry when I picked up the rod but within half a minute of starting to play the fish, it was blowing half a gale and pouring down. I'd got lucky. Feeding conditions had coincided with the main feeding time. How many times in a carp-fishing life does it happen the other way round, night after night?

Apart from the joy of hooking a winter carp and the pure theatre of the occasion, it was just another fish. A big scrapper, but no illuminated finger descended from the sky to announce 'It's you!' I was just out there on the exposed platform, getting blown to pieces, my legs and feet were getting soaked, and this fish out in the Mangrove high seas just scrapped and scrapped.

The water conditions were so heavy that I just didn't see or hear the fish at all when it broke surface. At one moment it was almost under the net which I was holding tight against the platform and was having trouble controlling in the big wind. I let the fish go, took a deep breath, and settled for taking however long it took to get the beast in the net. It came in under the rod tip again and this time I waited till it had virtually given up the ghost and was lying on its side before I dared to draw it over the mesh. I'll guess that all that took twenty minutes because it was quarter past eight when I got the torch from the bivvy.

I shone the torch down into the net in the water, and had a moment's confusion. It was another huge fish, but the flank was so light in the torch beam that I thought for a few moments that it was Conan again, the fish I'd caught on the previous session. It was certainly on the same size scale.

I lifted the mesh, staggered to the unhooking mat at the back of the platform and gently lowered the net. I flicked the torch on the fish and the huge gleaming scales stood out in the wavering beam: it was the mighty Scaley. I crouched there in the storm half stunned, half ecstatic, and had an affectionate conversation with the big mirror while I gently sacked it in the sack/sling. Scaley. The fish had weighed 38lb 8oz when Dave Treasure had caught him in the autumn so chances were I'd landed a new personal best. The Nash scales suspended on the tree trunk confirmed as much, and after a brief debate with myself I settled for the same weight as Dave's, 38lb 8oz, equalling the lake record (also held by Tony Baskeyfield and Conan at the same weight). You're on trust when you weigh a fish in those circumstances and 38lb 9oz was on, but at best you are approximating with the Nash 56lb scales, so I settled for equalling the record.

I wanted a picture and there was no chance of one in those conditions, so I lowered the sack into the margins, then went to ring Mary. I was exhilarated and we giggled like a couple of kids as I gave her the bare bones of the news; I told her I'd ring back when I'd got the end tackle back out there.

The rain had eased but the wind was still banging in. Preparing the end tackle and stringer set-up was a chore in the dripping bivvy, but the Kryston Meltdown has the twin attributes of being strong, and dissolving to order. I aimed left of the bed of bait and whacked the 2oz lead out into the gale. A check with the torch revealed that the end tackle hadn't finished up in the right place at all, so in it came, the stringer routine was repeated and back out it went.

This time the torch revealed that the line was pointing in the right direction so I set about making some sense of my soaked person and sodden bivvy. Towels over everything, change the undersuit, get the waterproofs on for the next weather front, put the kettle on. I looked at the luminous hand of the watch. Quarter to nine. I reached for the phone to complete the abbreviated conversation with Mary, at which moment the middle buzzer and the green LED burst into life again. A take on the recast rod!

Solid again on the strike, and the same protracted scrap in the heavy wind. Twenty anxious minutes later I carefully drew another big fish over the landing net and sat back on my haunches in

Ten minutes after I got the recast in position, the same rod roared off again with this super 26lb common on the end.

relief. Playing fish is an anxious business for me and a total forty minutes playing the two fish in the severe conditions had stretched my nerves. I propped the landing net over the front of the platform and went for the torch. The beam revealed a big common and I smiled. My driving force through the winter carping was the hope of a thirty-pound common – an objective which was keeping me on the Mangrove – and my immediate reaction was that I may have done it with this fish.

As it turned out the euphoria of the occasion had exaggerated my assessment. The fish was thick across the back but had nothing like the necessary depth for a thirty. The scales said 26lb, and I was as excited about the capture as I would have been about a thirty-pounder. In retrospect, Scaley and a thirty-pound common on one winter's night would have been too much euphoria! I had no complaints, and after I'd attended to the practicalities (including sorting out the end tackle and getting it back in position at the first attempt) I finally managed to get round to ringing Mary again to rejoice about Scaley and tell her about the latest fish. We shared a few moments of giddiness then I finally got round to making a hot drink to toast the evening's success.

I checked the sacks. Scaley had gone straight down to lie up as soon as I put him back in the water, but the common was lying just below the surface. It was the right way up and breathing comfortably so I had no anxiety, but I always keep checking them till they go down to rest, as the common eventually did.

Mary had rung my mate John Lilley with the news of Scaley and he was travelling up from Hereford in the morning to take the pictures, and Mary was coming across from Sheffield to see the great fish. Scaley was causing quite a stir.

Why? What's the big deal? I guess you've got to catch the fish – or see it – to understand. I'd caught it twice before, at 23lb in 1983 and 35lb 10oz in 1992. I wasn't fishing for it. On previous performance I was fishing in the wrong swims for both Conan (which I hadn't previously caught at any weight) and Scaley. I was fishing for a Mangrove winter capture, hopefully in the shape of a thirty pound common, but in the light of the Mangrove's previous winter history, anything really. As far as we know the 23lb mirror I caught in December 1993 was the only previous Mangrove December capture, so what happened this particular December was way beyond anyone's expectations (and certainly mine) which was why I was so excited by the events of that extraordinary December night.

After that super brace, what followed should have been gentle anticlimax: apart from any other considerations, winter feeding times are rarely protracted affairs and the conditions which triggered the earlier feeding had faded into gentler conditions altogether. I made one or two more phone calls and gradually came back down to earth, at which point the indicator to the right hand rod dropped back, bream-

like: up to that point, the absence of bream had been a blessing that evening. When I eventually caught up with the drop-back the bream had turned into a hard-fighting 16lb common. I thought the action had finished with the rain, but apparently I'd still got feeding fish in front of me. The finely tuned end-tackle trap went back out and I eased my way back into the inertia of bivvy life.

The moon had broken through the clouds while I was playing the double-figure common, and as the evening wore on the sky broke up and the bright half moon spasmodically lit the Mangrove and the surrounding countryside. The wind had eased and the memory of the half gale and torrential rain from eight till half past seemed to be of another night.

I had two more fish before midnight, a common of exactly 20lb, and a mirror of just over 23lb. Those are the statistics. If the captures feel anticlimactic now they certainly didn't seem so at the time. The excitement stayed at fever pitch and every sound of the buzzer had my heart thumping. For me, every carp capture is a memorable occurrence, but with the water already having produced two thirty-pounders for me during December, the thirty-pound common seemed well on the cards. The common came at twenty past eleven and the mirror at twenty to midnight. It occurred to me that despite the clearing sky and dropping temperature the carp seemed to be set for feeding all night. I was being overoptimistic: a bream broke the spell at half past midnight and the extraordinary carp feeding spell was over.

I slept till six, then drank coffee and reflected while I waited for the first of the arriving car lights to show coming down the fields across the water. Mary would have to get up at quarter past four to make it in time for first light. She had always wanted to see Scaley on the bank, and while early rising isn't really her bag, and the winter cold treats her cruelly, she would have been on the road soon after five. Scaley would be no stranger to John, but he knew the significance of the winter capture and I was delighted that he would be wielding the camera.

Looking back into the Lightning Tree swim from the area of the winter hot spot.

Mary made it about half seven and I went round to guide her over the flooded banks. John arrived soon after and made his way across by boat. We had a drink, I gave an incoherent account of the evening's fishing, John said he was delighted for me (but that if it had been anyone else, he would have been sick as a parrot) and we made the preparations for the photo session as the sun lifted clear of the fields at the back of the swim.

Mary gasped when I opened the sack. The great fish looked magnificent; absolutely flawless. The early morning sunlight made for brilliant photographic conditions, and John made the most of them. Then the moment was gone, the capture was over, and the marvellous mirror went back to its freezing home, looking huge as it swam slowly, apparently unconcernedly out of view.

Anticlimax set in after John and Mary had gone their separate ways. Your up-front reaction is that you have got it cracked and that the carp are queuing up for the bait, but deep inside you know that December evenings like that come your way just once. Not once a winter, or once every so often; just once. Make the most of it if and when it happens. Usually it's someone else sitting there when something like that happens, and the thought that it could just get even better will keep driving me back there, as it does hundreds of other winter carpers. You just keep getting it as right as possible and hope that, whatever your terms of reference are, somewhere, some time, the carp and the conditions will conspire to produce an occasion that will live with you for the rest of your life.

30 REFLECTIONS

I wrote this final section in mid-January 1997. A number of thoughts have occurred to me while finalizing what will almost certainly be my last major technical carp book, and I cannot really close without touching on them. I guess it will be my last technical carp book because it takes so long to accumulate enough experience and understanding to attempt a volume of this nature: I cannot imagine I will have enough patience to try and keep pace with the changing face of carp fishing over the next however many years it takes to make another such book possible. It was not till I came to write Chapter 17 on the Disappearing Food Source that the time scale of the development of a tactic was brought home to me. Three or four years to sense, think about, develop and 'refine' a method?! That's a small example, but the fact is that no writer goes into print to say ' Look, this works' until he or she has spent some seasons and hundreds of hours proving that it works, or that something is better than something else, or that another method is a waste of time.

The accumulated experience that lies behind the chapters in this books is massive, and I'm grateful to the talented carp angler/writers who have so expertly covered those areas of carp fishing I felt least able to tackle. I did not expect all the guest writers to see carp fishing as I see it. In areas where our chapters covered common ground there were undoubtedly some contradictions. On the other hand, I am equally sure that there were certain principles which we all emphasized the importance of. The points on which we have diverged do not mean that someone is wrong and someone else is right. It means that our perception of certain situations and our approach to them are different. There are a number of ways to get it right in carp fishing. I will emphasize that the best any of us can say is 'Here is a way. This works for me, it can work for you.' No one is claiming that their way is *the* way. Nor do we attempt to lay down any rules, because when it comes to catching carp, there are none. There are lines of thought and some standard practices. The further you can depart from the accepted lines of thought and the standard practices, and still catch carp, the more individualized your efforts will be.

On rigs, for example. My attitude to rigs is that they are best kept simple, provided the technicalities are adhered to. Kevin Nash talks sound sense on rigs (and has some original points to make) so I asked him to contribute a chapter a long time ago, to either contradict or reinforce what I had to say on the subject. But late in the day, it occurred to me that not everyone wants their rigs to be simple and as far as I am concerned, the market leader in keeping rigs complicated is my old mate Frank Warwick from Cheshire! Frank had already agreed to do the drawings for the book for me, so I asked him to contribute some alternative rigs to give the other side of the presentation picture too. I know that many anglers love messing around with rigs as much as many others enjoy experimenting with baits.

I hope the book has made you think, and has helped if you were in need of help. My carp fishing is at its best when I am most focused and have a clear line of attack in my mind. The point of the book is to try to give as comprehensive an overview of the key aspects of – and approaches to – carp fishing as possible. The contributors' chapters are in here because when it comes to carp fishing, no one person can possess that overview at any one time. The variation in waters, carp, pressure, available time, required bait knowledge, rig understanding, length and intensity of the sessions and a number of other key aspects means that carp fishing is inevitably different things to different people, a comment which applies to the writers and the readers alike. Somewhere, some time, Rod Hutchinson made the comment that there is no such thing as a carp-fishing expert, because no one person can have sufficient current knowledge of all aspects of carp fishing at any one time to aspire to that status. The book has been compiled on the basis of an acceptance of Rod's premise, although whether or not the combined efforts of the author and eight contributors add up to a collective carp fishing expert I will leave others to judge!

Carp fishing needs a big, new, original, technical book every few years. If you have an active carp-fishing mind, pick up your pen and start on the next big technical carp book. All you need is an open mind, a willingness to experiment, a few thousand hours to acquire the necessary experience, an understanding publisher, a few hundred hours sitting in front of a word processor, and some talented friends who will bail you out and cover those areas you know little or nothing about.

I see references in print to basic carp fishing and advanced carp fishing. Such references mystify me. To my mind 'basic' implies something easily understood, while 'advanced' suggests something more complicated, or harder to come to terms with. The reality is that you have to get it right to catch any carp. The more difficult the carp the harder you will have to work and the longer you may have to wait. The technology of fishing at one hundred and fifty yards is advanced carp fishing - unless all the carp are in the margins, in which case it's a waste of time! To succeed on any water you have to assess what

it will take to catch the fish and work towards getting it right. You can learn methods, and even tactics, from a book, magazine, or video, but you can only achieve consistent success from combining the lessons learnt with experience and understanding.

You cannot learn carp fishing overnight. I know from talking to people, and watching them in action – and from my own experiences – that it is possible to possess all the necessary experience and knowledge and still not understand. I commented in Chapter 1 that in certain circumstances, understanding can come to you in an instant, which I suppose is why so many carpers read magazines and books. They hope that somewhere, something they read will trigger understanding. With luck some of you may have found whatever it takes to trigger that understanding somewhere in this book. I hope you enjoyed reading it as much as I have enjoyed accumulating the experience and building the friendships to make it possible, and then putting it together.

In my book *Big Carp*, I quoted the following words of Ernest Hemingway. I'll close with them now because they have a relevance to everything practical and technical that is written about carp fishing. I offer them as a tribute to my contributors, who have paid for the accumulation of their carp-fishing knowledge and understanding with the precious commodity, time, and have passed on some of that knowledge and understanding within these pages. As it happens, Hemingway was a mighty angler, too.

There are some things which cannot be learned quickly, and time, which is all we have, must be paid heavily for their acquiring. They are the very simplest things and because it takes a man's life to know them the little new that each man gets from life is very costly and the only heritage he has to leave.

INDEX

INDEX